THEORIES OF SCIENTIFIC PROGRESS

When we look back at the scientific theories of the past and compare them to the state of science today, there seems to be little doubt that we have made progress. But how have we made this progess? Is it a continuous process which gradually incorporates past succcesses into present theories, or are entrenched theories overthrown by superior competitors in a revolutionary manner?

Theories of Scientific Progess presents the arguments for and against both these extremes, and the positions in between. It covers the interpretations of scientific progress from William Whewell through Karl Popper and Imre Lakatos to Thomas Kuhn and beyond, to the latest contemporary debates.

Along the way John Losee introduces and discusses questions about evidential support and the comparison of theories; whether scientific progress aims at truth or merely problem-solving effectiveness; what mechanisms underlie either process; and whether there are necessary or sufficient conditions for scientific progress. He ends with a look at the analogy between the growth of science and the operation of natural selection in the organic world, and the current ideas of evolutionary theorists such as Stephen Toulmin and Michael Ruse.

Theories of Scientific Progress is the ideal introduction to this topic. It is clearly organized, with suggestions for further reading which point the way to both primary texts and secondary literature. It will be essential reading for students of the history and philosophy of science.

John Losee is Emeritus Professor of Philosophy at Lafayette College, Pennsylvania. He is the author of *A Historical Introduction to the Philosophy of Science* (1972), which has been translated into eleven foreign languages and is currently in its fourth edition, and *Philosophy of Science and Historical Enquiry* (1987).

THEORIES OF SCIENTIFIC PROGRESS

An introduction

John Losee

Routledge
Taylor & Francis Group

NEW YORK AND LONDON

First published 2004
by Routledge
29 West 35th Street, New York, NY 10001

Simultaneously published in the UK
by Routledge
11 New Fetter Lane, London EC4P 4EE

Routledge is an imprint of the Taylor & Francis Group

© 2004 John Losee

Typeset in Garamond by
HWA Text and Data Management, Tunbridge Wells
Printed and bound by
MPG Books Ltd, Bodmin

Library of Congress Cataloging in Publication Data
A catalog record for this book has been requested

British Library Cataloguing in Publication Data
A catalogue record for this book is available from the British
Library

ISBN 0–415–32066–6 hbk
ISBN 0–415–32067–4 pbk

CONTENTS

List of illustrations   vii

Introduction   1

PART I
Progress as incorporation   5

1   Whewell's "tributary–river" image of scientific progress   7
2   Brewster on how not to do history of science   17
3   Mill's objections to Whewell's historicism   19
4   Progress through reduction   28
5   Lakatos' version of the "progress is incorporation" thesis   38
6   Progress and the asymptotic agreement of calculations   51
    Part I: Suggestions for further reading   56

PART II
Progress as revolutionary overthrow   63

7   I.B. Cohen on the identification of scientific revolutions   65
8   Kuhn's taxonomic criterion   68
9   Toulmin's "ideals of natural order"   73
10 Ideological upheaval and revolutionary change   75
11 Kuhn's three-beat pattern   76
12 Laudan's reticulational model of scientific change   82
13 Popper on progress through overthrow-with-incorporation   88
    Part II: Suggestions for further reading   92

PART III
Descriptive theories of scientific progress 95

14 Normative and descriptive theories 97
15 Scientific progress and convergence upon truth 98
16 Laudan on scientific progress as increasing
   problem-solving effectiveness 120
17 Kitcher on conceptual progress and explanatory progress 126
18 Normative naturalism 130
19 Scientific progress and the theory of organic evolution 140
   Part III: Suggestions for further reading 152

Conclusion 156

Notes 160
References 169
Index of names 175
Index of subjects 178

ILLUSTRATIONS

Figures

0.1	Incremental and discontinuous scientific progress	1
1.1	Whewell's "tributary–river" view of scentific progress	11
3.1	The composition of forces	23
5.1	A Lakatosian scientific research program	38
5.2	Lakatos' criterion of incorporation with corroborated excess content	39
5.3	The two electron-spin orientations of the hydrogen atom	40
5.4	Explanatory overlap of theories from research programs A and B	44
5.5	Lakatos on the evaluation of competing methodologies	46
6.1	Black-body radiation at various temperatures	54
11.1	History of science as a succession of "normal" and "revolutionary" stages	76
12.1	The reticulational model	82
12.2	Molières' elastic-vortex theory	83
13.1	Kuhn's successive periods of normal science following revolutions	88
15.1	Relationship of properties A and B	111
15.2	The caloric theory model of a gas	115
16.1	Brahe's theory of the universe	125

Tables

11.1	Kuhnian paradigm replacements	78
18.1	Laudanian hypothetical imperatives	134
18.2	Means-ends correlations and their failures	136
19.1	Toulmin on conceptual change as an evolutionary process	142

INTRODUCTION

There is nearly unanimous agreement that science is a progressive discipline. However, the nature of this progress has been, and continues to be, a matter of dispute.

"Progress" is a normative term.[1] A "progressive" sequence is constituted by stages each of which is superior to its predecessor. Such a sequence is upward-directed over time with respect to "goodness." The upward movement may be achieved in diverse ways (Figure 0.1). At the extremes, progress may be gradual and incremental (1) or sharply discontinuous (2).

Observers of science have disagreed about which pattern is appropriate. Those who accept pattern (1) emphasize the gradual incorporation of past achievements into present theories. Those who accept pattern (2) emphasize revolutionary episodes in which theories are overthrown and replaced by superior competitors.

Observers of science have disagreed, as well, about the nature of the "goodness" that increases over time. The list of recommended candidates includes predictive success, convergence upon truth (Peirce, Popper), consilience (Whewell), reduction (Nagel), incorporation-with-corroborated-excess-content (Lakatos), asymptotic agreement of calculations (Bohr), and problem-solving effectiveness (Laudan).

It is important to distinguish two aspects of the scientific enterprise. One aim of science is to describe the properties and relations of various substances.

Figure 0.1   Incremental and discontinuous scientific progress

A second aim is to formulate theories that explain why these properties and relations are what they are.

It is incontrovertible that there has been a growth of knowledge of the properties and relations of chemical compounds, plants, photons, tribes, and so forth. There also has been a growth of our knowledge of lawful regularities about those things, and an increase in precision in the determination of the values of the physical constants that appear in these regularities. In these respects, there has been an increase of scientific knowledge over time, and surely this counts as progress. Let's apply the label "descriptive progress" to this aspect of the growth of science.

But is the "accretion of knowledge" thesis also true of the successive theories about these substances? Is there a corresponding "theoretical progress?" Thomas Kuhn raised doubts. He declared that

> though the achievements of Copernicus and Newton are permanent, the concepts that made those achievements possible are not. Only the list of explicable phenomena grows; there is no similar cumulative process for the explanations themselves. As science progresses, its concepts are repeatedly destroyed and replaced.[2]

One response to Kuhn's challenge is to identify "progress in science" with "increasing descriptive knowledge," and to take an agnostic stance about "theoretical progress." From this standpoint, the focus is on the increasing range and success achieved by scientists in their forecasts. This is held to be what constitutes scientific progress. Whether or not successive theories are increasingly more adequate (or true) is irrelevant.

This position will not be examined further. It will be assumed—contrary to "theory-agnosticism"—that questions about theoretical progress are important and need to be answered. Many observers of science have insisted that successive theories in a domain of science typically are progressive. To take this position is to raise questions about the nature of this progress.

There have been two principal approaches to the interpretation of theoretical progress in science. The first is to identify the distinguishing feature of such progress— incorporation, revolutionary overthrow, etc.—and set forth the necessary and sufficient conditions of, for instance, "progress *qua* incorporation" or "progress *qua* revolutionary overthrow." This first approach is a normative undertaking. Its proponents seek to uncover those conditions that are necessary and/or sufficient for "good science." Once identified, these conditions are held to stipulate how science *ought to be* practiced. The first approach is the subject matter of Part I: "Progress as incorporation" and Part II: "Progress as revolutionary overthrow."

A second approach is to develop a theory of science. This second approach is the subject matter of Part III: "Theories of scientific progress."

A theory of science may take the form of an interpretation of the nature of the "goodness" that increases when progress is achieved. Two influential recommendations are:

1 scientific progress is the convergent approximation to truth achieved by successive theories (discussed in Chapter 15), and
2 scientific progress is the increasing effectiveness of problem-solving achieved by the application of successive theories (discussed in Chapters 16 and 17).

A theory of science also may take the form of an explanation of why science develops as it does. Just as scientists seek to uncover the underlying mechanisms responsible for the development of physical systems, philosophers of science seek to uncover the mechanisms responsible for scientific progress. The most widely promulgated theories about underlying mechanisms take progress in science to be analogous to biological evolution (discussed in Chapter 19).

A theory of science may or may not include normative pronouncements about how science ought be conducted. A purely descriptive theory of science issues no such pronouncements. The aim of such a theory is to discover and display those repeated patterns deemed progressive by the practitioners of science. This may be accomplished without claiming that some, or all, of these patterns ought be achieved by scientists today.

Part I

PROGRESS AS INCORPORATION

1

WHEWELL'S "TRIBUTARY–RIVER" IMAGE OF SCIENTIFIC PROGRESS

William Whewell was the first student of science to conduct a systematic investigation of the entire course of science from its inception to the time at which he was writing (1837). Whewell pursued the first approach to the interpretation of "theoretical progress." He sought to identify the nature of this progress and to uncover the conditions that make it possible.

Whewell shared the common nineteenth-century conviction that science was on an ascending path. Moreover, he was curious about the nature of this ascent. Whewell resolved to compile a history of the various sciences in order to see if there is a pattern within these developments. He was the first observer of science to seek to uncover the nature of scientific progress by means of an examination of the history of science.[1]

Whewell was well aware that to write a history one needs to make judgments about what is important and what is not. History requires interpretation. One cannot write the history of a war, for example, simply by compiling in chronological order official communiqués, the orders of field commanders, press reports, the diaries and letters of soldiers, factory output data, fuel consumption, and transportation data. To compile records in this way is to conduct a "scissors and paste" operation that falls short of historical reconstruction.

The same considerations apply to the history of science. The historian of science must assess the relative importance of the correspondence of scientists, their metaphysical commitments, and the organizational structure of scientific institutions. He or she must, in addition, assess the relative importance of the products of scientific research—theories, empirical generalizations and experimental results.

Without some convictions about what is important in science the historian can only apply the "scissors and paste" technique. Whewell acknowledged this.[2] He declared that he would interpret the history of science by reference to the basic polarity of "fact and idea." Indeed, Whewell took the relationship of fact and idea to be constitutive of all knowledge. Roughly speaking, facts provide the content of knowledge and ideas provide the form. To achieve knowledge is rather like baking a waffle—the grid of the iron (ideas) impresses form upon the batter (facts). Whewell referred to the binding together of facts by ideas as a "colligation of facts." For instance, Robert Boyle colligated facts about the variation of pressure and volume of confined samples of air at constant temperature by superimposing the idea of reciprocal proportionality ($P \propto 1/V$). Whewell declared that

> knowledge requires us to possess both Facts and Ideas;—that every step in our knowledge consists in applying the ideas and conceptions furnished by our minds to the facts which observation and experiment offer to us.[3]

Whewell conceded that the distinction between fact and idea is only a relative distinction. An idea at one level of interpretation may be a fact for a higher level of interpretation. For example, Kepler superimposed the idea of an ellipse upon the facts of successive planetary positions. These elliptic orbits subsequently became facts upon which Newton superimposed the ideas of inertial motion and gravitational attraction. Whewell noted, moreover, that there are no "pure facts." The simplest observation reports involve ideas of space, time and number. He maintained, nevertheless, that the fact-idea polarity is an appropriate foundation for writing a history of science.

Whewell assumed, further, that there exist discrete individual sciences. He held that the subject matter of each science is determined by a set of basic predicates, or "fundamental ideas," the meaning of which is given by general principles, or "axioms." Whewell declared that

> each science has for its basis a different class of Ideas; and the steps which constitute the progress of one science can never be made by employing the Ideas of another kind of science. No genuine advance could ever be obtained in Mechanics by applying to the subject the Ideas of Space and Time merely: —no advance in Chemistry, by the use of mere Mechanical Conceptions: —no discovery in Physiology, by referring to mere Chemical and Mechanical Principles. Mechanics must involve the Conception of *Force*; —Chemistry, the Conception of *Elementary Composition*; —Physiology, the Conception of *Vital Powers*. Each science must advance by means of its *appropriate* Conceptions.[4]

One way in which it does so is through an "explication of conceptions." The assignment of increasingly more precise meanings to "force," "instantaneous velocity," and "temperature", for instance, contributed to progress within physics.

Whewell applied these interpretive principles—the fact-idea polarity and the concept of hierarchically-organized individual sciences—in the composition of a *History of the Inductive Sciences* (1837). The assumptions Whewell made about science in order to write its history are quite robust. To construe science as Whewell does is to allow the achievement of finality within history. Each individual science has a structure determined by a set of axioms that state relations among its characteristic fundamental predicates. This structure exists whether or not scientists recognize it. In principle, scientists may achieve knowledge of the axioms of a particular science.

To achieve such knowledge would be to establish necessary truths about the universe. Whewell acknowledged that this is paradoxical. On the one hand, as Hume had emphasized, experience cannot prove universality or necessity. But on the other hand, certain scientific laws appear to be both universal and necessary. Whewell sought to resolve the paradox by distinguishing the "formal content" from the "empirical content" of necessary empirical truth.

Whewell believed that necessary empirical knowledge had been achieved for the science of mechanics. The appropriate axioms were formulated by Isaac Newton. They express the empirical content of the relation of cause and effect as these ideas apply to the motions of bodies under impressed forces.

Whewell maintained that "cause" and "effect" are fundamental ideas that are applicable within every individual science. He unpacked the "formal content" of these ideas in three axioms:

1 nothing takes place without a cause,
2 effects are proportional to their causes, and
3 reaction is equal and opposite to action.[5]

This "formal content" is apprehended by the mind *a priori*—no appeal to experience is needed.

Within the science of mechanics, historical developments culminating in the work of Newton uncovered the "empirical content" of these formal axioms. Newton established that

1* bodies have no intrinsic causes of acceleration,
2* accelerations are proportional to impressed forces ($F = ma$), and
3* momentum is conserved in collisions.

Whewell maintained that by specifying the empirical content of the axioms that relate "cause" and "effect," Newton established truths that were both empirical and necessary. He declared that

> the laws of motion borrow their axiomatic character from their being merely *interpretations* of the Axioms of Causation. Those axioms, being exhibitions of the Idea of Cause under various aspects, are of the most rigorous universality and necessity. And so far as the laws of motion are exemplifications of those axioms, these laws must be no less universal and necessary. How these axioms are to be understood; in what sense *cause* and *effect*, *action* and *reaction*, are to be taken,

experience and observation did, in fact, teach inquirers on this subject: and without this teaching, the laws of motion could never have been distinctly known. If two forces act together, each must produce its effect, by the axiom of causation; and, therefore, the effects of the separate forces must be *compounded*. But a long course of discussion and experiment must instruct men of what kind this *composition* of forces is. Again, action and reaction must be equal; but much thought and some trial were needed to show what *action* and *reaction* are.[6]

Whewell restricted to mechanics the claim that necessary empirical truths had been achieved within history. He conceded that chemists had not yet uncovered the empirical content of axioms about the fundamental idea of "elective affinity", and that biologists have not yet uncovered the empirical content of axioms about the fundamental idea of "vital force." Nevertheless, it is possible that scientists someday establish the empirical content of these axioms.

Whewell's conclusion about the history of mechanics provides motivation for the study of the history of the other sciences. Whewell noted that Newton's achievement was the culmination of earlier researches by Galileo, Descartes, Huygens, and others. Perhaps the histories of astronomy, chemistry, biology, and other sciences will reveal patterns of development similar to the early stages of the history of mechanics. If so, then knowledge of the factors that led to progress in mechanics may be of value in promoting progress in these other disciplines.

Armed with basic assumptions about the fact-idea polarity and the structure of an individual science, Whewell sought to reconstruct the historical development of the various sciences. His reconstruction of the history of astronomy emphasizes the colligation of facts by ideas. It may be represented, in part, by the following sequence:[7]

Facts—diurnal motions of the stars
1 Ideas—the celestial sphere—stars are embedded on the inner surface of a spherical shell rotating around the centrally located Earth
Facts—observed motions of the Sun, Moon, and planets on the celestial sphere
2 Ideas—the ecliptic—the Sun, Moon and planets travel along a line on the celestial sphere at an angle of 23½ degrees to the celestial equator
Facts—irregular motions of the planets along the ecliptic (including retrograde motions)
3 Ideas—mathematical models for each planet—epicycle and deferent circles, eccentric circles and equant points with the Earth placed at (or near) the center (Ptolemy)
Facts—Ptolemy's models
4 Ideas—the Earth revolves around the stationary Sun, rotating on an axis inclined 23½ degrees to its plane of revolution; Mercury, Venus, Mars, Jupiter and Saturn also revolve around the Sun (Copernicus)

Facts—examined telescopically, Venus displays a full range of phases (Galileo)

5 Ideas—only mathematical models that place Venus in an orbit around the Sun can be true of the universe

Facts—planets' observed motions along the ecliptic

6 Ideas—planets move in elliptical orbits, subject to a law of areas, with periods proportional to the 3/2 power of their distances from the Sun (Kepler)

Facts—planets moving in orbits that satisfy Kepler's laws

7 Ideas—a planet's motion is determined by the combination of its inertial motion and a $1/R^2$ central force directed toward the Sun (Newton)

Facts—deviations of the motions of Jupiter and Saturn from Keplerian ellipses

8 Ideas—universal gravitational attraction, which requires that the mutual attractions of Jupiter and Saturn be taken into account in the calculations of their orbits (Newton)

Facts—irregularities in the motion of the Moon

9 Ideas—the asymmetric mass distribution of the Earth—polar flattening, equatorial bulge (subsequently confirmed by measurements made in Peru and Lapland)

Whewell's emphasis throughout is on the incorporation of past results in present theories. He maintained that the historical development of astronomy resembles the confluence of tributaries to form a river.

The "tributary–river" view displays progress in science as a process of unification. (Figure 1.1) Joseph Priestley had emphasized this connection between progress and unification in the *History and Present State of Electricity* (1767). He concluded that the history of researches into electrical phenomena displays a progressive incorporation of diverse experimental findings under a decreasing

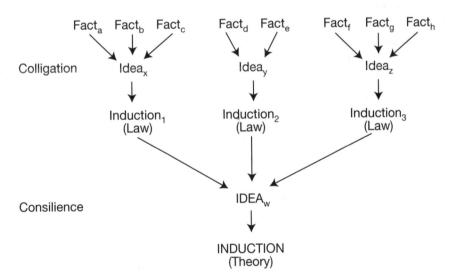

Figure 1.1 Whewell's "tributary–river" view of scientific progress

number of general principles.[8] Whewell did not refer to this anticipation of his view, although he did cite several of Priestley's accounts of particular discoveries of electrical phenomena.

Whewell insisted that even discredited theories may contribute tributaries to a river. Commenting on the "revolution" inaugurated by Copernicus, Whewell observed that Copernicus

> retained epicycles and eccentrics, altering their center of motion; that is, he retained what was *true* in the old system, translating it into his own.[9]

Whewell overstated the case for the Ptolemaic models. What is "true" about these models is only that they could be used to predict planetary positions along the zodiac. Copernicus needed to retain epicycles and eccentrics in order to achieve comparable predictive success.

Whewell's position seems to be that, because Copernicus made important contributions to astronomy, his applications of the ideas of his predecessors also must count as progressive. Whewell took a similar position on the relationship between Lavoisier's oxygen theory and the phlogiston theory it replaced.

According to the phlogiston theory, the burning of metals releases an invisible gaseous substance called "phlogiston" (φ), e.g.,

1   zinc   ⟶   calx of zinc + φ
       (calx of zinc + φ)

Lavoisier interpreted calcination by reference to the idea that there is a component of the atmosphere—oxygen—that combines with a metal to form its calx, *viz.*,

1*   zinc + oxygen   ⟶   zinc oxide
       (calx)

He claimed to have established a "revolution" in chemistry, in part by taking metals to be elementary substances and calces to be compounds.

In Whewell's reconstruction, emphasis is on continuity rather than revolutionary overthrow. He insisted that the phlogiston theory should receive credit for establishing that calcination, reduction and respiration are related processes. Phlogiston theorists interpreted the reduction of the calx of zinc to the metal as follows:

2   calx of zinc + charcoal   ⟶   zinc
       (rich in φ)   (calx of zinc + φ)

The phlogiston theory thus established facts subsequently interpreted correctly by the oxygen theory. Whewell maintained that the phlogiston theory was a contribution to progress in chemistry—a "tributary" to the "river"—even though there is no such thing as phlogiston.

Whewell's fundamental project was to construct a philosophy of science upon inspection of the history of science. The principal evaluative standard that he claimed to have found in the history of science is the "consilience of inductions."[10] Consilience is a criterion of progressive theory-replacement. It requires, as necessary conditions of the acceptability of the replacement of one theory by another that

1 the successor theory be consistent;
2 the successor theory be more inclusive than its predecessor. The range of facts subsumed by the successor theory must be greater than the range subsumed by its predecessor; and
3 the increase in subsumptive power be accompanied by a gain in simplicity.

Whewell recognized that a gain in subsumptive power may be achieved by conjoining two previously successful theories. He realized, however, that this is not what happens in the history of science. The confluence of tributaries to form rivers is accomplished by means of the superposition of ideas upon facts such that the facts are interpreted in a new way. Whewell maintained that when consilience is achieved

> particulars form the general truth, not by being merely enumerated and added together, but by being seen in a new light.[11]

A successor theory satisfies the simplicity requirement only if it integrates, and not just conjoins, the relevant facts. For example, Newton's theory of gravitational attraction achieves an integration of Kepler's laws. Kepler's third law, which correlates the periods and mean distances of the planets to the Sun—

$$\left(\frac{T_1}{T_2}\right)^2 = \left(\frac{D_1}{D_2}\right)^3$$ —is a successful colligation of observed planetary motions. But as

formulated by Kepler, the law had no theoretical rationale. It was only a mathematical regularity that "saves appearances." Kepler's first two laws—the law of elliptical orbits and the area law—also "save appearances." However, Kepler's "magnetic vortex" theory did provide a qualitative theoretical rationale for elliptical orbits.

Newton's integration of the three laws is a superposition of the ideas of inertial motion and $1/R^2$ central forces upon the facts of planetary motions. Newton showed that if a planet were a point-mass moving subject to a rectilinear inertial tendency and a $1/R^2$ force directed toward the Sun, conceived to be a stationary point-center of force, then Kepler's first two laws must hold. He also showed that any two non-interacting moving point-masses, subject to the principle of rectilinear inertia and a $1/R^2$ force directed toward the Sun, would conform to Kepler's third law. Before Newton's achievement, there was no connection known between Kepler's third law and the first two laws. Afterwards, a unification has been accomplished. Independent tributaries have been shown to merge into a river.

Of course, the assumptions that underlie Newton's analysis are false. The Sun is not a point center of force (there is a *reciprocal* gravitational force between the Sun and a planet), planets are not point-masses, and neither are they non-interacting. Newton himself was well aware of this. After deriving Kepler's laws from these false assumptions, he subsequently appealed to the idea of *universal* gravitational attraction to explain why the agreement between these laws and planetary motions is only approximate.

There has been nearly universal agreement that Newton's account of Kepler's laws qualifies as a superposition of ideas upon facts in which the laws are seen in a new light with a gain in simplicity and unification. Whewell maintained that consilience requires a gain in simplicity. But he failed to provide a criterion of simplicity.[12] In the absence of a suitable criterion, one must turn to Whewell's specific judgments about developments in the history of science.

Whewell praised Newton's theory of mechanics as the supreme example of the achievement of consilience within the history of science. Newton accounted for facts about planetary motions, the tides, the motions of pendulums, and so forth, by reference to a theory about inertial motion, the direct proportionality of force and acceleration, the equality of action and reaction, and universal gravitational attraction.

Newton's theory is immensely powerful. As noted above, it explains, not only why lower-level correlations hold, but also why they hold only approximately. Deviations from Kepler's laws by Jupiter, Saturn and the Moon are accounted for by applications of the theory itself. This is accomplished by taking account of the relevant conditions under which the theory is applied: the influence of a third body in the case of the motions of Jupiter and Saturn, and the asymmetry of the Earth in the case of the motion of the Moon. It would seem from this analysis that a theory qualifies as simple when its explanatory power is increased without introducing new assumptions into the theory itself.

But how is simplicity to be estimated in cases in which a theory is modified in its application to additional facts? Whewell noted that the Corpuscular Theory of Newton and the Wave Theory of Young and Fresnel both had been adjusted to fit the facts of diffraction, polarization and double refraction. He maintained that the modifications of the corpuscular theory were complex and disharmonious. Supporters of the corpuscular theory tacked on an assumption about "fits of easy transmission and reflection" (Newton) to account for the colors produced by the contact of thin plates, an assumption about the "asymmetrical sides" of a corpuscle to account for polarization, and an assumption about different forces exerted along different axes of a crystal to account for double refraction. To Whewell these assumptions seemed to be *ad hoc* devices to blunt the force of negative evidence. Whewell held that supporters of the wave theory, by contrast, had accounted for these phenomena by means of the "simple and harmonious" assumption that the propagation of light produces transverse waves. However, he did not develop a general criterion of comparative simplicity.

Because Whewell did not specify a criterion of simplicity, one cannot determine, in an arbitrarily selected case of theory-replacement, whether the conditions *necessary* for consilience are present. However, Whewell did specify a *sufficient* condition of consilience. That criterion is the achievement of "undesigned scope." He maintained that

> the evidence in favour of our induction is of a much higher and more
> forcible character when it enables us to explain and determine cases
> of a kind different from those which were contemplated in the formation
> of our hypothesis.[13]

Undesigned scope is a criterion of acceptability first recommended by Whewell's contemporary John Herschel.[14]

Herschel and Whewell took undesigned scope to involve both psychological novelty and logical novelty. Psychological novelty arises when an application of a theory is both successful and unexpected. Logical novelty arises upon successful application of a theory to cases different in kind from those taken into account when the theory was formulated. Unfortunately, neither Herschel nor Whewell specified an objective standard to determine when cases are "different in kind." Herschel, for instance, included among achievements of undesigned scope Fresnel's derivation from the wave theory that there is a bright spot at the center of the shadow cast by a metal disk illumined by a point source (a prediction confirmed experimentally by Poisson).[15] This consequence of the wave theory was surprising and unexpected, but the experimental confirmation of this consequence hardly could be said to be an application to a new kind of case. A better example of the application of a theory to a new kind of case is LaPlace's application of his theory of heat transfer to account for a puzzling discrepancy between calculated and observed velocities of sound.[16] Herschel and Whewell both emphasized that LaPlace had succeeded in extending the theory of heat to a new kind of phenomena.[17]

But even in this case, the "logical novelty" of the application may be challenged. Among the deductive consequences of the theory of heat is the consequence that heat is generated upon compression of an elastic fluid. What LaPlace did was to recognize that the propagation of sound involves the compression of an elastic fluid. In retrospect, he seems only to have made an obvious (once you see it) application of his theory.

In the absence of an objective standard of "newness" of applications, one must fall back upon the psychological impact of the application under consideration. Be that as it may, to judge that undesigned scope is achieved because an application of a theory was "unexpected" is to presuppose that the theory is more acceptable, given the display of undesigned scope, than if the newly-recognized application had been entertained at the time the theory was formulated.

Whewell defended this position by an appeal to the history of science. He claimed that no theory has displayed undesigned scope and subsequently been abandoned. Every theory that unexpectedly has accounted for a new range of phenomena, without specific adjustment for that purpose, has passed the test of survival. He insisted that if a theory

> of itself and without adjustment for the purpose, gives us the rule and reason of a class of facts not contemplated in its construction, we have a criterion of its reality, which has never yet been produced in favour of a falsehood.[18]

Whewell thus appealed to the history of science to justify a criterion of scientific progress. Those who disagree are invited to specify a case in which undesigned scope is realized, but the theory in question later is recognized to be false.

Unfortunately, given a reasonably strict standard of "unexpectedness," the achievement of undesigned scope is rare within the history of science. Thus even if Whewell's historical justification is successful, the criterion of undesigned scope singles out very few theories. Most questions about possible consilience must be answered by reference to the vague requirements of inclusiveness and simplicity.

It might seem that Whewell's analysis of scientific progress is circular. He begins with methodological assumptions about how science develops, formulates a history of science consistent with these assumptions, and then "discovers" upon investigation of the history of science that the consilience of inductions is a criterion of scientific progress. This procedure is not viciously circular. The initial assumptions are not identical with the subsequently discovered criterion. Nonetheless, Whewell's starting-point is consistent with, and points toward, an emphasis on inclusiveness and simplicity. Whewell begins with a fact-idea distinction and the Aristotelian concept of a series of distinct sciences, each with a set of axioms that state relations among the "fundamental ideas" of that science. Given this starting point, it is natural to view scientific progress as a continuing superposition of increasingly precise ideas upon an expanding factual base. Past results are subsumed and reinterpreted by present theories. The "consilience of inductions" is the evaluative criterion suggested by this "tributary–river" image of the history of science.

2

BREWSTER ON HOW NOT TO
DO HISTORY OF SCIENCE

David Brewster's review of Whewell's *History of the Inductive Sciences* in the *Edinburgh Review* (Brewster 1837) was unflattering. Brewster complained that Whewell's methodological prejudices had led him to misread important episodes in the history of science. In particular, Whewell was led astray by his commitment to the notion that each science has its own set of distinct and appropriate ideas.

In his section on Greek natural philosophy, Whewell attributes its failure to the indistinctness and inappropriateness of the ideas that were superimposed upon the facts. Brewster's evaluation of this claim is harsh:

> When Mr. Whewell ... states it as the cause of the failure of the Greek philosophers that the ideas which they possessed were not distinct and appropriate to the facts, he is merely using new expressions, and these somewhat cabalistic, to convey the trite information, that the Greek philosophers were ignorant ... of the art of investigating scientific truth.[1]

Brewster maintained that the failure of Greek natural philosophy was a failure to test ideas by further observations and experiments.

Whewell's "tributary–river" view of scientific progress suggests that once a distinct and appropriate idea is promulgated, scientists utilize this correct insight. Brewster called attention to Robert Hooke's neglected idea that the colors produced by thin glass plates are caused by interference of wave pulses from the first and second surfaces of the plate. Scientists at the time adopted instead Newton's inappropriate idea of "fits of easy transmission and reflection." It was not until Thomas Young's work on interference effects a century later that Hooke's "distinct and appropriate" idea was widely accepted.

Brewster also complained that Whewell's belief that all fundamental scientific discoveries require application of a "distinct and well pondered idea" led him to distort or ignore the historical record. Brewster pointed out that the history of optics reveals numerous important discoveries "in which no appropriate ideas had any share."[2] His list includes Bartholinus' discovery of double refraction, Huygens' discovery of polarization, and Malus' discovery of the polarization of light by reflection. "It cannot be questioned," he wrote, "that many of the finest discoveries in science have been the result of pure accident ."[3]

Brewster's concluding criticism of Whewell is his most effective. He argued that it is poor historiography to presume that one knows the "distinct and appropriate" ideas of the sciences, and to reconstruct the past on the basis of this presumed knowledge. Whewell was convinced that the idea of wave motion is fundamental to the science of optics. He praised the "harmonious" adjustments of the wave theory to new facts about diffraction and polarization, but criticized the "*ad hoc*" adjustments of the corpuscular theory to these same facts.

In his zeal to declare victory for the wave theory, Whewell either minimized or ignored certain recalcitrant phenomena. Whewell played down the inability of the wave theory to account for absorption. Since the rival corpuscular theory provides a plausible explanation of absorption, Whewell should have tempered his unequivocal support for the wave theory. Brewster noted, in addition, that Whewell ignored puzzling data about dispersion phenomena, metallic polarization, and the transverse fringes of grooved surfaces, data for which the wave theory had no rationale.

In defense of the wave theory, one may object that its defenders have not been allowed sufficient time to deal with this "ignored" evidence. Nevertheless, Brewster is entitled to criticize Whewell for failing to highlight these difficulties for the wave theory. Brewster concluded that we must ask

> Mr. Whewell how it happens that in a fair and honest estimate of the value of the undulatory theory, he has omitted all those discoveries which it is not able to explain?[4]

3

MILL'S OBJECTIONS TO WHEWELL'S HISTORICISM

On Whewell's appeal to *a priori* intuitions

John Stuart Mill found much to criticize in Whewell's theory of scientific progress. His basic objection was that Whewell had introduced *a priori* considerations into empirical science. Mill agreed with H.L. Mansel, an early critic of Whewell's position on necessary empirical knowledge. Mansel insisted that *a priori* principles and empirical generalizations differ in kind. According to Mansel

> the separation between the two classes of truths is such that no conceivable progress of science can ever convert the one to the other.[1]

Mill conceded to Whewell that fundamental ideas such as "force," "elective affinity," and "polarity" have been important in the historical development of the sciences. However, he held that these ideas arose within experience as a result of perceived resemblances and differences, analogical comparisons and abstraction.

Mill insisted that the appropriateness of general concepts depends on the accuracy of scientists' judgments about points of agreement and difference among phenomena. The appropriateness of concepts does not depend on an *a priori* intuition of the mind.[2] Nor does the clarity of concepts depend upon intuitive insight. Mill insisted that

> the principal requisites ... of clear conceptions are habits of attentive observation and extensive experience and a memory which receives and retains an exact image of what is observed.[3]

Scientists achieve the elimination of ambiguities, the reduction of vagueness, and the formulation of precise definitions during the course of empirical investigations. There is no place in the scientific enterprise for a Kantian *a priori* derivation of the meanings of fundamental ideas.

After purging the "tributary–river" image of its superfluous Kantian baggage, Mill took issue with Whewell's understanding of the process of successive inductive generalization responsible for creating the river. Mill registered three complaints against Whewell's position on induction:

1 Whewell fails to recognize the crucial role of inductive schemata in establishing the confluence of tributaries into rivers;
2 Not every process labeled "inductive" by Whewell qualifies as a *bona fide* inductive process; and
3 Whewell limits induction to the context of scientific discovery. He fails to recognize that inductive schemata are rules of proof appropriate within the context of justification.

On Whewell's "try it and see" theory of induction

Mill declared that

> I cannot help expressing astonishment that a philosopher of Dr. Whewell's abilities and attainments should have written an elaborate treatise on the philosophy of induction, in which he recognizes absolutely no mode of induction except that of trying hypothesis after hypothesis until one is found which fits the phenomena.[4]

Mill maintained that there are specific inductive methods that scientists implement in their search for causal relations. These methods—agreement, difference, concomitant variations, and residues—had been discussed earlier by David Hume and John Herschel, among others. Those inductive generalizations that pick out causal relations among phenomena contribute to scientific progress.

By "causal relation" Mill understood a correlation of two types of events that is both invariable and unconditional. He noted that Hume had taken causal relations to be nothing but constant sequential conjunctions of the members of the members of two classes of events.[5] Mill recognized that if Hume were correct to equate causal relation and constant conjunction, then all invariable sequences would be on a par. However, Mill believed that we know that some invariable sequences are causal and some are not. For example, cutting the stem of an apple is the cause of its subsequent fall to the Earth. But day is not the cause of night, despite the fact that our experience has revealed this sequence to be invariable. Mill thus distinguished causal regularities from non-causal regularities. Mill's insistence that causal relations are "unconditional" reflects his belief that there is something *necessary* about such relations. However, there is a certain vagueness in his account of unconditionality. We know a sequence to be "unconditional," he wrote, only if we believe

> not only that the antecedent condition always *has* been followed by the consequent, but that, as long as the present constitution of things endures, it always *will* be so.[6]

The "present constitution of things" presumably is determined by the "ultimate laws of nature." So long as these fundamental laws hold, certain invariant sequences are unconditional—bodies unsupported near the Earth are accelerated toward its surface, sodium samples react with chlorine, etc.

The sequence day-night is not unconditional on this understanding. It would not be a violation of the basic laws of the universe, for instance, if the Earth's rotation rate were one per revolution (like that of the Moon). Despite his failure to stipulate the "ultimate laws of nature" that circumscribe the possibilities for unconditional relations, Mill was optimistic about scientists' abilities to identify causal relations. He declared that

> it is experience itself which teaches us that one uniformity of sequence
> is conditional and another unconditional.[7]

A causal relation may be revealed upon application of the inductive method of agreement:

Instance	Circumstances	Phenomena
1	$A\,B\,E\,F$	p
2	$A\,C\,D$	p
3	$A\,B\,D\,E$	p
4	$A\,C\,F\,G$	p

$\therefore$ A is the cause (*qua* sufficient condition) of p.

For instance, substances of various composition and geometry are observed to sink in water. A listing of circumstances present reveals a common property—each body that sinks is heavier than an equal volume of water. Substitution into the agreement schema supports the conclusion that the greater density of sinking bodies is the cause of that behavior. The agreement schema also may be superimposed upon observations made of cud-chewing animals. Deer, cows, giraffes and oxen have a property in common. They all have cloven hooves. One might take that property to be the cause of the cud-chewing behavior. Aristotle had discussed this relationship. He pointed out that the aforementioned animals all have multiply-chambered stomachs as well. The method of agreement may mislead the investigator if there is an unlisted relevant circumstance in common to the instances considered.

Mill was aware of this limitation. He conceded that applications of the agreement schema are effective only if every relevant circumstance is listed. He noted that there is a further limitation, as well. In the above schema, there may be a plurality of causes of phenomenon p. It is possible that B causes p in instances 1 and 3, and that C causes p in instances 2 and 4. Because the possibility of a plurality of causes cannot be ruled out as a possibility, Mill directed the investigator to place greater reliance on the inductive method of difference:

Instance	Circumstances	Phenomena
1	$A\ B\ C$	p
2	$B\ C$	

$\therefore A$ is the cause (*qua* necessary condition) of p.

For instance, air confined over water supports combustion (for a time); air in which a candle has burned until extinction does not support combustion. Substitution into the difference schema supports the conclusion that the prior burning of the candle is the cause of the loss of the ability of air to support combustion.

The method of difference is not limited by the possibility of a plurality of causes. It does require, however, that a complete inventory of possibly relevant circumstances has been made. If there is some circumstance D that is present in instance 1 and absent in instance 2, it is possible that D, and not A, is the cause of p.[8]

The method of concomitant variations is a third inductive procedure for the discovery of causal relations:

Instance	Circumstances	Phenomena
1	$A^+\ B\ C$	p^+
2	$A^0\ B\ C$	p^0
3	$A^-\ B\ C$	p^-

$\therefore A$ is the cause of p.

Pascal's Puy de Dôme experiment fits this pattern. A barometer was carried up a small mountain. The height of mercury in the barometer decreased with increasing height. Pascal maintained that the relevant varying circumstances is the weight of the atmosphere above the surface of the mercury. He concluded that it is the decrease in pressure exerted by the "sea of air" during ascent of the mountain that is the cause of the decrease in mercury level.

The method of residues is a fourth inductive procedure for the discovery of causal connections:

Instance	Circumstances	Phenomena
1	$A\ B\ C$	$a\ b\ c$
2	B is known to be the cause of b	
3	C is known to be the cause of c	

$\therefore A$ is the cause of a.

Mill cited Arago's demonstration that a magnetized needle, suspended by a twisted thread and released, comes to rest sooner when placed over a sheet of copper as an application of the method of residues.[9] Arago subtracted the known damping effect in air alone from the observed damping effect in the presence of the copper plate. He attributed the cause of the increased damping of the needle's vibrations to the presence of the copper plate.

At one point, Mill made an extreme claim for these four inductive methods. In response to criticism by Whewell, he declared that if any discoveries ever were made by observation and experiment, "it was by processes reducible to one or other of those methods."[10] However, this was a slip on Mill's part. He frequently emphasized that the most impressive scientific achievements were the results of applications of a hypothetico-deductive method. Newtonian mechanics is a case in point. Its success depends on hypotheses about inertial motion and the relationship between force and motion, and not upon application of inductive schemata.

Mill noted that if two or more causal agents combine to produce an effect of the same kind that each separately would produce, then the inductive methods are unavailing. For example, one cannot use the inductive schemata to establish the causes of a resultant force. This is because numerous component-force combinations may produce a given resultant force. In Figure 3.1 resultant force F_R may be the effect of component forces F_1 and F_2, or F_3 and F_4, or countless other possible combinations.

Mill shared Whewell's conviction about the importance of wide-ranging theories like Newtonian mechanics. Since such theories do not arise upon application of inductive methods, Mill concluded that

> to the Deductive Method ... the human mind is indebted for its most conspicuous triumphs in the investigation of nature. To it we owe all the theories by which vast and complicated phenomena are embraced

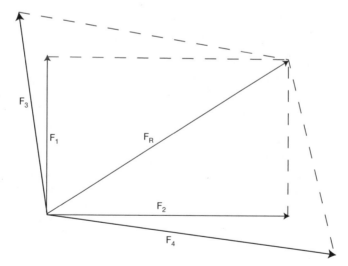

Figure 3.1 The composition of forces

under a few simple laws, which, considered as the laws of those great phenomena, could never have been detected by their direct study.[11]

Given Mill's position on the importance of the hypothetico-deductive method, he is entitled to criticize Whewell only for neglecting to credit the role of inductive methods in the formulation of low-level generalizations like the laws of Galileo, Snel and Boyle.

On Whewell's failure to distinguish induction from description

Mill's next complaint about Whewell's theory of scientific discovery is that Whewell's conception of induction is too broad. According to Mill, Whewell is guilty of taking the mere description of observed phenomena to be an induction. Mill and Whewell engaged in an extended debate over the status of Kepler's first law. Whewell took Kepler's achievement to be a superposition of the simplifying and unifying idea of an ellipse upon the facts of planetary locations. According to Whewell, this colligation of facts is a *bona fide* inductive generalization.

Mill disagreed. He insisted that, although every induction involves a colligation of facts, some colligations of facts are mere descriptions that do not qualify as inductions. Mill maintained that Kepler merely described a set of data points as an ellipse. Mill asked the reader to assume the vantage point of an observer in space above the plane of revolution of the planets. Suppose a planet left a visible track behind in space. The observer then would see an ellipse. No induction is required. Mill declared that

> if the path was visible, no one I think would dispute that to identify it with an ellipse is to describe it.[12]

According to Mill, Kepler's first law is basically a description. The only inductions involved are 1) to generalize that a planet continues to trace out a given elliptical path, and 2) to interpolate intermediate positions along the ellipse between observed locations.

Mill's analysis is flawed. John Venn, commenting on the Whewell–Mill debate, emphasized that a planet only approximates motion in an ellipse.[13] Mill surely was aware that LaPlace and others had applied a theory of perturbations to account for irregularities in the motions of Jupiter and Saturn. Mill's hypothetical observer, possessed of super-keen eyesight, would not "see" an ellipse in the trail left by a planet. Kepler's achievement was not to produce a straightforward description of what is, or could be, seen.

Inductive schemata as rules of proof

Mill also complained that Whewell had failed to account for the role of induction in the context of justification. He insisted that scientific inquiry is a search for causal connections, correlations that are both invariable and unconditional. He maintained that, although the history of science may provide evidence that a correlation has been invariable, it cannot establish that the correlation will continue to be invariable, much less that it is unconditional. Whewell was wrong to suggest otherwise.

It is inductive logic, and not the history of science, that warrants causal connections. Mill declared that

> the business of Inductive Logic is to provide rules and models ... to which, if inductive arguments conform, those arguments are conclusive, and not otherwise.[14]

He insisted that

> even if they [the Inductive Methods] were not methods of discovery, it would not be the less true that they are the sole methods of proof.[15]

Just as *modus ponens* and *modus tollens* stipulate the form of valid deductive arguments, so also the inductive schemata stipulate the form of those inductive arguments that succeed in proving causal connections.

Mill began his discussion of the context of justification in the *System of Logic* with the claim that all four inductive schemata are rules of proof of causal connections. However, he soon retreated to the position that only the method of difference can prove causal connections.[16]

But how can the difference schema provide proof of causal connection? Suppose the schema is instantiated as follows:

Instance	Circumstances	Phenomena
1	$A\ B\ C$	p
2	$B\ C$	—

To establish that A causes p one would have to prove that

1 A, B, and C are the *only* possible causes of p, and
2 the schema is instantiated in the same way whenever circumstances of type ABC and BC are present (and not just for instances "1" and "2" above).

Mill maintained that these two conditions are fulfilled in certain cases. However, he cited just one instance, Newton's derivation of Kepler's law of areas. According to Mill, instantiation of the difference schema proves that a $1/R^2$ force emanating from the Sun is the cause of a planet's obeying Kepler's second law (given that a planet would move rectilinearly in accordance with

Newton's law of inertia in the absence of the central force directed toward the Sun). In this instantiation

Instance	Circumstances	Phenomena
1	$A\ B\ C$	$a\ b\ c$
2	$B\ C$	$b\ c$

A is a $1/R^2$ central force directed toward the Sun,
B, C are all the circumstances applicable to a planet other than exposure to a $1/R^2$ central force
a is the direct proportionality between the area swept by the planet-Sun line and the time taken to traverse the corresponding segment of its orbit, and
b, c are all motions of the planet other than a.[17]

Mill held that Newton proved that, given circumstances B, C, no force law other than A could produce a. Given $F \propto 1/R^{2+d}$, increasing positive or negative values of d produce increasing divergences from Keplerian ellipses and the law of areas. Mill concluded that Newton had established that the Sun's $1/R^2$ attractive force is invariably and unconditionally responsible for Kepler's law of areas (again, given the inertial tendency of a planet). Mill emphasized that the warrant for this claim is logic—instantiation of the difference schema—and not history.

Mill's instantiation of the difference schema is suspect, however. He has not described circumstances B and C. He merely uses "B, C" to stand for "every relevant circumstance except A."

This will not do. To use the difference schema to prove a causal connection one must *prove* that A, B and C are the only relevant circumstances. Mill could not do this. Condition 1 above is not fulfilled.

Mill was unsuccessful as well in his attempt to justify condition 2. He sought to justify this condition by appeal to the general principle of the uniformity of nature. But "nature is uniform" is itself the conclusion of inductive reasoning. Our evidence for uniformity is individual observed regularities. It would seem that Mill's justification is circular. Inductive arguments are cited to support the conclusion that inductive reasoning is sound.

Mill conceded the circularity involved in his justification. He insisted, however, that the inductive method of simple enumeration possesses unique advantages that enable the theorist to establish the uniformity postulate. He maintained that

> the precariousness of the method of simple enumeration is in an inverse ratio to the largeness of the generalization. The process is delusive and insufficient, exactly in proportion as the subject matter of the observation is special and limited in extent. As the sphere widens, this unscientific method becomes less and less liable to mislead; and the most universal class of truths, the law of causation for instance ... [is] duly and satisfactorily proved by that method alone.[18]

Enumerative induction may mislead in the case of individual generalizations (e.g., "all swans are white"), but not in the case of the all-inclusive generalization that "for every phenomenon there is some set of circumstances upon which it is invariably and unconditionally dependent." Mill declared that no exception is known to this uniformity postulate; every seeming exception has been traced either to the presence of a circumstance normally absent or to the absence of a circumstance normally present.[19]

Mill's appeal to experience to prove that nature has been and will continue to be uniform is not successful. Even if it were true that there never has been a *bona fide* exception to the principle of uniformity, it would not follow that no exception is possible. David Hume had insisted on this point a century before before Mill's attempted justification.[20]

4

PROGRESS THROUGH REDUCTION

Incorporation was an important emphasis within logical empiricist philosophy of science. Logical empiricism was the dominant philosophy of science during the period immediately after World War II. Its program was based on the following assumptions about science and its interpretation:

1 The theories, laws and experimental findings of science are (or may be expressed as) declarative sentences;
2 These sentences may be reconstructed in the symbolism of formal logic;
3 The task of philosophy of science is to specify criteria for the evaluation of laws and theories. Once suitable criteria have been formulated, they may be applied, for instance, to assess the adequacy of proposed explanations, to determine the degree of evidential support provided a law by observational evidence, or to gauge the rationality of theory choice;
4 An important part of the task of formulating an evaluative criterion is to specify an "explication" of the appropriate epistemological term, e.g., "law," "theory," "confirmation," "explanation," "reduction," *et al.* An explication is a logical relationship among sentences.
5 The evaluation of theories is possible because one can formulate observation reports that are logically independent of the theories compared.
6 Questions about the rationality of developments in the history of science can be decided by comparing the theories which were dominant within a domain of science at different times; and
7 Although the history of science may provide clues about the relations among theories, laws, and observation reports, what is important to the philosophy of science is the *logic* of these relations.[1]

Logical empiricists took scientific progress to consist, in part, in the replacement of theories by superior competing theories. They sought to develop criteria to assess the relative acceptability of theories. Ernest Nagel, for instance, formulated a theory of "reduction" that stipulates formal and empirical criteria for the replacement of one theory by a second, more inclusive, theory.

Nagel's conditions for heterogeneous reduction

Often the reduced theory includes terms not found in the reducing theory. Nagel labeled such cases instances of "heterogeneous reduction." The relationship between kinetic molecular theory and classical thermodynamics is an example. The terms "temperature" and "pressure" do not occur in the axioms of kinetic molecular theory. A requirement for the reduction of classical thermodynamics is that these terms be linked to the theoretical terms of the reducing theory, e.g., "number of molecules" and "velocity of a molecule."

In addition, successful reduction requires that the laws of the reduced theory be derivable from the interpreted axioms of the reducing theory. In the case of thermodynamics, the axioms of kinetic molecular theory, in conjunction with statements that link molecular motions to temperature and pressure, imply the classical laws of Boyle, Charles and Gay-Lussac. Nagel emphasized that the derivability requirement is fulfilled only if the terms common to both theories have the same meaning in each theory.[2]

Nagel conceded that satisfaction of the two formal necessary conditions— connectability and derivability—is not sufficient to establish reduction. There are empirical requirements as well.

The reducing theory must be supported by evidence over and above the evidence that supports the reduced theory. This requirement blocks putative "reducing" theories invented solely to imply the laws of the original theory. The kinetic molecular theory qualifies on this score. There is abundant evidence for it from domains other than thermodynamics.

The reducing theory also must prove fertile. Its theoretical assumptions must give rise to further developments of the original theory. The kinetic molecular theory qualifies on this score as well. It was modified subsequently by van der Waals to take account of intermolecular forces and the finite size of molecules. Van der Waals derived a formula[3] from these assumptions that reproduces observed pressure–volume–temperature data over a wider range of values than does the ideal gas law of the original kinetic molecular theory.

Nagel conceded that his theory of reduction is applicable only to theories which are , or can be, formalized as deductive systems. Despite this limitation, he insisted that the four conditions of reduction are fulfilled by important episodes in the history of science. Such episodes are important contributions to scientific progress. Nagel declared that

> the phenomenon of a relatively autonomous theory becoming absorbed
> by, or reduced to, some other more inclusive theory is an undeniable
> and recurrent feature of the history of modern science.[4]

However, he supported this claim about the history of science primarily by a detailed application of the criteria for reduction to the transition from classical thermodynamics to statistical mechanics.

Feyerabend on reduction within the history of science

Paul Feyerabend noted that other *prima facie* candidates for reduction fail to fulfill Nagel's criteria. He pointed out that the transition from Galileo's law of falling bodies to Newton's gravitation theory, for example, does not satisfy the derivability requirement. Galileo's law is not a deductive consequence of Newton's theory. In Newtonian mechanics, gravitational force, and hence the mutual acceleration of two bodies, increases with decreasing distance. A body in free fall toward the earth has a motion in which acceleration continually is increasing. But Galileo's law states that the acceleration is constant. The Newtonian laws imply Galileo's law only in conjunction with the factually false claim that distance of fall / radius of earth = 0.[5]

Nor does Newtonian mechanics reduce to general relativity theory. The transition from Newtonian mechanics to general relativity fails to satisfy Nagel's criterion of connectability. The term "length" is a property term in Newtonian mechanics. "Newtonian length" is independent of signal velocity, gravitational attraction, and the motion of the observer who measures it. "Relativistic length," by contrast, is a relational term which is dependent on signal velocity, gravitational fields, and the motion of the observer.[6] Feyerabend concluded that, since "Newtonian length" and "relativistic length" are concepts of different logical type, Newtonian mechanics is not reducible to general relativity theory. He also maintained that Newtonian mechanics cannot be reduced to quantum mechanics.[7]

Feyerabend even raised doubts about the supposed reduction of classical thermodynamics to statistical mechanics. He maintained that "temperature" in classical thermodynamics is not the same concept as "temperature" in statistical mechanics. The former concept is defined with reference to reversible processes "operating between two levels, L^* and L^{**}, each of these levels being characterized by one and the same temperature throughout."[8] The latter concept, by contrast,

> allows for fluctuations of heat back and forth between two levels of temperature and, therefore, again contradicts one of the laws implicit in the "established usage" of the thermodynamic temperature.[9]

Feyerabend thus argued that several *prima facie* cases of reduction do not satisfy Nagel's criteria. He was concerned to establish that successive high-level theories in the history of science are not related by a relation of incorporation. Marshall Spector agreed with Feyerabend that Nagel's criteria of reduction are too restrictive. However, he maintained that there are genuine instances of reduction—acknowledged to be such by practicing scientists—which ought, but do not, qualify on Nagel's criteria. Spector declared that an example of reducibility without deducibility is provided by "tide theory," which no one would deny is reducible to mechanics—Newton's great unification accomplished this. Yet specific tidal regularities (for particular places) simply cannot be deduced from basic mechanical laws (plus boundary conditions).[10]

Spector's objection is off-target. Nagel restricted the reduction relation to theories that can be formalized as deductive systems. "Tide theory" does not meet this restriction.

Hilary Putnam responded to Feyerabend's challenge by suggesting that what is involved in reduction is only the deduction from the new theory of a suitable approximation of the old theory. For example, classical geometrical optics is not deducible from (and hence is not reducible to) electromagnetic field theory, but a suitable approximation of classical geometrical optics is so deducible. Putnam emphasized that all that should be expected from a theory of reduction is a set of criteria for the reduction of an approximate version of the replaced theory.[11] If approximate versions are permitted, then transitions from Newtonian mechanics to special relativity theory, and to quantum mechanics, qualify as instances of "reduction" as well.

Feyerabend replied that this is not enough. Consider the transition from geometrical optics (G) to electromagnetic theory (E). Putnam had conceded that G and E are inconsistent, but had insisted that there exists a theory G^* which does follow from E. Feyerabend was unimpressed. He pointed out that of course all the deductive consequences of E follow from E. This is trivial. But the original interest in reduction had been an interest in relationships between actual scientific theories. Feyerabend maintained that transitions between theories, *qua historical realities*, do not satisfy the requirements of Nagelian reduction.[12]

Surveying the dispute, Nagel responded that a focus on actual scientific practice supports Putnam's position. He noted that, the derivation of laws from theories often involves simplification or approximation. For example, the law of the simple pendulum[13] is derived from Newtonian theory only on the assumptions that all the mass of the pendulum is concentrated at a point in its bob, that the distance of this point from the center of the Earth is constant during oscillations, and that the angle of oscillation is small. Similarly, Kepler's third law[14] is derived from Newtonian theory only on the assumptions that the mass of the Sun is infinite in comparison to the masses of the two planets under consideration, and that no third planet is present to perturb their motions around the Sun. It is not a telling objection to the theory of reduction to call attention to the fact that the reduced laws are only good approximations to the deductive consequences of the reducing theory. According to Nagel, it suffices that

in homogeneous reductions the reduced laws are either derivable from the explanatory premises, or are good approximations to the laws derivable from the latter.[15]

31

Feyerabend's incommensurability thesis

Feyerabend replied that it is heterogeneous reductions that are of greatest interest. He insisted that successful high-level theories do not incorporate their predecessors. The Chinese-box view of scientific progress is incorrect. Indeed Feyerabend recommended the following incommensurability thesis:

> what happens when transition is made from a restricted theory T^* to a wider theory T (which is capable of covering all the phenomena which have been covered by T^*) is something more radical than incorporation of the *unchanged* theory T^* into the wider context of T. What happens is rather a complete replacement of the ontology of T^* by the ontology of T, and a corresponding change in the meanings of all descriptive terms of T^* (provided these terms are still employed).[16]

Although Feyerabend did not specify explicitly what counts as a "change of meaning," he did indicate that the meaning of a term is a function of the theory in which it occurs.[17] To his critics it appeared that Feyerabend was committed to the position that any change in the structure of a theory is also a change in meanings of the terms of the theory.

Nagel maintained that Feyerabend had overstated the case for meaning variance. He insisted that not every term is

> so deeply embedded in the totality of assumptions constituting a particular theory that they can be understood only within the framework of the theory.[18]

Nagel contrasted the term "electron spin," which is "deeply embedded" in quantum theory, and the term "electron charge," which is not bound to a specific theory, but retains a meaning that is invariant across various theories. Since many scientific concepts are like "electric charge" in this respect, Feyerabend's thesis is false. Dudley Shapere complained that alternative axiomatization ought not count as a change in the meanings of the terms of a theory.[19] Peter Achinstein emphasized that it would be stretching the phrase "change of meaning" beyond all usefulness if every alteration of a theory were to count as a "change of meaning" of its terms. He suggested a number of cases of theory-modification that presumably do not change the meanings of the terms involved. His best illustration is perhaps the alteration of the Bohr theory of the hydrogen atom to permit the electron to describe elliptical orbits around the nucleus. Surely the inclusion of elliptical orbits among those orbits permitted the electron does not alter the meaning of "electron."[20]

Achinstein and Shapere professed to be unable to see how incommensurable theories can be compared. Achinstein pointed out that if theories T and T'' are incommensurable, if no term in T has the same meaning as a term in T'', then T'' cannot contradict T. But it would appear that a theory may deny what is asserted by some other theory. For example, the Bohr theory, in which the angular momentum of an electron is quantized, appears to be a denial of the classical theory of the electrodynamics of moving charged bodies.[21]

In reply to Achinstein, Feyerabend correctly stated that Achinstein had attempted to defend the following thesis:

> it must be possible for two theories employing many of the same terms to be incompatible .... And this presupposes that at least some of the common terms have the same meaning in both theories.[22]

Feyerabend sought to refute this thesis by citing examples of pairs of competing theories which do not share any element of meaning. But surely this is not enough. Achinstein's thesis is that it is *possible* for competing theories employing common terms to be incompatible. This thesis cannot be refuted by citing examples of competing, but incommensurable, theories.

However, in the course of his discussion of specific incommensurable theories, Feyerabend did sharpen the issue. He conceded that not every change in theory produces a change of meaning. For instance, given T = classical celestial mechanics, and T^* = classical celestial mechanics with a slightly changed value of the strength of the gravitation potential, the transition from T to T^* does not involve any changes in meaning. Feyerabend noted that although T and T^* assign different force-values in a given application, the difference in values is not due to the action of different kinds of entities.[23] He contrasted this "transition" with a transition from T to T', where T' is general relativity theory. In this latter transition, the meaning of "spatial interval" does change, supposedly because the entities referred to differ in T and T'.

Consistent with this contrast, Feyerabend suggested the following criterion of "change of meaning":

Transition	Type of change in theory	Change of meaning of the terms of T_1 that occur in T_2
From T_1 to T_2	1 Alteration of the system of classes to which the concepts of T_1 refer.	Yes
	2 Alteration of the extensions of the classes, but not the way in which the classes are stipulated.	No

Feyerabend insisted that before this criterion can be applied we need to decide how to "interpret" theories. His own choice was to decide questions about meaning-change by appeal to the principles of the respective theories and not by appeal to similarities or differences at the observational level.[24]

He noted that this way of interpreting theories makes possible the analysis and correction (from above) of the ways we express the results of observation. By contrast, the orthodox interpretation protects the "observation language" from the possibility of theoretical reinterpretation. Feyerabend maintained that the scientific revolutions of the seventeenth and twentieth centuries reflect his "interpretation" and not that of orthodoxy.

But even if Feyerabend's proposed interpretation is accepted, the criterion of meaning-change is useful only if unique and definite rules of classification can be specified for the "entities" referred to by theories. Shapere emphasized the difficulties that arise upon application of this criterion. The rules must be sufficiently definite to permit an unambiguous classification. And if competing rules of classification are available, then it must be clear which rule is used implicitly by the theory in question. Shapere expressed doubt that this can be achieved in the case of high-level theories.

> Are mesons different "kinds of entities" from electrons and protons, or are they simply a different subclass of elementary particles? Are the light rays of classical mechanics and of general relativity (two theories which Feyerabend claims are "incommensurable") different "kinds of entities" or not? Such questions can be answered either way, depending on the kind of information that is being requested ... for there are differences as well as similarities between electrons and mesons, as between light rays in classical mechanics and light rays in general relativity.[25]

An important residual problem for Feyerabend is how theories can be compared. He conceded that low-level theories may be evaluated by comparing their consequences with "what is observed." This can be done because there exist background theories to provide a common interpretation for the observational consequences of low-level theories. The background theories have a status that is independent of the fate of individual low-level theories. But high-level theories cannot be compared in this way. No theory-neutral observation language is available at this level. Rather, each high-level theory specifies its own observation language.

Nevertheless, Feyerabend maintained that there are rational procedures for the evaluation of conflicting high-level theories. He suggested three procedures of theory-evaluation.

The first procedure for assessing competing theories is to formulate a still more general theory within which occur statements that can be used to test the competing theories.[26]

The second procedure is to compare the internal structures of the competing theories. Two theories may differ with respect to the length of derivation from postulates to observation statements. They also may differ with respect to the number and severity of approximations made in the course of the derivations.

Feyerabend suggested that, other things being equal, a smaller length of derivation and a smaller number of approximations is preferable.[27] Why this should be, he did not say.

The third procedure is to compare the observational consequences of theories with "human experience as an actually existing process."[28] Feyerabend recommended a "pragmatic theory of observation," according to which

> a statement will be regarded as observational because of the *causal* context in which it is being uttered, and not because of what it means. According to this theory, "this is red" is an observation sentence, because a well-conditioned individual who is prompted in the appropriate manner in front of an object that has certain physical properties will respond without hesitation with "this is red"; and this response will occur independently of the *interpretation* he may connect with the statement.[29]

An observer is caused to respond in certain ways by the characteristics of the observational situation and his prior conditioning. Feyerabend declared that

> we can ... determine in a straightforward manner whether a certain movement of the human organism is correlated with an external event and can therefore be regarded as an indicator of this event.[30]

Feyerabend proposed to use these verbal "event-indicators" to evaluate high-level theories. A given "event-indicator" may be consistent with one theory and inconsistent with a second theory.

Shapere complained that, although Feyerabend denied that there could exist a theory-independent observation language, he made use of theory-independent observations to evaluate theories.[31] But Shapere denied that these theory-independent observations could perform the function that Feyerabend assigned to them. Even if observation sentences do issue from certain situations as conditioned responses of the observer, they are mere uninterpreted noises. They have no more linguistic content than a burp.[32] Before such a sentence can count as a test of a theory, it must be interpreted. Feyerabend had maintained, however, that observational findings are subject to reinterpretation at the hands of successful new theories. If this is so, then observation sentences cannot decide the issue between competing theories. In short, Feyerabend cannot have it both ways. *Either* an appeal to observation sentences can decide the issue between competing theories and observation sentences are not subject to reinterpretation by the theories compared, *or* an appeal to observation sentences cannot decide the issue between competing theories and observation sentences are subject to reinterpretation by the theories compared.

Of course, one can decide to reject a theory upon the occurrence within experience of a conflict between expectations derived from the theory and an observer's response to an observational situation. This is to decide not to interpret the response from the standpoint of the theory. But Feyerabend can select this option only at the risk of introducing disharmony into his methodology, since he repeatedly emphasizes the importance of theoretical reinterpretation of statements about what is observed.

In later essays, Feyerabend suggested that the evaluation of incommensurable theories may rest on aesthetic considerations. Matters of taste are involved. But matters of taste are not beyond the reach of argument. Feyerabend compared the evaluation of high-level scientific theories with the evaluation of poems.

> Poems, for example, can be compared in grammar, sound structure, imagery, rhythm, and can be evaluated on such a basis .... Every poet who is worth his salt compares, improves, argues until he finds the correct formulation of what he wants to say. Would it not be marvelous if this free and entertaining process played a role in the sciences also?[33]

Nickles on two concepts of reduction

Very few observers of science accepted Feyerabend's position on theory-assessment. The consensus was that there are distinctions to be drawn between the justification of theory-change and the evaluation of poems.

Thomas Nickles, for instance, maintained that certain of Nagel's intuitions about theory-change were sound, even though his theory of reduction requires revision.[34] Nickles noted, first of all, that scientists often speak of the more inclusive theory of a pair as the theory "reduced." For example, special relativity theory is said to be reduced to Newtonian mechanics in the limiting case where $v / c \Rightarrow 0$. In Nagel's usage, on the other hand, it is the less inclusive theory that is said to be "reduced" as it is incorporated into a theory of greater scope. He held, for example, that Galileo's theory of falling bodies is reduced to Newtonian gravitation theory, and that classical thermodynamics is reduced to statistical mechanics. Nickles concluded that two concepts of "reduction" are required for the analysis of theory-replacement.

He labeled the incorporation of one theory into a second theory of greater scope "reduction$_1$." Reduction$_1$ is a relation between mutually consistent theories belonging to different domains. The paradigm case of reduction$_1$ is the relationship between classical thermodynamics and statistical mechanics.

"Reduction$_2$," is a relation in which a more inclusive theory approaches its predecessor in that domain by some process of limitation or approximation. The paradigm case of reduction$_2$ is the relationship between special relativity theory and Newtonian mechanics as $v / c \Rightarrow 0$.

Nickles held that Nagel had blurred the distinction between these distinctive types of reduction by treating instances of reduction$_2$ as if they were instances of reduction$_1$. This enabled critics such as Feyerabend to claim that, since the theories related in reduction$_2$ typically are mutually inconsistent, the notion of "reduction" does not fit developments in the history of science. Nickles emphasized that Feyerabend's demonstrations of violations of the consistency condition are irrelevant to cases of reduction$_2$. Predecessor and successor theories within a domain are not required to be mutually consistent to achieve reduction$_2$. It suffices that calculations made from the successor theory by some limiting process agree with those of the predecessor theory.

Many of the criticisms of Nagel's theory of reduction, including that of Nickles, neglect Nagel's emphasis on the empirical requirements for reduction. The critics attack Nagel's view as if he had proposed connectability and derivability as conditions jointly sufficient for reduction. But Nagel insisted that the mere deduction of the laws of a theory is insufficient for reduction. There must be additional evidential support for the second theory, and it must prove fertile of further progress. Moreover, Nagel acknowledged that the "derivation" necessary for reduction often makes use of simplification and approximation.

5

LAKATOS' VERSION OF THE "PROGRESS IS INCORPORATION" THESIS

Reduction$_1$ shares with Whewell's tributary–river view an emphasis on incorporation. Imre Lakatos sought to adapt the concept of incorporation to the more restricted context of individual scientific research programs. According to Lakatos, a scientific research program consists of a central core of axioms and principles and an evolving collection of auxiliary hypotheses adopted in the course of applying the core.[1] The central core is taken to be inviolable by those working within the research program.

Lakatos cited post-Newtonian planetary astronomy as an historically important scientific research program. In this Newtonian research program the three axioms of motion and the law of gravitational attraction were shielded from modification or replacement. Divergences that arose between calculations and observations were removed by making changes in a protective belt of auxiliary hypotheses. Thus when the motion of the Moon was observed not to conform to calculations made from the Newtonian axioms, agreement was restored by adding an auxiliary hypothesis to the protective belt. This auxiliary hypothesis attributes to the Earth an asymmetrical distribution of mass (the Earth bulges at the equator and is flattened at the poles). Given the fact that the Earth's axis of rotation is

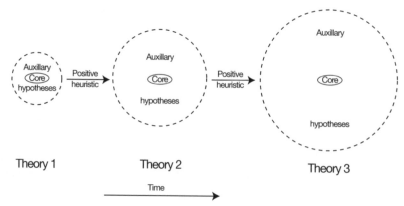

Figure 5.1 A Lakatosian scientific research program

inclined 23½ degrees to the plane of its orbit, this asymmetrical mass distribution affects the Earth's gravitational pull on the orbiting Moon. And when the motion of the newly discovered Uranus was observed to deviate from the orbit required by theory, another hypothesis was added to the protective belt. This hypothesis posited the existence of a trans-Uranic planet, and the hypothesis subsequently was confirmed.

Lakatos insisted that the refusal to accept apparently negative evidence as counting against the core principles of a research program often *promotes* progress. So long as modifications of the protective belt generate theories that incorporate their predecessors and achieve additional successes, the research program is progressive. The Newtonian program achieved a string of successes in the eighteenth and nineteenth centuries, and should be appraised as "progressive" during this period.

Lakatos declared that

> within a research programme a theory can only be eliminated by a better theory, that is, by one which has excess empirical content over its predecessors, some of which is subsequently confirmed. And for this replacement of one theory by a better one, the first theory does not even have to be "falsified" in Popper's sense of the term. Thus the progress is marked by instances verifying excess content rather than by falsifying instances; empirical "falsification" and actual "rejection" become independent.[2]

Lakatos maintained that the replacement of theory T_{n-1} by theory T_n within a research program is justified provided that

1 T_n accounts for the previous successes of T_{n-1};
2 T_n has greater empirical content than T_{n-1}; and
3 Some of the excess content of T_n has been corroborated.[3]

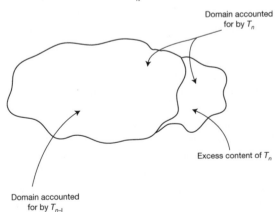

Domain accounted for by T_n

Excess content of T_n

Domain accounted for by T_{n-1}

Figure 5.2 Lakatos' criterion of incorporation with corroborated excess content

Figure 5.3 The two electron-spin orientations of the hydrogen atom

It is not difficult to find instances of theory-replacement that fulfill these requirements. One such instance that fulfills Lakatos' criterion is the replacement of Bohr's theory of the hydrogen atom by Sommerfeld's theory that takes account of the two possible spin orientations of the electron with respect to the nucleus. On Sommerfeld's theory the two orientations in Figure 5.3 are states of different energ.

Sommerfeld's theory accounted for the previously unexplained fact that the spectral lines of hydrogen occur as closely spaced doublets. It thus has confirmed empirical content over and above that of the Bohr theory.

A second instance of justified theory replacement is the conversion of Mendeleeff's theory that correlates the periodic variation of the chemical properties of the elements with their weights to Moseley's theory that correlates the periodic variation of properties with their atomic numbers (the positive charge of the nucleus). Mendeleeff could explain most observed periodicities by reference to weight relations. However, certain periodic relationships were anomalies within his theory. Iodine, for example, has chemical properties similar to chlorine and bromine. Unfortunately, a periodic table based on weight relations associated tellurium, and not iodine, with chlorine and bromine. Moseley's theory, on the other hand, places iodine in the "correct" group, since the atomic number (but not the atomic weight) of iodine is greater than that of tellurium. Since Moseley's theory removes the iodine–tellurium anomaly (and other anomalies), and still accounts for the successes achieved by Mendeleeff's theory, this transition also is justified on Lakatos' criterion.

Lakatos' criterion—"incorporation-with-corroborated-excess-content"—is not a necessary condition of progress within a scientific research program. Progress also is achieved within a program by improving the fit between theory and observations without increasing the range of phenomena covered. And sometimes progressive theory-replacement involves a *reduction* of scope. An example is the research program to account for the properties of solutions of electrolytes (substances that separate—wholly or in part—into positively and negatively charged ions in water). Arrhenius proposed a theory (1887) to explain the colligative effects of electrolytes—vapor pressure lowering of the solvent, freezing point lowering, boiling point elevation, and osmotic pressure. The theory was proposed for all electrolytes, but was in agreement only with the behavior of weak electrolytes (an electrolyte is "weak" if its percent decomposition into ions in water is low).[4] Debye and Hückel (1923) and Onsager (1926) improved agreement with measured values of colligative properties and conductance by narrowing the scope from electrolytes in general to strong electrolytes.[5]

Lakatos applied the incorporation criterion as if it were a sufficient condition of progress within a scientific research program. However, this criterion is not a sufficient condition of progress within a research program either. This conclusion is supported by both logical considerations and historical evidence.

The logical point is that if X is a well-confirmed theory consistent with the central core of a research program, then the transition from T_1 to T_2, where $T_2 = (T_1 \,\&\, X)$, is progressive on the incorporation criterion. But *ad hoc* conjunctions of this sort do not contribute to progress in science.

An historical countercase to the sufficient-condition thesis is Galileo's extension of his astronomical research program to comets. Galileo's program was to account for the motions of the heavenly bodies by reference to uniform circular motions. He took seriously the myth (which he attributed to Plato) that God formed the Solar System by successively imposing circular motions on the planets as they "fell" through space in straight-line motions:

> let us suppose God to have created the planet Jupiter, for example, upon which He had determined to confer such-and-such velocity, to be kept perpetually uniform forever after. We may say with Plato that at the beginning He gave it a straight and accelerated motion; and later, when it had arrived at that degree of velocity, converted its straight motion into circular motion whose speed thereafter was naturally uniform.[6]

Galileo was anxious to include the Earth among the "heavenly bodies" and postulated that circular motions equidistant from the Earth's center would remain constant in the absence of external retarding influences.

The motions of comets posed an obstacle to Galileo's research program. Critics of heliostatic astronomy, pre-eminently Tycho Brahe, directed the following argument against that position:

1　If comets follow roughly circular paths around the Sun and if the Earth too revolves around the Sun, then comets display periods of retrograde motion.
2　Comets follow roughly circular paths around the Sun.
3　Comets do not display periods of retrograde motion.

∴ The Earth does not revolve around the Sun.

Galileo's response to this argument was interesting. He did not consider rejecting premise 2 (so far as we know). Uniform circular motion was a core principle of his research program. So much so that he sought to extend the principle to the terrestrial realm. Instead Galileo denied that comets were *bona fide* celestial objects to which the principle of uniform circular motion applies. Comets, he suggested, are pseudo-objects like rainbows and halos.[7] Adding the pseudo-object hypothesis increased the range of "successful" explanations within Galileo's heliostatic research program. On the incorporation criterion this counts as progress (assuming the absence of retrograde motions is taken to "corroborate" the augmented theory).

A second countercase is the Proutian research program discussed by Lakatos himself. Prout's program (1815) was to show that the atomic weights of the chemical elements are exact multiples of the atomic weight of hydrogen.[8] Given that the atomic weight of hydrogen is 1.0 gm./gm.atom, Prout's program required that the atomic weights of other elements be integral multiples of this value.

The program achieved some early successes—nitrogen = 14, oxygen = 16, sulfur = 32 ... — but anomalies soon became apparent. For example, successively more accurate determinations of the atomic weight of chlorine converged upon the value 35.5 gm./gm.atom.

The French chemist J.B.A. Dumas sought to rescue Prout's program by adding the auxiliary hypothesis that the basic building block of the elements is not hydrogen but a yet-to-be-discovered substance whose atomic weight is precisely one-half that of hydrogen. Dumas' theory accounts for all the successes achieved by Prout's theory, and the case of chlorine as well. As more accurate data on atomic weights became available, Dumas suggested that perhaps the basic building block of the elements has an atomic weight of one-fourth that of hydrogen.[9] But why stop there? Perhaps the basic chemical building block has an atomic weight one-eighth or one-sixteenth that of hydrogen. To adopt auxiliary hypotheses of this type is to bring the weights of additional elements into agreement with the Proutian research program. But surely this type of "incorporation-with-corroborated-excess-content" is not progressive.

Satisfaction of the incorporation criterion thus is neither necessary nor sufficient for progress. Lakatos nevertheless applied the criterion to appraise the careers of scientific research programs. He held that a program is "progressive" only so long as it generates successive theories that incorporate their predecessors and are supported by evidence that confirms their excess claims. A research program that fails to advance in this way is "degenerating."

Lakatos conceded that the appraisal of a research program may change over time. Once again, the Newtonian program is a good example. Adams and Leverrier postulated the existence of a transUranic planet to account for discrepancies between Newtonian calculations and the observed motion of Uranus (1846). This turned out to be a progressive move, since Neptune was found at the predicted position along the zodiac.

Several years later, Leverrier advanced a similar hypothesis to account for a discrepancy in the motion of Mercury. The major axis of Mercury's elliptical orbit revolves 43 seconds of arc per century in excess of the value calculated from Newtonian theory. Leverrier postulated the existence of a small planet

(Vulcan) inside the orbit of Mercury. But no such planet has been identified (although several "sightings" have been claimed). Efforts to explain Mercury's anomalous motion by reference to Newtonian calculations invoking unobserved masses have turned out to constitute a degenerating research program.

Einstein showed in 1915 that the theory of general relativity requires the addition of a "$1/r^4$" term to Newton's law of gravitational attraction ($F = Gm_1m_2 / r^2 + A / r^4$). [10]

He applied this relativistic equation for gravitational attraction to the problem of Mercury's orbit. The result was elimination of the 43 seconds-of-arc discrepancy. To accept Einstein's conclusion is to abandon a core principle of the Newtonian research program. The astronomer Fred Hoyle, reflecting on Leverrier's two applications of the Newtonian research program declared that

> I learned this story when I was young and drew a moral from it: that it is unwise to attempt to repeat one's successes! [11]

Lakatos noted as well that a "degenerating" research program subsequently may stage a comeback. This happened in the case of William Prout's research program (1815) that interpreted the atoms of the chemical elements to be made up of multiple units of hydrogen. Prout's program received a new lease on life in the twentieth century. It was discovered that many elements occur in nature as mixtures of isotopes. Chlorine, for example, is a mixture of two isotopes. Every chlorine atom has 17 protons in its nucleus, but one isotope has 18 neutrons and the second isotope has 20 neutrons. Since naturally-occurring Chlorine contains three atoms of isotope Cl^{35} to one atom of Cl^{37}, its atomic weight turns out to be 35.5. The Proutian research program was revived, but applied to isotopes of elements rather than to elements themselves.

At a given point in time, one can apply the incorporation criterion to appraise the status of a scientific research program. However, a positive appraisal is no guarantee of success for continued application of the program. A hitherto progressive program may be about to run aground. Similarly, a negative appraisal does not make irrational the efforts of scientists to revive a degenerating program. A hitherto degenerating program may be about to stage a comeback. Lakatos emphasized the distinction between the appraisal of a research program and the decision to pursue or abandon the program. He insisted that the philosopher's task is one of appraisal. It is not part of the evaluative task of the philosopher of science to issue recommendations to scientists about research strategies. [12]

Transitions between research programs

There remains the problem of gauging progress in the case of transitions between research programs. Paul Feyerabend noted that such transitions sometimes display explanatory overlap, as shown in Figure 5.4. [13]

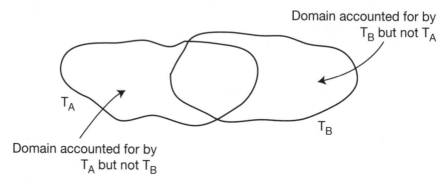

Figure 5.4 Explanatory overlap of theories from research programs *A* and *B*

In such cases, T_B has corroborated excess content, but accounts only for most— but not all—the successes of T_A . An example of explanatory overlap is the transition from Descartes' vortex program to Newton's gravitational attraction program. The Newtonian program achieved corroborated excess content. It accounted for Kepler's laws of planetary motion (approximately). By contrast, the principles of the vortex theory are inconsistent with Kepler's laws. But the vortex theory had an explanatory success that the Newtonian program did not match. It explained why the planets all travel in the same direction around the Sun. Given that there is an invisible whirlpool of aether within which the planets float, their revolutions are unidirectional. There was no corresponding explanation of unidirectional motions provided within Newton's original program.[14]

Lakatos maintained that competing research programs should be appraised by reference to their relative rates of progress. If one program is stagnant, having failed to generate new confirmed consequences over a period of time during which a second program has been fertile, then the second program is superior to the first. In cases where two programs both have been progressive, as certified by applications of the incorporation criterion, appraisal requires an assessment of the relative importance of these achievements.

As indicated above, Lakatos emphasized that the appraisal of a scientific research program is given at a specific time in its history. The comparative status of competing programs may change over time. A currently progressive program may become degenerating, and a currently degenerating program may become progressive.

The justification of evaluative criteria

Lakatos put forward the methodology of scientific research programs as a rational reconstruction of scientific progress. He held that rational reconstructions of scientific progress, his own included, can be evaluated by appeal to the history of science. He declared that all methodologies function as historiographical (or meta-historical) theories (or research programmes) and can be criticized by criticizing the rational reconstructions to which they lead.[15]

Thus, inductivist rational reconstructions emphasize the discovery of facts and the formulation of inductive generalizations. Popperian reconstructions emphasize bold, "content-increasing" conjectures and dramatic refutations. And Lakatosian reconstructions emphasize the rivalry and succession of research programs.

Lakatos distinguished two "historical entities": the historical record of scientific developments and the philosopher's rational reconstruction of scientific progress. The historical record includes both Darwin's theory of evolution by natural selection and Lysenko's theory of inheritance; a rational reconstruction may include the former but exclude the latter.

Lakatos left unresolved the problem of the proper relationship between the history of science and its rational reconstruction. Historical episodes must be treated with respect. They must not be converted onto mere illustrations of the principles of some methodology. Clearly there is a point at which a rational reconstruction is at such variance with the history of science that it is no longer a reconstruction of *science*.

Lakatos conceded that there will be divergences between the reconstruction dictated by a methodology and the actual course of science. A methodological reconstruction is always something different from a mere repetition of historical developments. He stated that all *normative* reconstructions have to be supplemented by *empirical* external theories to explain the residual non-rational factors. The history of science is always richer than its rational reconstruction.[16] But even though every rational reconstruction establishes a division between "internal history of science"—science that conforms to the methodological principles in question—and "external history of science," it still is possible to assess competing methodologies (see Figure 5.5).

Insofar as different philosophies of science stipulate different criteria of theory-replacement, they generate different reconstructions of scientific progress. Lakatos recommended the following procedure for the evaluation of competing methodologies.[17] First, one selects a set of competing methodologies and elaborates the rational reconstruction of scientific progress "implied" by each methodology. Next, one compares each rational reconstruction against the history of science. If methodology M_2 reconstructs all the historical episodes reconstructed by M_1, and additional episodes besides, then M_2 is the superior methodology. This is an application of the incorporation criterion to the justification of competing methodologies.

Lakatos argued that his own methodology of scientific research programs is the winner in a competition with inductivism and Popperian methodological falsificationism. He insisted that his methodology renders rational more of the history of science than do either of these competing methodologies. Unlike inductivism, the methodology of scientific research programs accounts for theories

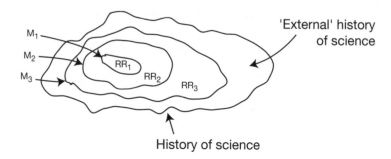

Figure 5.5 Lakatos on the evaluation of competing methodologies. RR_1, RR_2, RR_3 indicate rational reconstructions

about unobservables such as "point masses" and "electromagnetic waves." And unlike Popperian methodological falsificationism, the methodology of scientific research programs accounts for scientists' continuing pursuit of research programs that have encountered dramatic falsifications (for example, pursuit of the Newtonian program in the face of evidence of the anomalous motion of Mercury). Since "incorporation-with-corroborated-excess-content" is the criterion of theory-replacement within Lakatos' methodology, the triumph of this methodology over its competition is a vindication of this criterion as well.

Circularity in the evaluation of competing methodologies

The incorporation criterion is inapplicable to cases of partial overlap in which methodology M_2 reconstructs episodes not reconstructed by M_1, but methodology M_1 reconstructs episodes not reconstructed by M_2. To deal with cases of overlap, it would be necessary to develop a measure of the relative importance of the historical episodes reconstructed by M_2 but not M_1, and *vice versa*.

There is an additional problem raised by Lakatos' proposal for the evaluation of competing methodologies. There is no methodologically neutral history of science against which to measure rational reconstructions of scientific progress. Every history of science is an interpretation of the available records. Historians must decide which journal articles, letters, notebook entries, *et al.*, are important to the development of science. They need to reconstruct a sequence of human actions and to place those actions correctly as stages within the long-term projects of scientists. This accomplished, they next need to determine whether or not scientists are pursuing a specific research program, and, if so, what is its nature. If they do succeed in characterizing a research program, they then need to ascertain the content, scope and evidential support of successive theories generated by the program.

It is indisputable that historical reconstruction requires judgment of importance on the part of historians. They need to assess the relative significance of experimental investigations and speculative flights of fancy. They also need to decide how important it is to deal constructively with the anomalies that arise during application of a research program. Given the inevitability of these judgments of importance in historical inquiry, the question arises whether there is an important element of circularity in Lakatos' proposal for the evaluation of competing methodologies. This circularity arises with respect to the following argument:

1 M_3 is justified only upon appeal to a history of science.
2 Every history of science presupposes some methodological standpoint M^*

∴ M_3 is justified only if M^* is presupposed.

As written, the argument is not circular. M^*, the methodology presupposed in the formation of a history of science, need not imply M_3, the winner of the justificatory competition. However, Lakatos insisted that the history of science ought be written from the standpoint of the best available methodology. Hence M^* should be identical to M_3.

There is no doubt that Lakatos' justificatory strategy involves an element of circularity. The superior methodology is that methodology whose rational reconstruction of scientific progress best conforms to a history of science formulated according to the canons of that same methodology.

However, the circularity is open-ended. At a given point in time, M_3 may be superior to M_1 and M_2 when their respective rational reconstructions of scientific progress are compared to a history of science formulated according to the principles of M_3. Subsequently, methodology M_4 may be formulated, such that, given a history of science that reflects its assumptions, M_4 accounts for all the episodes accounted for by M_3, and additional episodes besides. Lakatos' justificatory strategy thus is independent of any particular methodology (including his own). Nevertheless, every argument to justify a methodology is subject to the above circularity.

Lakatosian case studies

Several case studies were undertaken in the 1970s to assess the ability of the methodology of scientific research programs to account for progressive historical developments.[18] Success in this enterprise requires identification of

1 a central core of propositions held inviolable by a community of practitioners;
2 a positive heuristic that directs investigators to formulate auxiliary hypotheses that expand the range of application of the core principles; and
3 a sequence of theories that satisfy the "incorporation-with-corroborated-excess-content" criterion.

Peter Clark suggested that the career of the kinetic-molecular theory of gases is an instance of a progressive Lakatosian scientific research program.[19] The central core of the program is the assertion that macroscopic phenomena are to be attributed to the behavior of microscopic particles subject to the laws of Newtonian mechanics. The positive heuristic of the program directs the theorist to make assumptions about the properties and relations of the particles such that predictions derived from the model of the micro domain increasingly approximate the behavior of real gases. The research program was implemented by theories formulated by Joule, Krönig, Clausius, Maxwell and van der Waals, among others. These theories made different assumptions about molecules and the distribution of molecular motions. Clausius, for example, introduced the concept of "mean-free-path" between molecular collisions, and Maxwell introduced a statistical distribution pattern for molecular velocities.

The kinetic-molecular research program was "progressive" in the required sense. Successive theories incorporated their predecessors and exhibited corroborated excess content. Clausius' theory (1857) accounted for the prior successes of the Joule-Krönig Theory and displayed corroborated excess content—an account of Dalton's Law of partial pressures and the evaporation of gases. Maxwell's theory (1859) accounted for the successes of Clausius' theory, and predicted that the viscosity of a gas is independent of its density, an unexpected result subsequently confirmed experimentally by Maxwell and O.E. Meyer. The transition from Maxwell's theory to van der Waals' theory also was progressive, exhibiting both incorporation and corroborated excess content. Van der Waals' theory better accounts for the pressure–volume–temperature behavior of gases near their critical points (at which the distinction between gaseous and liquid phases disappears). Clark concluded that a Lakatosian rational reconstruction of kinetic-molecular theory fits the historical record.

Alan Musgrave came to a different conclusion about the value of Lakatosian rational reconstructions.[20] He noted that Lakatos had cited the development of Newtonian mechanics as an illustration of a progressive scientific research program. Musgrave insisted that to interpret the career of Newtonian mechanics in this way is to distort the historical record.

Musgrave pointed out that there were several attempts by professed Newtonians to alter the supposedly "hard core" law of universal gravitational attraction. Alexis Clairaut suggested (1747) addition of a "$1/r^4$" term to the law to account for anomalies in the motion of the Moon. Leonhard Euler and J.L. Lagrange (1750) agreed that some modification of the law was necessary. A century later George Airy and Friedrich Bessel recommended that the law be modified to account for anomalies in the motion of Uranus (1846). And Asaph Hall and Simon Newcomb (1910) suggested that the value of the exponent "2" in the Newtonian law be increased slightly to account for the anomalous motion of Mercury. Musgrave concluded that some Newtonians at some points did take a methodological decision to retain Newton's laws unchanged in the face of an anomaly, and some did not. The former were usually sucessful and the latter were not. But it is only by ignoring half of the actual history that it can be made to fit Lakatos' methodology.[21]

Henry Frankel shared Musgrave"s misgivings about the fit between Lakatosian rational reconstructions and historical developments. Frankel surveyed the history of theorizing about a horizontal drift of continents, from the initial suggestion of Alfred Wegener (1910) to the plate-tectonics version of Harry Hess, Fred Vine, Drummond Matthews and Tuzo Wilson (1960s).

Frankel claimed that all continental-drift theorists accepted the core principle that

> the continents have displaced themselves horizontally with respect to each other. Certain continents, now separated by vast oceans, were once combined.[22]

However, individual drift-theorists accepted quite different assumptions about the mechanism responsible for the horizontal movement of continents. Frankel held that these assumptions about the causes of continental drift were equally basic core principles.

The historian sympathetic to Lakatos' recommendations has a choice. He or she may identify discrete research programs advanced by 1) Wegener, who held that, although continents are less dense than the ocean floor, they nevertheless plough through that floor; 2) Arthur Holmes, who held that "continents move passively on top of the upper mantle and lower level of crust as sea floor is stretched due to convection currents"[23]; and 3) Hess, who held that sea-floor spreading is the basic mechanism of continental drift. Alternatively, he or she may maintain that there is a single research program whose core principles were modified during its implementation.

Frankel opted for the latter alternative. He held that there was a continuous continental-drift research program in competition with two other research programs: one that postulates a "periodic contraction of the earth," and the other that assumes that "continents are permanent (after an initial process of formation)."[24]

Frankel and Musgrave agreed that historical episodes are distorted by their reconstruction as scientific research programs that have inviolable central cores. Frankel suggested that a modified "methodology of scientific research programs" is a valuable model for the identification and interpretation of progressive episodes in the history of science. A needed modification is a relaxation of the restrictions on the core principles of a program. Frankel's "more flexible" methodology permits changes in the core principles that one must accept in order to work within a program. He counseled, however, that although a more flexible "methodology of scientific research programs" is of value for historical reconstruction, this does not mean that it is the definitive, or even the best, model for the analysis of scientific progress.[25]

Musgrave, by contrast, argued that the failure of Lakatos' methodology of scientific research programs to fit important historical episodes is a good reason to reject it. The concept "scientific research program" is of no value for the interpretation of scientific progress if one and the same program can contain different inviolable principles at different times.

Musgrave complained, in addition, that Lakatos' concept of "positive heuristic" is too vague to be useful.[26] In a Lakatosian rational reconstruction, the interpreter must decide whether scientists developed the theories they did in the process of implementing the positive heuristic of a research program. For a reconstruction to be convincing, the interpreter needs to show that scientists were committed to a narrow range of permitted ways to develop a program.

Musgrave pointed out that the positive heuristic of a scientific research program provides only vague hints about how to proceed. It directs the scientist to add auxiliary hypotheses to the core principles so that implications of the resultant theory are in agreement with observations. But the positive heuristic does not instruct the scientist on the avoidance or resolution of specific anomalies that arise in the development of a research program.

6

PROGRESS AND THE ASYMPTOTIC AGREEMENT OF CALCULATIONS

Lakatos' criterion of justified theory-replacement is vague. One of its requirements is that T_n "accounts for the previous successes of T_{n-1}."[1] It is unclear what qualifies as "accounting for previous successes." A weak requirement is that calculations from T_n are in agreement with calculations from T_{n-1} for that area of experience for which T_{n-1} had achieved agreement with observations.

Niels Bohr emphasized the importance of asymptotic agreement in his theory of the hydrogen atom (1913). Axioms of Bohr's theory include:

1   The electron moves in one of a set of circular orbits around the nucleus;
2   The orbital motion of the electron obeys both Newton's second law— $F = ma$—and Coulomb's law of electrostatic attraction—$F = q_+q_- / r^2$;
3   The orbital angular momentum is subject to a quantum condition. Its values are restricted to integral multiples of a minimum value $h / 2\pi$, viz., $m v = n h / 2\pi$, where h is a constant, and n is an integer; and
4   Energy is absorbed or emitted only upon transition from one orbit to another, such that $E_i - E_f = (n_i - n_f) h c / \lambda$, where λ is the wavelength of the radiation.

Rules of correspondence correlate values of n and λ within the axiom system with lines observed in the emission and absorption spectra of hydrogen gas. For instance, transitions from orbits for which $n = 3, 4, 5 \ldots$ to $n = 2$ are in agreement with that series of spectral lines whose wavelengths were determined experimentally by Balmer. No rules of correspondence are specified, however, for locating an electron either within an orbit or between orbits during a transition.

Bohr noted that calculations obtained from the theory approach asymptotically the results calculated from classical electromagnetic theory in that region of application for which the classical theory had achieved success. There is an asymptotic limit toward which the orbital energy of an electron decreases as the radius of its orbit increases. This limit is the energy possessed by a free electron no longer bound to the nucleus, as calculated from the equations of classical electromagnetic theory.

Bohr made asymptotic agreement a basic principle of his quantum theory of the hydrogen atom. He labeled it the "correspondence principle." This principle stipulates that, as electron-nucleus distance increases, the equations of motion for discrete electron orbits approach asymptotically the classical equations for the motion of a free electron.

Bohr elevated the correspondence principle to the status of a general methodological directive. As a methodological directive, the principle directs the theorist to establish asymptotic agreement of calculations between a proposed new theory and its predecessor for that domain in which the earlier theory is in agreement with observations. Ernest Hutten and Joseph Agassi championed the correspondence principle as an important criterion of acceptability for theory-replacement.[2]

Support for "asymptotic agreement with calculations" as a criterion of theory-replacement came principally from developments in early twentieth-century physics. Both Schrödinger's quantum theory and Einstein's special relativity theory exhibit asymptotic agreement to Newtonian mechanics. In the limiting case in which the quantum of action may be neglected, Schrödinger's equation for the probability distribution of quantum mechanical particles yields the same results as the Newtonian equations of motion. And in the limiting case in which the velocity of a system is negligible with respect to the velocity of light, Einstein's relativistic equations yield the same results as the Newtonian equations of motion.

Of course, there are other reasons to accept quantum theory and the special theory of relativity. But the fact that calculations from both theories are in agreement with those of Newtonian mechanics in the appropriate limiting cases presumably makes these theories more acceptable than they would be otherwise.

As an evaluative standard, "asymptotic agreement of observations" is neither a necessary nor a sufficient condition of justified theory-replacement. No one would promote the standard as necessary for justified theory-replacement. After all, there do exist non-quantified theories. For example , the theory of the organic origin of fossils is an acceptable theory even though it is not in asymptotic agreement with the earlier theory that fossils are inorganic mineral remains produced by a "plastic force" within the earth.

"Asymptotic agreement" is not a sufficient condition of justified theory-replacement either. Given an equation, a theorist can construct numerous more complex equations that reduce to the original equation under specified conditions. Suppose there is an equation

$$AB = kC$$

which has received empirical support. It is clear that the equation

$$(A + D/B^2)(B - E) = k\,C$$

is in asymptotic agreement with the original equation in the limiting case in which D and E, approach zero. But why would anyone pay attention to this relation of asymptotic agreement?

Something more than the asymptotic agreement of calculations is required. There must be theoretical considerations that support the replacement of the first formula by the second. For example, if A stands for the pressure of a gas, B for its volume, C for its absolute temperature, D for the magnitude of intermolecular forces and E for the ratio of the collective volume of all the molecules of the gas to the volume of the gas, then the asymptotic agreement is between the ideal gas law and the van der Waals Equation.

Scientists accept van der Waals' Equation in part because of its asymptotic agreement with the ideal gas law at moderate pressures and temperatures. Moreover, on the above interpretation of the symbols, there are good reasons to accept the van der Waals formula. These reasons are supplied by the kinetic theory of gases. If it is correct that gases are comprised of tiny, rapidly moving molecules, then it is to be expected that the ideal gas theory, which takes molecules to be point-masses and denies the presence of intermolecular forces, requires modification under conditions of high compression. The transition from ideal gas theory to van der Waals' Theory has a theoretical basis.

Max Planck's formula for black-body radiation (1900), by contrast, initially lacked theoretical support. A black body is an idealized isothermal radiator that absorbs 100 percent of the energy incident upon it. A very good approximation to this ideal is a box lined with lampblack which has a small hole in one of its walls. Nearly all the radiation received upon heating such a box is absorbed within the box and radiated from it as electromagnetic energy.

The variation of energy emitted with wavelength of such bodies was determined experimentally for a variety of temperatures (see Figure 6.1). Two equations were formulated to account for the energy-wavelength curves.[3]

The first equation was developed by Wilhelm Wien in 1896:

$$E_\lambda = a \, / \, \lambda^5 \exp^{b/\lambda T}$$

where E_λ is the energy radiated at wavelength λ, T is the absolute temperature of the heated cavity and a and b are constants. The Wien equation successfully reproduces the experimentally-derived curves at short wavelengths. Unfortunately, the Wien formula becomes increasingly inaccurate as the wavelength of the radiation increases.

The second equation was developed by Rayleigh and Jeans in 1900:

$$E_\lambda = 2 \, \pi \, k \, T \, / \, c \, \lambda^4$$

where k is Boltzmann's constant, and c is the velocity of light.

The Rayleigh–Jeans formula successfully reproduces the experimentally-derived curves at long wavelengths. The formula fails, however, at short wavelengths. Indeed, it predicts that the emitted energy increases without limit as wavelengths decrease. Paul Ehrenfest referred to this failure as the "ultraviolet catastrophe."[4] Contrary to the Rayleigh–Jeans formula, the experimentally-derived curve for a specific temperature displays a maximum energy output at a particular wavelength. For wavelengths shorter that this, the energy output decreases.

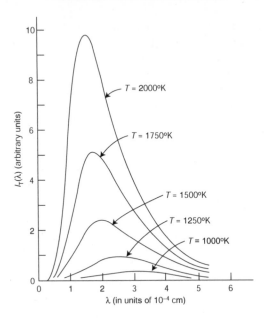

Figure 6.1 Black-body radiation at various temperatures

Max Planck was one of a distinguished group of physicists who sought to reconcile theory and experiment for black-body radiation. Planck hypothesized that the source of the radiation emitted by a heated black body is a collection of linear harmonic oscillators. He subjected the oscillators to the laws of classical electrodynamics and statistical mechanics, but was unable to reproduce the experimentally-derived radiation curves. Planck then decided (1900), for purposes of calculation, to distribute the total energy of a black body among the oscillators such that each oscillator of frequency n can assume only quantized energy values 0, $h\nu$, $2h\nu$, $3h\nu$ ... where h is Planck's constant (6.62×10^{-27} erg-sec). On this quantum hypothesis, the emission or absorption of energy is a transition between states of an oscillator such that $\Delta E = nh\nu$, where n is an integer.

By adopting the hypothesis of energy quantization, Planck was able to derive the equation

$$E_\lambda = 2\,\pi\,h\,c^2\,/\,\lambda^5\,\exp^{\,(ch/\lambda kT-1)}$$

Planck's equation is in asymptotic agreement with the Wien equation at short wavelengths and the Rayleigh–Jeans equation at long wavelengths.

If achieving asymptotic agreement of calculations were sufficient to establish the acceptability of a theory, then one would expect that the community of physicists would immediately endorse Planck's reconciliation of the Wien and Rayleigh–Jeans formulas. However, this did not happen. Planck had no rationale for assuming that energy is quantized. Within classical electromagnetic theory there is a continuum of possible energy values, and the distribution of total energy can be distributed among the oscillators in an infinite number of ways.

The historian of physics Max Jammer observed that

> Planck's introduction of h seems to be regarded at that time as an expedient mathematical device of no deeper physical significance, although his radiation law was repeatedly subjected to experimental test.[5]

Eventually scientists came to accept the quantization of energy as an essential aspect of the structure of the universe. But this acceptance was achieved only after the quantization of energy was featured in other successful theories: Einstein's theory of the photoelectric effect (1905) and Bohr's theory of the hydrogen atom (1913).

PART I: PROGRESS AS
INCORPORATION

Suggestions for further reading

Theorists of scientific progress

WILLIAM WHEWELL

Whewell, William (1857 [1967]) *History of the Inductive Sciences*, 3rd edn. London: Cass.
—— (1847 [1967]) *Philosophy of the Inductive Sciences*, 2nd edn. London: Cass.

Butts, Robert E. (ed.) (1968) *William Whewell's Theory of Scientific Method*.Pittsburgh: Pittsburgh University Press. Contains selections from Whewell's writings, a bibliography of works by and about Whewell, and an introductory essay by Butts.

Achinstein, Peter (1990) "Hypotheses, Probability, and Waves", *Brit. J. Phil. Sci.* 41: 73–102. An evaluation of the competing views of Whewell and Mill.
Brewster, David (1837)"Whewell's *History of the Inductive Sciences,*" *Edinburgh Review* 66: 110–51.
Butts, Robert E. (1965) "Necessary Truth in Whewell's Philosophy of Science", *Am. Phil. Quart.* 2: 161–81.
Ducasse, C.J. (1951) "Whewell's Philosophy of Scientific Discovery", *Phil. Rev.* 60: 56–69; 213–34; reprinted in R.M. Blake, C.J. Ducasse and E.H. Madden (eds) (1960) *Theories of Scientific Method : The Nineteenth Century*, Chapter 9. Seattle: University of Washington Press.
Fisch, Menachem (1991) *William Whewell, Philosopher of Science*. Oxford: Clarendon Press.
Morrison, Margaret (1997) "Whewell on the Ultimate Problem of Philosophy", *Stud. Hist. Phil. Sci.* 25: 417–37.
Snyder, Laura (1991) "It's *All* Necessarily So: William Whewell on Scientific Truth", *Stud. Hist. Phil. Sci.,* 25: 785–807.

JOHN STUART MILL

Mill, John Stuart (1963) *Works*, F.E.L. Priestley, J.M. Robinson, *et al.* (eds). Toronto: University of Toronto Press.
—— (1970) *A System of Logic*, 8th edn. London: Longman.

Ducasse, C. J. (1960) "John Stuart Mill's System of Logic", in R.M. Blake, C.J. Ducasse and E.H. Madden (eds) *Theories of Scientific Method: The Renaissance Through the Nineteenth Century,* 212–38. Seattle: University of Washington Press.
Jevons, W.S. (1890) "John Stuart Mill's Philosophy Tested" in *Pure Logic and Other Works*. London: Macmillan.
Losee, John (1983) "Whewell and Mill on the Relation Between Philosophy of Science and History of Science', *Stud. Hist. Phil. Sci.* 14: 113–21.

Scarre, G. (1998) "Mill on Induction and Scientific Method", in J. Skorupski (ed.) *The Cambridge Companion to Mill,* 112–38. Cambridge: Cambridge University Press.

ERNEST NAGEL

Nagel, Ernest (1961) *The Structure of Science.* New York: Harcourt, Brace & World.
—— (1971) "Theory and Observation" in M. Mandelbaum (ed.) *Observation and Theory in Science.* Baltimore: The Johns Hopkins Press.

Feyerabend, P.K. (1962) "Explanation, Reduction, and Empiricism" in H. Feigl and G. Maxwell (eds) *Minnesota Studies in the Philosophy of Science,* Vol. III, 28–97. Minneapolis: University of Minnesota Press.
—— (1965) "On the 'Meaning' of Scientific Terms", *J. Phil.* 62: 266–74.
Nickles, Thomas (1975) "Two Concepts of Intertheoretic Reduction", *J. Phil.* 70: 181–201.
Putnam, Hilary (1965) "How Not to Talk About Meaning" in R. Cohen and M. Wartofsky (eds) *Boston Studies in the Philosophy of Science,* Vol. II, 205–22. New York: Humanities Press.

IMRE LAKATOS

Lakatos, Imre (1970) "Falsification and the Methodology of Scientific Research Programmes" in I. Lakatos and A. Musgrave (eds) *Criticism and the Growth of Knowledge,* 91–195. Cambridge: Cambridge University Press.
—— (1971) "History of Science and its Rational Reconstructions" in R.C. Buck and R.S. Cohen (eds) *Boston Studies in the Philosophy of Science,* Vol. VIII, 91–182. Dordrecht: Reidel. Includes critical appraisals by T.S. Kuhn, H. Feigl, R.J. Hall and N. Koertge, and a reply by Lakatos.

Clark, Peter (1976) "Atomism *versus* Thermodynamics" in C. Howson (ed.) *Method and Appraisal in the Physical Sciences,* 41–105. Cambridge: Cambridge University Press.
Frankel, Henry (1979) "The Career of Continental Drift Theory: An Application of Imre Lakatos' Analysis of Scientific Growth to the Rise of Drift Theory" *Stud. Hist. Phil. Sci.* 10: 21–66.
Fricke, Martin (1976) "The Rejection of Avogadro's Hypothesis" in C. Howson (ed.) *Method and Appraisal in the Physical Sciences,* 277–307. Cambridge: Cambridge University Press.
Kuhn, Thomas S. (1980) "The Halt and the Blind: Philosophy and History of Science" *Brit. J. Phil. Sci.* 31: 181–92.
Musgrave, Alan (1976a) "Why Did Oxygen Supplant Phlogiston? Research Programmes in the Chemical Revolution" in C. Howson (ed.) *Method and Appraisal in the Physical Sciences,* 187–207. Cambridge: Cambridge University Press.
Musgrave, Alan (1976b) "Method and Madness?" in R. S. Cohen, *et al.* (eds) *Boston Studies in the Philosophy of Science,* Vol. 39. Dordrecht: Reidel.
Zahar, Elie (1973) "Why Did Einstein's Programme Supersede Lorentz's?" *Brit. J. Phil. Sci.* 24: 95–123, 223–61.

NIELS BOHR

Bohr, Niels (1934) *Atomic Theory and the Description of Nature*. Cambridge: Cambridge University Press.
—— (1958) *Atomic Theory and Human Knowledge*. New York: Wiley.

French, A.P. and Kennedy, P.J. (eds) (1985) *Niels Bohr: A Centenary Volume*. Cambridge, MA: Harvard University Press. Includes excerpts from Bohr's writings, reminiscences by Heisenberg, von Weizsacker, and others and critical essays by Bohm, Mermin, A. Petersen, *et al.*
Folse, Henry J. (1985) *The Philosophy of Niels Bohr*. Amsterdam: North-Holland.
Harre, Rom (1986) *Varieties of Realism*, 301–6. Oxford: Blackwell, 1986.
Murdoch, Dugald (1987) *Niels Bohr's Philosophy of Physics*. Cambridge: Cambridge University Press.

Episodes from the history of science

ATOMIC THEORY

Dalton, John (1808 [1964]) *A New System of Chemical Philosophy*. New York: The Citadel Press.
Perrin, Jean (1913 [1922]) *Atoms* (D Hammick, trans.). London: Constable. Includes a discussion of various determinations of the value of Avogadro's number.
Thackray, Arnold (1972) *John Dalton: Critical Assessments of His Life and Science*. Cambridge, MA: Harvard University Press.
—— (1970) *Atoms and Powers*. Cambridge, MA: Harvard University Press. A study of Newtonian matter theory and the origins of atomic theory.

COPERNICAN ASTRONOMY

Encyclopedia Britannica (1952) *Ptolemy, Copernicus, Kepler* Great Books of the Western World, Vol. XVI. Chicago: Encyclopedia Britannica. Contains Ptolemy, *Almagest*; Copernicus, *On the Revolutions of the Heavenly Spheres*; Kepler, *Epitome of Copernican Astronomy*, Book 5.
Rosen E. (trans.) (1959) *Three Copernican Treatises*, 2nd edn. New York: Dover. Contains Copernicus, *Commentariolis, Letter Against Werner*; Rheticus, *Narratio Prima*.
Curd, Martin V. (1982) "The Rationality of the Copernican Revolution", *PSA 1982*, Vol. 1, 3–13. East Lansing: Philosophy of Science Association
Drake, Stillman and O'Malley, C.D. (eds) (1960) *The Controversy on the Comets of 1618*. Philadelphia: University of Pennsylvania Press. Includes writings by Galileo, Grassi, Guiducci and Kepler.
Kuhn, Thomas S. (1985) *The Copernican Revolution*. Cambridge, MA: Harvard University Press.
Thoren, Victor E. (1990) *The Lord of Uraniborg: A Biography of Tycho Brahe*. Cambridge: Cambridge University Press.

CORPUSCULAR VERSUS. WAVE THEORIES OF LIGHT

Achinstein, Peter (1991) *Particles and Waves*. New York: Oxford University Press.

—— (1993) "Waves and Scientific Method", *PSA 1992*, Vol. 2, 193–204. East Lansing: Philosophy of Science Association.

Buchwald, Jed Z. (1989) *The Rise of the Wave Theory of Light*. Chicago: University of Chicago Press.

Eliasmith, Chris and Thagard, Paul (1997) "Waves, Particles and Explanatory Convergence", *Brit. J. Phil. Sci.* 48: 1–19.

Whewell, William (1857 [1967]) *History of the Inductive Sciences*, 3rd edn. London: Cass. Part II, 269–373, 480–3.

Worrall, John (1994) "How to Remain (Reasonably) Optimistic: Scientific Realism and the 'Luminiferous Ether'", *PSA 1994* Vol. 1, 334–2. East Lansing: Philosophy of Science Association. An analysis of Fresnel's and Maxwell's versions of wave theory.

EINSTEIN'S THEORIES OF SPECIAL AND GENERAL RELATIVITY

Einstein, Albert (1961) *Relativity*. New York: Crown.

—— (with Leopold Infeld) (1961) *The Evolution of Physics*. New York: Simon and Schuster.

Holton, Gerald (1986) *The Advancement of Science and its Burdens*, 3–138. Cambridge: Cambridge University Press.

—— (1973) *Thematic Origins of Scientific Thought: Kepler to Einstein*, 165–380. Cambridge, MA: Harvard University Press.

Miller, Arthur I. (1983) "On Einstein's Invention of Special Relativity", *PSA 1982*, Vol. 2, 377–402, East Lansing: Philosophy of Science Association.

Norton, John D. (2000) "'Nature is the Realisation of the Simplest Conceivable Mathematical Ideas': Einstein and the Canon of Mathematical Simplicity", *Stud. Hist. Phil. Mod. Phys.* 31B: 135–70.

KINETIC MOLECULAR THEORY

Brush, Stephen G. (1965) *Kinetic Theory*, 2 vols. Oxford: Pergamon Press. Contains an *Introduction* by Brush, and excerpts from the writings of Boyle, Newton, D. Bernoulli, Mayer, Joule, Helmholtz, Clausius, Maxwell, Boltzmann, and others.

Clark, Peter (1976) "Atomism *versus* Thermodynamics" in C. Howson (ed.) *Method and Appraisal in the Physical Sciences*, 41–105. Cambridge: Cambridge University Press, 1976.

NEWTONIAN MECHANICS

Cohen, I. Bernard, (1985) *The Birth of the New Physics*, revised edn. New York: W. W. Norton. An historical survey of the transition from Aristotelian physics to Newtonian physics.

——(1980) *The Newtonian Revolution*. Cambridge: Cambridge University Press.

Grosser, Morton (1962) *The Discovery of Neptune*. Cambridge, MA.: Harvard University Press.

Fauvel, J *et al.* (eds) (1988) *Let Newton Be*. Oxford: Oxford University Press. A collection of essays designed to introduce Newton's achievements in mathematics, physics, alchemy, theology and public service.

McMullin, Ernan (2001) "The Impact of Newton's *Principia* on the Philosophy of Science", *Phil. Sci.* 68: 279–310.

Westfall, Richard S. (1980) *Never At Rest: A Biography of Isaac Newton*. Cambridge: Cambridge University Press.

Worrall, John (2000) "The Scope, Limits, and Distinctiveness of the Method of 'Deduction from the Phenomena': Some Lessons from Newton's 'Demonstrations' in Optics", *Brit. J. Phil. Sci.* 51: 45–80.

PERIODIC TABLES OF THE CHEMICAL ELEMENTS

Mendeleeff, Dmitri (1879, 1880) "The Periodic Law of the Chemical Elements", *Chemical News*. Reprinted in David M. Knight (ed.) *Classical Scientific Papers— Chemistry, Second Series*, 273–302. New York: American Elsevier.

Van Spronsen, J.W. (1969) *The Periodic System of Chemical Elements*. New York: Elsevier.

PHLOGISTON THEORY

Conant, James B. (1956) *The Overthrow of the Phlogiston Theory: Harvard Case Studies in Experimental Science, Case 2*. Cambridge, MA.: Harvard University Press.

Musgrave, Alan (1976) "Why Did Oxygen Supplant Phlogiston? Research Programmes in the Chemical Revolution", in C. Howson (ed.) *Method and Appraisal in the Physical Sciences*, 187–207. Cambridge: Cambridge University Press.

Priestley, Joseph ([1961]) "Experiments and Observations on Different Kinds of Air", in *The Discovery of Oxygen, Part 1* Alembic Club Reprint No. 7. Edinburgh: Alembic Club.

PLATE TECTONICS

Frankel, Henry (1981) 'The Non-Kuhnian Nature of the Recent Revolution in the Earth Sciences" *PSA 1978*, Vol. 2, 197–214. East Lansing: Philosophy of Science Association.

Hallam, A. (1973) *A Revolution in the Earth Sciences: From Continental Drift to Plate Tectonics*. Oxford: Clarendon Press.

Vine, Fred (1966) "Spreading of the Ocean Floor: New Evidence", *Science* 154: 1405–6.

PROUT'S HYPOTHESIS

Knight, David M. (ed.) (1970) *Classical Scientific Papers—Chemistry, Second Series*. New York: American Elsevier. Papers by W. Prout, 62–8; J.B. Dumas, 352; and J.H. Gladstone, 353–20.

Dumas, J.B. (1859) "Memoir on the Equivalents of the Elements", *Ann. Chim. Phys.* 55: 129–210.

Lakatos, Imre (1970) "Falsification and the Methodology of Scientific Research Programmes" in I. Lakatos and A. Musgrave (eds) *Criticism and the Growth of Knowledge* 138–40. Cambridge: Cambridge University Press.

Prout's Hypothesis, Alembic Club Reprint No. 20 (1932). Edinburgh: Alembic Club. Contains papers by W. Prout, J.S. Stas and C. Marignac.

Part II

PROGRESS AS
REVOLUTIONARY
OVERTHROW

Progress through revolutionary overthrow is the principal alternative to progress by incorporation. Revolutionary progress involves discontinuity. Science presumably is practiced at a higher level under the victorious theory. The paradigm case of a successful revolution is perhaps the replacement of Aristotelian physics by Newtonian physics.

Not every replacement of one theory by another rises to the status of a "scientific revolution." At a minimum we require that a "revolutionary" replacement involve

1 activities of human beings that result in
2 an important change, which involves
3 the replacement (overthrow) of a current interpretation—theory, methodological rule, evaluative practice ..., such that
4 scientists subsequently utilize (for a time) the replacement in their work.

This characterization is quite vague. Scientific revolutions are held to be important changes that have an impact on the subsequent practice of science. But scientific achievements vary widely in importance. To restrict revolutions to those developments that are important is to provide a fuzzy demarcation at best.

Requirement 3) excludes from the class of scientific revolutions those new developments which emerge in the absence of competition. Revolution entails conflict. Of course, theories are never put forward in a total theoretical vacuum, but it is arguable that the theories of radioactive decay, superconductivity and DNA structure are not "replacement theories" in any straightforward sense. On the above understanding of "scientific revolution" these theories are not "revolutionary."

7

I.B. COHEN ON THE IDENTIFICATION OF SCIENTIFIC REVOLUTIONS

I.B. Cohen has maintained that scientific revolutions can be identified despite the vagueness of the above characterization of "scientific revolution." He declared that it is

> possible to have a working test for the occurrence of revolutions in science, even without a clear-cut definition.[1]

Cohen suggested four tests of revolutionary status:

1 the testimony of contemporary witnesses;
2 references to the achievement in subsequent documents in the field;
3 the judgments of competent historians of science; and
4 the opinions of scientists working in that field today.[2]

The publication of Newton's *Principia*, for example, passes each test. Fontenelle, Clairaut, Bailly, and others, lauded the work as "revolutionary." Eighteenth- and nineteenth-century textbooks on physics and astronomy give Newton's achievement pride of place. And both historians and working scientists today concur in this assessment.

Cohen's procedure for identifying scientific revolutions is subject to severe limitations. The most obvious limitation is cases of overt disagreement. Evidence relevant to the revolutionary status of Copernicus' achievement includes both the affirmative pronouncement of Kuhn and the negative pronouncement of Cohen himself.[3] Evidence relevant to the revolutionary status of Darwin's achievement includes both the affirmative testimony of August Weismann and Ernst Mayr[4] and the negative testimony of Adam Sedgwick and Richard Owen.[5] Of course, one may survey opinions at a particular point in time and accept the judgment of the majority. But the greater the disagreement present the less secure the conclusion that a revolution has occurred.

A further problem for Cohen's identification procedure is that observers of science may agree that a particular episode is revolutionary but disagree about why it is important. For instance, *A*, *B*, *C*, and *D* may agree that publication of Copernicus' *De revolutionibus* constitutes a scientific revolution. They may do so, however, for quite different reasons. Critic *A* labels publication of *De revolutionibus* "revolutionary" because Copernicus repudiated the Ptolemaic–Thomistic distinction between "saving appearances" and putting forth candidates for physical truth. Critic *B* labels publication "revolutionary" because Copernicus interpreted the earth to be a planet, thereby displacing the earth from the center of the universe. Critic *C* labels the publication "revolutionary" because Copernicus formulated a theory of the solar-system-as-a whole to replace Ptolemy's individual mathematical models for each planet. And critic *D* labels the publication "revolutionary" because Copernicus provided a rationale for known facts about the frequency and extent of retrograde motions.

A, *B*, *C*, and *D* agree that Copernicus achieved a revolution but disagree about its "revolution-making" features. The disagreement admittedly is hypothetical. I am not concerned to argue that there have been observers of science who maintain, for instance, that Copernicus achieved a revolution *solely because* he repudiated the distinction between saving appearances and claiming truth (the position of *A*). However, Edward Grant and Edward Rosen have defended positions similar to that of *A*.[6] Thomas Kuhn, like *B*, has stressed the importance of the shift in world-view inaugurated by Copernicus.[7] Derek Price, like *C*, has emphasized that Copernicus recognized a common feature of Ptolemy's separate mathematical models and used this feature to create a single model of the Solar System.[8] And Imre Lakatos and Elie Zahar, like *D*, have emphasized Copernicus' conversion of "mere facts" into "facts required by the heliostatic system." [9]

Given these diverse perspectives, the fact that each critic labels "revolutionary" Copernicus' achievement counts for little. What is far more important are the reasons why the predication is made.

In my hypothetical dispute, *A*, *B*, *C*, and *D* disagree about the revolution-making features of Copernicus' achievement, but not about the events that make up this achievement. It is the publication of *De revolutionibus* whose revolutionary status is in dispute. However, in many disputes about scientific revolutions, the participants disagree about the scope or extent of the revolution in question. In the above hypothetical example, *A* might have claimed that it was the circulation of Copernicus' *Commentariolis* that was revolutionary and *B* might have claimed that no revolution occurred until the results of Galileo's telescopic observations were disseminated.

A 1988 issue of *Osiris*, for instance, contains two quite different appraisals of "the chemical revolution." J.B. Gough viewed the work of Lavoisier as the culmination of a "Stahlian revolution" which emancipated chemistry from the domination of physics. Gough suggested that the chemical revolution began with Stahl's opposition to the Newtonian theory that matter is comprised of inertially homogeneous particles and reached fruition in Lavoisier's identification of qualitatively distinct chemical elements.[10] Robert Seigfried, by contrast, interpreted the work of Lavoisier to be a preliminary stage of a revolution achieved by Dalton. Seigfried suggested that the chemical revolution began with Lavoisier's gravimetric studies to show that metals are simple substances (and their calces compound) and reached fruition in Dalton's assignment of relative atomic weights to elementary species.[11]

Cohen has maintained that the chemical revolution passes all the tests for a revolution in science."[12] Gough and Seigfried might well agree with this assessment. However, they predicate "the chemical revolution" of different collections of events.

This is not an unusual situation. Historians of science often disagree about which events comprise a given revolution. Given a sequence of scientific achievements, S_1—S_2—S_3, one observer may label "revolutionary" the sequence as a whole. A second observer may interpret the sequence to be a succession of three individual revolutions.

A.R. Hall, for example, has authored an influential book on *The Scientific Revolution: 1500–1800*.[13] The achievements of Copernicus, Newton and Lavoisier fall within this period.

Hall maintained that developments during this period created science as we know it today. By 1800 science was an ongoing enterprise. Prior to 1500 science, properly speaking, did not exist. From this standpoint, *the* scientific revolution is that set of human actions that created the methodological and valuational commitments whose implementation constitutes scientific inquiry.

Thomas Kuhn has written about both *the* scientific revolution and diverse individual revolutions. In *The Essential Tension* (1977) he suggested that *the* scientific revolution is a union of two traditions—a mathematical tradition practiced in astronomy, optics, statics and harmonics, and a Baconian experimental tradition practiced in such disciplines as electrostatics, magnetism, pneumatics and microscopy. Kuhn noted that Newton participated in both traditions, but that his achievements gave rise to separate eighteenth-century traditions, one deriving from the *Principia* and one deriving from the *Opticks*. A lasting union of the two traditions was achieved only during the first half of the nineteenth century.[14]

In *The Structure of Scientific Revolutions*, by contrast, Kuhn discussed a number of individual revolutions, with particular emphasis on the Copernican, Newtonian, chemical, and Einsteinian revolutions.[15] More recently, I.B. Cohen has included among scientific revolutions the achievements of Descartes, Harvey, Galileo, Lyell, Darwin, Maxwell, Freud and Bohr.[16]

Cohen has suggested that we can tell whether a scientific revolution has occurred without becoming involved in an explication of the phrase "scientific revolution." However, his project to identify revolutions by reference to the testimony of qualified observers is unsatisfactory for the reasons given above.

8

KUHN'S TAXONOMIC CRITERION

The question about which developments in the history of science are revolutionary remains. An alternative to Cohen's approach is to begin by formulating criteria of revolutionary status and then to apply the criteria to determine which historical episodes qualify. The formulation of criteria is the sort of inquiry that engages philosophers.

Thomas Kuhn suggested that scientific revolutions involve changes in the ways in which entities or processes are classified. He claimed, moreover, that revolutionary taxonomic changes are "holistic." They involve replacement of "an integrated picture of several aspects of nature."[1] Moreover, the change of categories occurs, not piecemeal, but all at once. Kuhn maintained that the transitions from Aristotelian to Newtonian physics, from electrostatic to electrochemical theories of the Voltaic cell, and from Boltzmann's "resonators" to Planck's "oscillators" exemplify the types of taxonomic changes that characterize scientific revolutions. He noted, moreover, that these transitions involve a "central change of model, metaphor, or analogy."[2]

Kuhn restricted revolutionary developments to those changes that modify or replace taxonomic categories. He held that the mere addition (or deletion) of members to a class is an activity proper to "normal science." Kuhn's characterization of revolutionary episodes excludes Humphrey Davy's classification of iodine as an element and William Herschel's realization that what he initially took to be a comet instead is a planet.

To apply a taxonomic criterion is to identify classes newly introduced or modified. Consider Copernicus' achievement, an achievement that Kuhn himself labeled "revolutionary." What are the relevant classes? Kuhn suggested that Copernicus introduced a new taxonomic category, the category "satellite." In Ptolemy's taxonomy of astronomical bodies there are just "stars" and "planets." Copernicus augmented this taxonomy by creating a new category for the Moon. On this reading Copernicus did introduce a holistic taxonomic change.

However, it is unclear that Kuhn's reading of taxonomic change is correct in this case. There are other ways to interpret Copernicus' innovation. One such interpretation is that Copernicus accepted without modification Ptolemy's subdivision of heavenly bodies into those that revolve and those that do not.

On this interpretation, Copernicus' achievement may be dismissed as the addition of the Earth to the former class and the deletion of the Sun and the stars from the latter class. The earlier taxonomy remains unchanged and no revolution has occurred.

A second alternative interpretation is that Copernicus did achieve a taxonomic change, but that the important change is a change in the taxonomy of spherical bodies, and not the introduction of a new category "satellite." Whereas geostatic theorists implicitly distinguished two types of spherical bodies—those that rotate around an axis (like the Moon) and those that do not (like the Earth). Copernicus denied this distinction. According to Copernicus, it is of the nature of a spherical body to rotate on its axis. From an historical perspective, however, there would be something forced about basing the revolutionary status of Copernicus' achievement on that particular taxonomic change. Geostatic theorists would have agreed that the Moon displays the same face to the Earth, but would have attributed this not to an axial rotation, but to the "fact" that the Moon is embedded in a rotating crystalline shell.

A third alternative interpretation is that the relevant taxonomic change associated with the transition to a Sun-centered astronomy is the abandonment of the Aristotelian distinction between separate terrestrial and celestial realms, each with its own appropriate laws. This surely is the most important taxonomic change associated with the triumph of heliostatic astronomy. But this change was accomplished by Newton. One likely result of applying Kuhn's criterion would be to credit Newton, and not Copernicus, with accomplishing a revolution in astronomy.

Emphasis on holistic taxonomic change also may require a reevaluation of Lavoisier's work. C.E. Perrin has shown that Lavoisier's oxygen theory emerged piecemeal over an extended period of time. Moreover, according to Perrin, influential contemporaries at first adopted one or another component feature of Lavoisier's system without adopting others. Perrin declared that

> detailed studies of individual conversions ... show they followed a gradual and stepwise pattern, with successive adaptation of new components into a modified traditional framework.[3]

Kuhn, however, had demanded holistic change. He maintained that

> in revolutionary change one must either live with incoherence or else revise a number of interrelated generalizations together. If these same changes were introduced one at a time, there would be no immediate resting place. Only the initial and final sets of generalizations provide a coherent account of nature.[4]

Applications of the Kuhnian criterion thus may exclude the achievements of Copernicus and Lavoisier from the class of scientific revolutions. This would be a controversial result, but perhaps not an unacceptable result. Our "pre-criterial" intuitions about the revolutionary status of the work of Copernicus and Lavoisier are not strong; there has been considerable disagreement among historians of science about the importance of their achievements.

A more serious difficulty is the inclusiveness of the Kuhnian criterion. Judgments about holistic impact are judgments about extensiveness and interdependence. How is one to establish a non-arbitrary division of taxonomic changes into those that have sufficiently widespread repercussions (and hence are revolutions) and those that do not? Since questions of degree are involved, it is to be expected that interpreters of science who apply a "holistic taxonomic change" criterion will disagree about specific episodes.

A case in point is Geoffroy's classification of acids and bases by reference to "elective affinities" manifested in displacement reactions (1718).[5] This classification achieved a significant measure of interconnection and integration. Should Geoffroy receive credit for inaugurating a revolution on that account? Or is his taxonomic scheme to be excluded from the ranks of genuine revolutions on the grounds that its holistic impact is insufficient? To be revolutionary a change of taxonomy must have widespread repercussions within a scientific discipline. But a chemist could accept Geoffroy's taxonomy without abandoning a commitment to either the Newtonian doctrine of the inertial homogeneity of matter or the doctrine of distinct chemically elementary atoms.

The following sequence of stellar classification systems illustrates the difficulty about extensiveness that arises in applications of Kuhn's taxonomic criterion.[6]

1   William Herschel subdivided double stars into binary star systems and non-binary, optically-double stars;
2   Angelo Secchi classified stars by reference to four basic spectral types: whitish-blue (strong hydrogen absorption lines), yellow (spectra similar to that of the Sun), red (dark bands present), and faint red (hydrocarbon absorption bands), (1863–80), and
3   Ejnar Hertzsprung and Henry Norris Russell located stars on a two-dimensional grid whose axes are spectral type and absolute magnitude, (1905–14).

Herschel's new taxonomy was associated with an important theoretical achievement, the application of Newton's gravitational theory to calculate elliptical orbits for binary star systems. Herschel's achievement thus satisfies Kuhn's requirement that a revolutionary change display an analogy or metaphor. Binary star systems are viewed as analogues of the Earth–Moon system. Moreover, Herschel's dichotomous division of double stars must be accepted or rejected as a whole. Supporters of Herschel's taxonomy have come to see the universe in a new way. Line-of-sight, non-binary star-pairs are not really "double stars" at all. This episode would seem to satisfy Kuhn's "holistic taxonomic change" criterion rather well. Of course, one might argue that since the taxonomy applies only to double stars, and not to all stars, it is not sufficiently extensive to count as "revolutionary."

Secchi's classification is more extensive, since the overwhelming majority of stars can be assigned to his four spectral classes. This classification too displays an analogy. Secchi's system was taken to specify an evolutionary sequence from youth (blue-white) to old age (red). The same sequence of colors is observed during the cooling of a hot piece of metal.

It might seem that Secchi's taxonomy is just an alternative way of assigning stars to categories on the basis of their observed colors. Were this the case, Secchi's system would not be a replacement of a prior system, and for that reason would not be a revolutionary change. However, the terms "blue-white," "yellow," etc., are mere labels of spectral types. It is the position and intensity of spectral lines that determine classification. These spectral lines are measures of absolute surface temperatures and not observed colors. The observed color of a star depends not only on surface temperature but also on distance (due to the reddening effect produced by scattering from interstellar dust). Some "optically red" stars turn out not to be "red" in Secchi's taxonomy. Hence Secchi's taxonomy did not just restate an earlier system based on observed colors, and on Kuhn's criterion would appear to qualify as a revolution.

The Draper star catalog, compiled by E.C. Pickering and others (1882–90) subdivided the Seechi blue-white class into types A and B, and the Seechi yellow class into types F, G, and K. This taxonomy lacked theoretical significance. Only after terrestrial helium was discovered (1895) and helium-rich O-type stars were added was the sequence O, B, A, F, G, K, M, N shown to be a natural system. The above sequence was recognized to be in the order of decreasing surface temperature. This ordering was achieved only after visually-reddish O-type stars were discovered to be distant from the Solar System, and hence subject to significant reddening from absorption by interstellar dust.

Hertzsprung and Russell plotted the above sequence of spectral types against absolute visual magnitudes on a two-dimensional grid (1905–14). They noted that stars cluster in certain regions of the plot—e.g., main sequence stars, red giant stars, white dwarfs, etc.—and interpreted the clustering as evidence for stellar evolution. Russell, in particular, interpreted the class of red giant stars to be newly-formed stars in the process of moving toward the main sequence.

The Hertzsprung–Russell taxonomy facilitated the formulation of an integrated picture of stellar evolution, a picture that incorporates mass-luminosity data and theories of nuclear energy generation. One implication of this picture is that Russell's initial interpretation of red giant stars was incorrect. These stars are moving away from, and not towards, the main sequence. The Hertzsprung–Russell classification is impressively holistic, extensive, and displays an analogy to organic evolution. It thus would appear to satisfy Kuhn's requirements for revolutionary change.

Looking back over the history of astrophysics, it seems clear that Secchi's spectral classification was more important than Herschel's dichotomous classification of double stars, and that the Hertzsprung–Russell taxonomy was more important than Secchi's spectral classification. If each of these developments qualifies as a holistic taxonomic change, then it will be necessary to distinguish "more important revolutions" from "less important revolutions." The suspicion arises that extensive application of Kuhn's criterion would lead to a proliferation of scientific revolutions, many of which are of minor importance.

This suspicion is reinforced by an examination of successive theories of acidity.[7] Within the taxonomy of Arrhenius (1887), a given chemical species can be an acid or a base, but not both. Within the Brønsted–Lowry taxonomy (1923), by contrast, one and the same chemical species may be both a proton donor and a proton acceptor, and hence may be both an acid and a base.[8] The transition from Arrhenius to Brønsted–Lowry is a holistic taxonomic change, but neither chemists nor historians of chemistry speak of the transition as "revolutionary."

G.N. Lewis subsequently interpreted acids to be electron-pair acceptors, rather than proton donors. Within the Lewis taxonomy, the oxygen atom and the boron trichloride molecule qualify as acids.[9]

9

TOULMIN'S "IDEALS OF NATURAL ORDER"

Stephen Toulmin's concept 'replacement of an ideal of natural order' might appear at first glance to be an appropriate criterion of revolutionary status. According to Toulmin

> "ideals of natural order" mark off for us those happenings in the world around us which do require explanation, by contrasting them with "the natural course of events"—i.e., those events which do not.[1]

An ideal of natural order provides a background against which events or relations are unexpected and puzzling. Such deviations from "the way things should go" are regarded as anomalies. For example, if one accepts Steno's principle of original horizontality, then uptilted sedimentary strata are anomalies to be explained by reference to forces operating subsequently to deposition. And if one accepts the LaPlacian ideal of accounting for all motion by reference to attractive or repulsive central forces, then electromagnetic induction is an anomaly. One might appropriate Toulmin's concept by stipulating that only those historical episodes that involve the replacement of one ideal of natural order by a second qualify as scientific revolutions.

Toulmin himself stressed the importance of the transition from Aristotle's ideal of natural order to that of Newton. Aristotle's ideal takes rest to be the natural state of affairs in the terrestrial region. This ideal stipulates that instances of motion are anomalies that require explanation. Newton's ideal, by contrast, requires only that changes in motion be explained. Whereas motion *per se* is anomalous within Aristotelian physics, only changes of motion are anomalous within Newtonian physics. Inertial motion—motion that is uniform and linear—is (or, rather, would be) self-explanatory. Newtonian physics thus appears to satisfy the requirement that a scientific revolution introduce a new ideal of natural order.

So far, so good. But any two competing theories have different deductive consequences (given the same auxiliary hypotheses, boundary conditions and initial conditions). Acceptance of T^* in place of T changes our expectations..

This is true not only for Newton's inertial physics, but also for Avogadro's modified atomic theory, which postulates polyatomic gas molecules and changes expectations about volume relations in gas phase reactions, and Sommerfeld's modified theory of the hydrogen atom, which permits elliptical electron orbits and changes expectations about the spectrum of hydrogen. If changes in expectations about the order of nature indicates that a scientific revolution has taken place, then it would be difficult to include Newton's achievement but exclude the achievements of Avogadro and Sommerfeld. What is needed, it seems, is some measure of the importance of revised expectations.

But if cases of theory-replacement vary more or less continuously with respect to importance, then there is no clear-cut demarcation of revolutionary episodes. Given the difficulties that beset I.B. Cohen's proposal for identifying scientific revolutions, prospects for agreement about judgments of importance are not good.

Scientific revolutions may well involve changes in expectations about the natural course of events. However, the appeal to a change of expectations does not provide a means to distinguish scientific revolutions from less exalted scientific achievements.

10

IDEOLOGICAL UPHEAVAL AND REVOLUTIONARY CHANGE

Another approach might be to require that all and only those changes in science that produce "ideological upheaval" are revolutionary. There is general agreement that Copernicus, Darwin, Freud, and Einstein created theories whose acceptance altered man's understanding of himself and his place in the universe.

However, "ideological upheaval" is probably too vague to serve as a criterion of revolutionary status. It also may be too exclusive. Applications of this criterion presumably would disqualify the "chemical revolution" associated with the work of Lavoisier and Dalton and the "geological revolution" associated with the development of plate-tectonic theory. Moreover, one could include or exclude Cartesian physics and Newtonian physics depending on what is taken to count as "ideological change." In the last-mentioned case, one also would have to distinguish the "ideology of Newton's physics (within which God plays an active role as governor of the universe), from the "ideology of Newtonian physics" (as exemplified by Laplace).

11

KUHN'S
THREE-BEAT PATTERN

To adopt "holistic taxonomic change," "replacement of an ideal of natural order," or "ideological upheaval" as a criterion of revolutionary status does violence to our preanalytic convictions. These proposed criteria are unsatisfactory. But even if there is no condition that is necessary or sufficient for a scientific revolution, it yet may be the case that there is a unique pattern of development displayed by revolutionary episodes.

Thomas Kuhn suggested that scientific revolutions have a distinctive "fingerprint"—a three-beat sequence of stages.[1] The pattern begins with a period of "normal science," within which scientists apply and extend a dominant "paradigm." The second stage is a period of conflict within which supporters of a second paradigm seek to overthrow the hitherto dominant paradigm. And the third stage is a new period of normal science under the victorious second paradigm.

The transition between normal science and a revolutionary interlude is marked by an accumulation of anomalies. In Kuhn's usage, anomalies are phenomena that resist explanation by reference to the categories of the dominant paradigm.

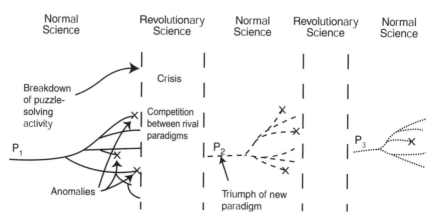

Figure 11.1   History of science as a succession of "normal" and "revolutionary" stages

Examples include projectile motion for Aristotelian physics, the motion of Mercury for Newtonian physics, partial reflection for the wave theory of light, and the atomic weights of tellurium and iodine for the periodic classification of the chemical elements.

Kuhn's "revolutionary fingerprint" is useful for historical analysis only if it is clear what counts as a "paradigm." In the second edition of *The Structure of Scientific Revolutions*, Kuhn introduced the concepts "exemplar" and "disciplinary matrix" to stand for a narrow and a broad sense of "paradigm."[2]

An exemplar is an influential application of a scientific theory. Examples are Newton's explanation of planetary motions, Bohr's explanation of the hydrogen spectrum, and Mendel's explanation of the distribution of phenotypes in hybrid pea plants. Transitions from one exemplar to another are not the sorts of changes traditionally labeled "revolutions." For example, Newton, d'Alembert, LaGrange, and Hamilton proposed influential exemplars for mechanics. However, historians of science do not speak of a "LaGrangean revolution" or a "Hamiltonian revolution" in physics.

It is the broad sense of "paradigm" that is relevant to discussions about revolutions in science. Unfortunately, the concept "disciplinary matrix" is quite vague. A disciplinary matrix includes commitments to all or some of the following:

1   certain kinds of inquiry (e.g., *in vivo* vs. *in vitro* examinations, neutral-observer vs. participant-observer studies ...),
2   certain patterns of explanation (e.g., deductive, inductive; statistical, teleological ...)
3   certain types of theories (e.g., contact-action vs. field theories),
4   the existence of theoretical entities (e.g., absolute space, atoms, microbes ...),
5   principles held to be inviolable (e.g., conservation principles, extremum principles ...), and
6   exemplars.

If fulfillment of the three-beat pattern is necessary for an historical episode to qualify as a scientific revolution, four conditions must be satisfied:

1   in the process of application and extension, a dominant paradigm (P_1) is beset by a number of anomalies,
2   a second paradigm (P_2) is introduced,
3   P_2 is believed by scientists to resolve some of the anomalies that thwarted P_1, and
4   scientists abandon P_1 in favor of P_2.

A number of historical developments traditionally labeled "revolutions" appear to fit the Kuhnian pattern. Transitions from Aristotelian physics to Newtonian physics, from phlogiston chemistry to oxygen chemistry, from Newtonian

Table 11.1 Kuhnian paradigm replacements

Initial paradigm	Anomalies	Successor paradigm
Aristotelian physics	Free fall; projectile motion	Newtonian physics
Phlogiston chemistry	Weight calx > weight metal	Oxygen chemistry
Newtonian mechanics	Precession of perihelion of Mercury	General relativity theory
Classical physics	Stability of nuclear atom; black-body radiation	Quantum physics

mechanics to general relativity theory, and from classical physics to quantum physics all conform to the general requirements of the pattern, as shown in Table 11.1

Unfortunately, Kuhn's pattern is at variance with certain of our pre-analytic beliefs about scientific revolutions. In at least one case, a *prima facie* revolutionary change took place without a prior accumulation of anomalies. Many historians, including Kuhn himself, credit Copernicus with inaugurating a scientific revolution. But the preceding period of Ptolemaic normal science did not produce an accumulation of anomalies. There were discrepancies between predictions drawn from the theory and observations, to be sure, but the discrepancies were addressed within the paradigm by adjusting the very flexible parameters of its mathematical models. Moreover, Copernicus did not introduce a new type of inquiry or pattern of explanation, nor did he posit new theoretical entities or inviolable principles. And the quantified theory of Books II–VI of *De revolutionibus* is not different in kind from its Ptolemaic predecessor (save for the absence of equant points).[3]

If this analysis is correct, then we have a choice. We can insist that Copernicus' achievement is a *bona fide* revolution and that Kuhn's three-beat pattern does not fit all scientific revolutions. On the other hand, we can affirm Kuhn's pattern as a necessary condition of revolutionary status, and exclude Copernicus' achievement from the class of scientific revolutions. Some interpreters of science, among them I.B. Cohen, have insisted that Copernicus played only a minor role in the revolution in astronomy. According to Cohen,

> if there was a Copernican Revolution, it occurred in the seventeenth and not in the sixteenth century and was associated with the names of Kepler, Galileo, Descartes and Newton.[4]

The three-beat pattern fails to fit historical episodes in another respect. Kuhn was wrong to claim that a higher-level theory is rejected only when a competing theory is available. Kuhn takes theory-rejection to be a triadic relation—T_1, e, T_2—where T_2 is a competing theory and e is a statement recording evidence. He declared that once it has achieved the status of paradigm, a scientific theory is declared invalid only if an alternative candidate is available to take its place.[5]

Imre Lakatos echoed Kuhn's claim. According to Lakatos,

contrary to naive falsificationism, no experiment, experimental report, observation statement or well-corroborated low-level falsifying hypothesis alone can lead to falsification. There is no falsification before the emergence of a better theory.[6]

Kuhn's thesis appears to fit the career of Newtonian gravitation theory, a long-lived paradigm for planetary astronomy. Late nineteenth-century scientists were aware that various applications of the Newtonian theory had failed to explain the anomalous precession of Mercury's orbit. Nevertheless, they did not reject the Newtonian theory until after the development of Einstein's general theory of relativity (1916).

A.S. Eddington observed that after Einstein formulated the Special theory of relativity (1905), physicists were aware of an additional tension.[7] The special theory accounted for the null result of the Michelson–Morley experiment (1887), but required a reformulation of the classical concepts of space and time. Einstein's theory, unlike Newton's mechanics, took mass and distance to be velocity-dependent. How then is one to decide which theory to implement to specify mass and distance values in the Newtonian gravitational formula— $F = G \, m_1 \, m_2 / r^2$?

Eddington noted that scientists continued to apply Newtonian gravitation theory despite the success achieved by the special theory of relativity. In one respect, the two theories are not in competition. The special theory is applicable only to non-accelerated motion and planetary orbits are cases of accelerated motion. Nevertheless, the fundamental concepts of the two theories do conflict. "Mass" and "distance" are univocal predicates in Newtonian mechanics but dyadic predicates in the special theory of relativity.

The situation changed with the formulation of Einstein's general theory of relativity. The general theory is applicable to cases of accelerated motion. This places the general theory in direct competition with Newtonian gravitation theory. Inferences drawn from the general theory differ from those drawn from Newtonian theory. One such inference is that there should be a small perturbation in Mercury's Newtonian-calculated orbit. Einstein's general theory received credit for removing an anomaly that had plagued Newtonian gravitation theory.

A second inference is that the path of a light ray is bent passing through the gravitational field of a large mass. Eddington was a participant in the solar eclipse expedition to the Isle of Principe in 1917. Its purpose was to test the general-theory prediction of a measurable deflection of starlight by the Sun. The expedition provided the first "new" confirmation of the general theory of relativity.

In addition, since calculations derived from the general theory of relativity approach asymptotically calculations derived from Newtonian theory in the limiting case of velocities small with respect to the velocity of fight, a reasonable degree of conceptual harmony is restored. Scientists now can say " yes, Newtonian mechanics is false, but its calculations suffice for slowly moving bodies, just as Galileo's false law of falling bodies suffices for the motions of objects near the earth's surface." [8]

Kuhn restricted his theory about theory-rejection to high-level theories which achieve status as "paradigms." "Paradigms," in this context, are "disciplinary matrices," which include shared beliefs, values and techniques, as well as commitments to theoretical entities and relations.

It is clear that low-level hypotheses often are rejected upon receipt of negative evidence in the absence of any alternative hypothesis. For example, the chemist who hypothesizes that a white powder is aspirin will reject the hypothesis if the powder fails to melt at 134°C. The melting points of organic compounds are characteristic "fingerprints." Failure to display the appropriate melting point is taken to be a sufficient reason to reject a hypothetical identification, despite the absence of any alternative hypothesis.

But even if we restrict our attention to paradigms, Kuhn's claim does not fit the history of science. There are a number of episodes in which a paradigm was rejected in the absence of a viable competing paradigm.

Perhaps the most striking example is the rejection of the principle that mass is conserved in all physical interactions. This conservation principle was abandoned in the face of evidence about radioactive decay processes. It subsequently was replaced by a new conservation principle—the conservation of mass-energy. But at the time that scientists "declared invalid" the principle of conservation of mass, there was no competing theory on the horizon. Rather the evidence from radioactive decay was taken to be a sufficient reason to reject the principle of conservation of mass.

A supporter of Kuhn's position might argue that the principle of the conservation of mass was not rejected, but only reinterpreted. However, it was not the case that the theory of special relativity was available alongside the principle of conservation of mass at the time of the discovery of radioactive decay. Conservation of mass was rejected before a theory became available that hypothesized the interconvertibility of mass and energy. Of course, one can insist that there is always a competing theory present in a test situation— namely, the negation of the theory under test. But Kuhn's thesis is of interest only if we exclude the case where $T_2 = -T_1$, from the possibilities for T_2 in the triad [T_1, e, T_2].

In the mid 1950s, the principle of conservation of parity met a similar fate. The principle, which states that all physical processes display a mirror-symmetry, was widely accepted by physicists prior to 1956. Experiments suggested by C.N. Yang and T.D. Lee in that year revealed that parity is not conserved in so-called "weak interactions."[9] The conservation principle, *qua* universally applicable, was quickly rejected. Yang and Lee received a Nobel Prize for this result in 1957. At the time no well-developed alternative theory of electroweak interactions had been formulated. Kuhn's picture of a high-level theory being rejected only when a rival theory is available does not fit this historical episode either.

12

LAUDAN'S RETICULATIONAL
MODEL OF SCIENTIFIC
CHANGE

Larry Laudan complained that "Kuhnian holism" introduces an unacceptable evaluative relativism into the interpretation of scientific revolutions. Before a revolutionary episode, a Kuhnian disciplinary matrix includes theories T, methodological rules M and cognitive aims A. After the revolution, the disciplinary matrix includes T^*, M^* and A^*. The transition cannot be justified by appeal to M^* or A^*. Such a "justification" would involve an unacceptable circularity. Moreover, according to Kuhn, there is no paradigm-neutral standpoint available from which to appraise the transition.

Laudan claimed that his own "reticulational model" is superior to "Kuhnian holism" in which theories, methodological rules and cognitive aims are replaced all-at-once (see Figure 12.1).

On the reticulational model, the tensions that arise among theories, methodological rules and cognitive aims are kept in dynamic equilibrium through a process of gradual, piecemeal adjustment. Laudan stressed the reciprocity of the adjustment process. The tension between two apices of the triangle may be resolved by adjustment of either apex. No subset of propositions is to be taken as foundational.

Laudan's reticulational model fits scientific practice rather well. Consider the relationship between theories and methodological principles.

Theories sometimes are modified to accommodate methodological principles. A case in point is the response of vortex theorists to Newton's criticism. Newton had argued that Descartes' vortex theory of the Solar System fails to conform to an important methodological principle. The principle in question is that an acceptable theory ought to subsume deductively the relevant laws within its

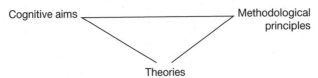

Figure 12.1 The reticulational model[1]

domain of application. Newton proved that the period of revolution of a planet carried by the Cartesian vortex would be proportional to the square of its distance from the Sun. This result is at variance with Kepler's third law, which states that the period of revolution of a planet is proportional to the three-halves power of its mean distance from the Sun.

Descartes' successors accepted the nomic subsumption principle and sought to alleviate tension by modifying Descartes' theory. Leibniz, for instance, developed a complicated theory in which a planet is affected by both a "solar vortex" and a "harmonic vortex." The aethereal particles of the two vortices are required to move through the same space without interacting, and yet to combine in such a way that Kepler's laws are obeyed.

J.P. de Molières (1677–1742) also sought to reconcile vortex theory and Kepler's laws. He suggested that the solar vortex contains bands of rotating elastic vortices, bounded on either side by nonelastic vortices, arranged so that the bands are located at the observed distances of the planets from the Sun. The small elastic vortices expand and contract as they move around the Sun.[2]

Molières hypothesized that a planet is carried in its orbit by small elastic vortex T (see Figure 12.2). As T moves from A to C, increasing its distance from the Sun's position F, it slows down and rotates more rapidly, thereby expanding against the constraining force of the non-expanding vortices on the inside and outside of its path. At C it is furthest form the Sun. As T moves from C to A, its distance from F decreases, it gains speed and rotates less rapidly, thereby contracting in size. N is the vortex T at perihelion and Q at aphelion. R and P represent the size of vortex T at points D and B of its elipical orbit. Molières

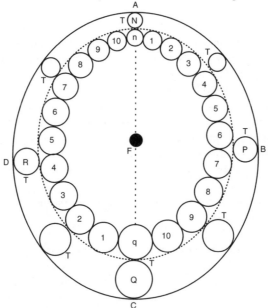

Figure 12.2 Molières' elastic-vortex theory

reduced the tension between theory and methodology by means of this elaborate modification of Descartes' vortex theory.

There also are occasions within the history of science in which methodological principles are modified in response to the success of theories. For example, the success of the quantum theory of Bohr and Heisenberg led scientists to abandon a principle of completeness. The methodological principle abandoned required that a *complete* explanation of a physical process must specify a causal relationship which accounts for the continuous spatio-temporal evolution of the process.

Just as a disparity between a theory and a methodological principle may be overcome by revising either the theory or the principle, so also a disparity between a theory and a cognitive aim may be overcome by revising either the theory or the aim. In some historical episodes the cognitive aim takes precedence over individual theories. For example, Cartesian natural philosophers affirmed as a cognitive aim that physical processes be explained by reference to contact action. They believed that to appeal to "action-at-a-distance" is to cross the boundary that separates natural philosophy from superstition. Astrologers, for instance, attribute the causes of events on Earth to the operation of "astral forces" that derive from the relative positions of the planets. Cartesians sought to exclude reference to such "forces" from the domain of natural philosophy.

Given this cognitive aim, Newton's concept of gravitational attraction was suspect. Cartesians conceded that Newton had been able to "save the appearances" of planetary motions by means of the hypothesis of gravitational attraction. Cartesians denied, however, that he had explained planetary motions. Some Cartesians drew an analogy between Newton's achievement and Ptolemy's success in reproducing the zodiacal motions of the planets by means of epicycle-deferent models. Commitment to the cognitive aim of contact-action explanations led Cartesian theorists to reject the theory of gravitational attraction as an explanation of planetary motions.

Other historical episodes reveal the modification of a cognitive aim to accommodate the success of a theory. The success of quantum theory led Niels Bohr to reinterpret the cognitive ideal of unambiguous communication. Bohr took unambiguous communication to require that the concepts of classical physics be applied (subject to important limitations) to the behavior of quantum systems between observations. As Max Born expressed this ideal:

> scientific results should be interpreted in terms intelligible to every thinking man.[3]

Bohr believed that the cognitive aim of unambiguous communication can be realized by providing mutually exclusive, but complementary, wave and particle pictures applicable to quantum systems between observations. He noted that, for a given experimental arrangement, either a wave picture is appropriate or a particle picture is appropriate, but not both. For instance, in the case of the diffraction of electrons or photons at a single slit in a diaphragm, it is possible to set up apparatus to measure accurately either the path[4] of a particle or the diffraction pattern produced. If the diaphragm is rigidly anchored to a massive frame, the transverse component of the position of the particle passing through the slit can be determined by means of the position of the slit. The transverse component of the momentum of the particle then may be determined only with very low accuracy, although the *distribution* of particles striking a photographic plate can be calculated from the Schrödinger equation upon substitution of a specific distance between diaphragm and plate. At the pictorial-language level, the wave picture is appropriate. The pattern on the photographic plate is "explained" by reference to the diffraction of a wave at the slit. Bohr pointed out that if the diaphragm instead is connected to the frame by an elastic spring,

> it should, in principle, be possible to control the momentum transfer to the diaphragm and, thus, to make more detailed predictions as to the direction of the electron path from the hole to the recording point.[5]

This increase in accuracy with which the path of a particle may be determined is achieved only at the expense of a blurring of the diffraction pattern. At the pictorial-language level, the particle picture is appropriate. The electron is pictured as a particle whose path is determined by the momentum transfer at the slit.

The experimental arrangement in which an interpretation in terms of "wave language" is applied (the diaphragm is rigidly connected to the frame), does not lend itself to an interpretation in terms of "particle language," and the experimental arrangement in which an interpretation in terms of "particle language" is applied (the diaphragm is connected to the frame by an elastic spring), does not lend itself to an interpretation in terms of "wave language." Bohr placed a restriction on linguistic usage at the pictorial level—the results of a particular experiment may not be interpreted in terms of both a "particle picture" and a "wave picture." Thus, although the wave-picture and the particle-picture are mutually exclusive descriptions of what happens between measurements made on a system, the pictorial level of language does not contain logically incompatible claims. In the case of the passage of electrons through a slit, for instance, the "Copenhagen interpretation" restricts the wave-picture to one experimental arrangement and the particle-picture to a second experimental arrangement. Given a specific experimental arrangement, it does not follow from the "Copenhagen interpretation" that both "a wave passed through the slit" and "a particle exchanged momentum with the slit."

Bohr insisted that individual pictorial-level interpretations are perfectly coherent. In particular, descriptions of quantum processes by reference to conservation laws are both consistent and appropriate. What is incoherent is the combining of mutually exclusive pictures of the same experimental arrangement. Although superposition of spatio-temporal description and causal analysis upon a particular experimental arrangement is a consistent interpretation within classical physics, this superposition is not a consistent interpretation within quantum physics.

Bohr defended a principle of complementarity which stipulates that two mutually exclusive descriptions of a quantum process, in which two different experimental arrangements are employed, are complementary and combine to produce an exhaustive interpretation of the process. He maintained that wave-picture and particle-picture are of equal importance. This equivalence is based ultimately on the uncertainty relations, Einstein's equation $E = h \nu$, and de Broglie's equation $p = h \nu / c$. If the equations expressing energy and momentum in terms of frequency are substituted into the uncertainty relations $\Delta p \, \Delta q \geq h / 4 \pi$ and $\Delta E \, \Delta t \geq h / 4 \pi$, it is evident that there is a formal symmetry between the specification of spatio-temporal coordinates and the specification of wave-like properties. Bohr emphasized that these symmetry properties are the foundation of quantum mechanics.

Tensions between cognitive aims and methodological principles also have been resolved by modifying one or the other. Eighteenth-century natural philosophers resolved the tension between Newton's pronouncements on behalf of "experimental philosophy" and his practice of an axiomatic methodology in favor of the latter. Newton had urged that the content of natural philosophy be restricted to statements about "manifest qualities" and their relations, theories "derived from" these relations, and "queries" directive of further inquiry. But the methodology of the *Principia* is a successive formulation and application of axiom systems—the axioms of motion and gravitational attraction, combined with progressively more complex auxiliary hypotheses. Laudan observed that one indication of the demise of the ideal of "experimental philosophy" was the proliferation of theories about "non-manifest" entities such as caloric, aether and phlogiston.

Einstein's "suspension of disbelief" in the face of Walter Kaufmann's apparent experimental disproof of the special theory of relativity might be cited as an example of a resolution of tension in favor of cognitive aims. Gerald Holton has argued that Einstein gave precedence to the cognitive ideals simplicity, invariance and symmetry. Of course, Einstein did not repudiate the methodological principle that requires agreement between theory and experiment. But he was willing to set aside this principle of behalf of the above cognitive ideals.[6]

Laudan claimed normative-prescriptive status for the reticulational model. He declared that this model

> is intended to be more than descriptive of existing practices. It purports to give a normatively viable characterization of how discussions about the nature of cognitive values should be conducted.[7]

86

Critics objected that the reticulational model, like Kuhn's holistic model, is a recipe for relativism.[8] The reticulational model requires that a change in one component that disturbs the triadic equilibrium be accommodated by a compensating change in one (or both) of the other components. But the Model does not specify how the equilibrium is to be reestablished.

Laudan responded to this objection. He superimposed on the relationships among the apices of the triangle two constraints on cognitive aims. The cognitive aims of science are required to be both consistent and realizable. He held that these constraints are inviolable, thereby providing fixed standards for the appraisal of possible adjustments within the triangle.

However, these constraints are too weak to be of much assistance to the methodologist. The methodologist is directed to restore equilibrium in such a way that consistency and realizability are satisfied. But tensions within the triad may be alleviated by modifying any one component, or combination of components. In many evaluative contexts there are numerous consistent and realizable adjustments that can be made to restore equilibrium. The methodologist needs to know, for a specific situation, whether to modify a theory, an evaluative standard or a cognitive aim. The reticulational model merely restricts the numerous permissible modifications to those that preserve consistency and realizability.

Moreover, the realizability constraint is subject to challenge. Philip Quinn pointed out that there may be correct methodological rules for pursuing an electrodynamic theory of action-at-a-distance, despite the fact that instantaneous electromagnetic action-at-a-distance is physically impossible.[9] More generally, one might object that it is not irrational to pursue the cognitive aim of the complete reproducibility of experimental results in spite of the unrealizability of this aim.

If the realizability constraint is abandoned, then Laudan's only constraint on adjustments within the triangle is that the cognitive aims of science be consistent. Under this single external constraint, there is no way to discriminate among numerous alternative modifications of theories, methodological rules and (lesser) cognitive aims.

The reticulational model is valuable as a description of scientific evaluative practice. However, the model does not provide an effective means to distinguish acceptable from unacceptable developments. It is inadequate as a normative theory that prescribes appropriate evaluative decisions in specific contexts, and hence does not stipulate the specific conditions required for scientific progress.

13

POPPER ON PROGRESS THROUGH OVERTHROW– WITH–INCORPORATION

Kuhn interpreted the history of science to be a succession of periods of normal science, punctuated by occasional revolutionary episodes. According to Kuhn, there is progress within both normal science and revolutionary science. Within normal science progress is growth by incorporation. A successful revolution, on the other hand, accomplishes a discontinuous elevation of the level at which science is practiced (see Figure 13.1)

Karl Popper, also held that progress involves both growth by incorporation and revolutionary overthrow. However, whereas Kuhn maintained that some developments are progressive because of incorporation and other developments are progressive because of revolutionary overthrow, Popper maintained that progress is achieved when one and the same episode displays *both* incorporation and overthrow. Popper set forth two conditions for progressive theory-replacement:

> first, in order that a new theory should constitute a discovery or a step forward it should conflict with its predecessor; that is to say, it should lead to at least some conflicting results. But this means, from a logical point of view, that it should contradict its predecessor: it should overthrow it. In this sense, progress in science, although revolutionary rather than merely cumulative, is in a certain sense always conservative:

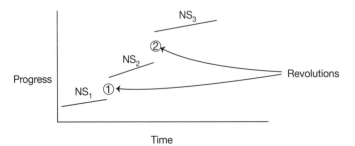

Figure 13.1 Kuhn on periods of normal science following revolutions. NS$_1$, NS$_2$, NS$_3$ indicate periods of normal science

a new theory, however revolutionary, must always be able to explain fully the success of its predecessor. In all those cases in which its predecessor was successful, it must yield results at least as good as those of its predecessor and, if possible, better results. Thus in those cases the predecessor theory must appear as a good approximation to the new theory; while there should be, preferably, other cases where the new theory yields different and better results than the old theory.[1]

Thus for progress to be achieved in science the following requirements must be met:

1 There is some evidence statement e implied by T_2, but not by T_1,
2 e falsifies T_1 but not T_2, and
3 T_2 reproduces all the explanatory successes of T_1, and
4 T_2 achieves some explanatory success not achieved by T_1.

These requirements combine emphases on explanatory incorporation and overthrow by falsification. However, some amplification is required.

With respect to requirement 1), it should be noted that e is not implied by theory T_2 directly. Rather, e is implied only by the conjunction of T_2 and statements about boundary conditions and initial conditions, and (usually) auxiliary hypotheses about the operations of instruments. For example, the ideal gas theory implies a 50 percent decrease in the volume of a gas only from a set of premises that includes, for instance, statements about the doubling of pressure and the constancy of mass and temperature. In addition there are implicit assumptions about the operation of devices used to record values of the relevant variables. Popper was well aware of the complex relationship between a theory and a statement recording evidence.

With respect to requirement 2), Popper emphasized in other works that arguments to prove false a logically consistent theory never are decisive.[2] As noted above, the truth of e falsifies only a conjunction of premises and not T_1 itself. Moreover, the truth of e is always subject to challenge.

Popper labeled statements recording evidence "basic statements."[3] A "basic statement" specifies that an intersubjectively observable event takes place in a certain region of space and time. Examples are "that liquid now is cloudy," "that substance now has melted" and "the top of the mercury column now is on 6.7." Basic statements are not incorrigible. Popper conceded this. He acknowledged that to test a theory it is necessary to accept some basic statements as true. We decide to accept statement e as true despite our realization that it always is possible to raise questions about whether the event indicated really occurred. In the *Logic of Scientific Discovery* Popper declared that

the testing of a theory depends upon basic statements whose acceptance or rejection, in its turn, depends on our *decisions* .... I differ from the conventionalist in holding that the statements decided by agreement are *not universal but singular*. And I differ from the positivist in holding that basic statements are not justified by our immediate experiences, but are, from the logical point of view, accepted by an act, a free decision.[4]

The "falsification" of T_1 stipulated in requirement 2) is relative both to assumptions about the truth of basic statements and to the truth of statements about relevant conditions and auxiliary hypotheses.

Thus amplified, Popper's first two requirements for progressive theory-replacement are reasonable. Requirement 3), however, is untenable. There are numerous *prima facie* progressive transitions in the history of science that would be denied this status by the requirement that a successor theory account for *all* the successes of its predecessor. Among them are the following:

1   Aristotle's theory of the universe, in which the Earth is centrally-located and stationary, explains why bodies, when released, fall straight to the base of towers. Copernicus' theory of the universe, in which the Earth rotates on an axis and revolves around the Sun, does not.
2   Descartes' vortex theory of the Solar System explains why the planets all revolve in the same direction around the Sun. Newton's gravitation theory does not.
3   The phlogiston theory explains why all metals are shiny. It is because they all contain phlogiston. Lavoisier's oxygen theory does not explain the common physical properties of metals.

Of course, one could argue that Aristotle, Descartes and phlogiston theorists did not "really explain" the phenomena in question. However, this is a view achieved only in the wisdom of hindsight. Moreover, to generalize this approach is to deny that an appeal to false premises ever can explain. We then would have to say that Galileo did not explain free fall, Newton did not explain the motion of the planets, and the kinetic molecular theory does not explain the laws of Boyle, Charles and Gay-Lussac. If Nancy Cartwright is correct that the fundamental laws enshrined in high level theories all are "born false," and if we disqualify putative explanations that appeal to false premises, then there is no theoretical explanation in science. Such a position on explanation is untenable. The objection to Popper's third requirement must be sustained. To be acceptable, requirement 3) must be weakened to require only that T_2 account for *most* of the explanatory successes of T_1.

"Progressive theory-replacement" clearly is not a purely logical relationship. Rather, the phrase records a three-part verdict rendered by scientists. The first part of the verdict is that the relevant assumptions about evidence and the relevant conditions under which T_1 is applied are sufficiently reliable to establish its "falsification." The second part of the verdict is that the successor theory account for *most* of the explanatory successes of its predecessor. And the third part of the verdict is that the successor theory achieves some improvement on the explanations offered by its predecessor.

As a contribution to a philosophical analysis of "scientific progress," the above characterization is too vague to be of much value. To speak of "sufficiently reliable" assumptions and "most" of a theory's explanatory successes is to provide a very imprecise demarcation of "progressive theory-change."

PART II: PROGRESS AS
REVOLUTIONARY OVERTHROW

Suggestions for further reading

Theorists of scientific progress

I. BERNARD COHEN

Cohen, I.B. (1966) *Franklin and Newton*. Cambridge, MA: Harvard University Press.
—— (1980) *The Newtonian Revolution*. Cambridge: Cambridge University Press.
—— (1985) *The Birth of a New Physics*, revised edn. New York: Norton.
—— (1985) *Revolution in Science*. Cambridge, MA: Harvard University Press.
Westfall, R. S. (1986) "Review of *Revolution in Science*", *ISIS* 77: 109–10.
Williams, L. P. (1986) "Review of *Revolution in Science*", *Brit. J. Phil. Sci.* 19: 340–2.

THOMAS S. KUHN

Kuhn, Thomas S. (1970) *The Structure of Scientific Revolutions* 2nd edn. Chicago:
    University of Chicago Press.
—— (1977) *The Essential Tension*. Chicago: University of Chicago Press.
—— (1978) *Black-Body Radiation and the Quantum Discontinuity, 1894–1912*.
    Oxford: Clarendon.

Conant, J. and Haugeland, J (eds) (2000) *The Road Since "Structure": Philosophical
    Essays, 1970–93*. Chicago: University of Chicago Press.. Includes a bibliography
    of Kuhn's writings.
Caneva, Kenneth, L. (2000) "Possible Kuhns in the History of Science", *Stud. Hist.
    Phil. Sci.* 31: 87–124.
Horwich, Paul (ed.) (1993) *World Changes*. Cambridge, MA: MIT Press. Essays on
    Kuhn's work by McMullin, Cartwright, Hacking, and others, with a response by
    Kuhn.
Hoynigen-Huene, Paul (1993) *Reconstructing Scientific Revolutions: Thomas S.
    Kuhn's Philosophy of Science*. Chicago: University of Chicago Press.
Meiland, Jack W. (1974) "Kuhn, Scheffler and Objectivity in Science", *Phil. Sci.* 41:
    179–87.
Musgrave, Alan (1971) "Kuhn's Second Thoughts", *Brit. J. Phil. Sci.* 22: 287–306. A
    critique of Kuhn's *Postscript* in the 2nd edition of *The Structure of Scientific
    Revolutions*.

STEPHEN TOULMIN

Toulmin, S. (1953) *Philosophy of Science*. New York: Harper Torchbooks.
—— (1961) *Foresight and Understanding*. New York: Harper Torchbooks.
—— (1972) *Human Understanding*. Oxford: Clarendon Press.

—— (1974) "Rationality and Scientific Discovery" in K. Schaffner and R. S. Cohen (eds) *Boston Studies in the Philosophy of Science,* Vol. XX. Dordrecht: Reidel, 387–406.

Cohen, L. Jonathan (1973) "Is the Progress of Science Evolutionary?", *Brit. J. Phil. Sci.* 24: 41–61.
McMullin, Ernan (1974) "Logicality and Rationality: A Comment on Toulmin's Theory of Science" in R. J. Seeger and R. S. Cohen (eds) *Philosophical Foundations of Science.* Dordrecht: Reidel, 415–30.

LARRY LAUDAN

Laudan, L. (1981) *Science and Hypothesis.* Dordrecht: Reidel. Includes essays on Whewell, Mach, Locke, Hume and Reid.
—— (1984) *Progress and its Problems.* Berkeley: University of California Press.
—— (1984) *Science and Values.* Berkeley: University of California Press.
—— (1990) *Science and Relativism.* Chicago: University of Chicago Press.
—— (1996) *Beyond Positivism and Relativism.* Boulder: Westview Press. Includes essays on Kuhn, Feyerabend, normative naturalism and the underdetermination of theories by evidence.

Donovan, A., Laudan, L., and Laudan, R. (eds) (1988) *Scrutinizing Science.* Dordrecht: Kluwer. A collection of essays on important episodes in the history of science. It is alleged that these analyses provide support for a "problem-solving" model of scientific progress.
Musgrave, Alan (1979) "Progress with Progress", *Synthese* 42: 443–64.
Quinn, Philip L. (1986) "Comments on Laudan's 'Methodology: Its Prospects'", *PSA 1986* Vol. 2, 355–8. East Lansing: Philosophy of Science Association.
Worrall, John (1988) "The Value of a Fixed Methodology", *Brit. J. Phil. Sci.* 39: 263–75. A critical analysis of Laudan's *Science and Values.* Laudan replied (1989) in "If it Ain't Broke, Don't Fix It", *Brit. J. Phil. Sci* 40: 369–75. Worrall responded (1989) with "Fix it and Be Damned: A Reply to Laudan" *Brit. J. Phil. Sci.* 40: 376–88.

KARL R. POPPER

Popper, Karl (1950) "Indeterminism in Quantum Physics and in Classical Physics", *Brit. J. Phil. Sci.* 1: 117–33, 173–95.
—— (1959) *The Logic of Scientific Discovery.* New York: Basic Books.
—— (1959) "The Propensity Interpretation of Probability", *Brit. J. Phil. Sci.* 10: 25–42.
—— (1963) *The Open Society and its Enemies,* 2 vols., 4th edn. New York: Harper Torchbooks.
—— (1963) *Conjectures and Refutations.* New York: Basic Books.
—— (1972) *Objective Knowledge.* Oxford: Clarendon Press.
—— with Eccles, J. (1983) *The Self and its Brain.* London: Routledge & Kegan Paul.

Ackermann, R. J. (1976) *The Philosophy of Karl Popper.* Amherst: University of Massachusetts Press.
Bunge, Mario (ed.) (1964) *The Critical Approach to Science and Philosophy.* Glencoe, IL: Free Press. A collection of essays on Popper's work, with a bibliography of Popper's publications.

Newton-Smith, W.H. (1981) *The Rationality of Science,* Chapter 3. London: Routledge & Kegan Paul.

Nola, Robert (1987) "The Status of Popper's Theory of Scientific Method", *Brit. J. Phil. Sci.* 38: 441–80.

O'Hear Anthony (1980) *Karl Popper.* London: Routledge & Kegan Paul.

Salmon, Wesley (1981) "Rational Prediction", *Brit. J. Phil. Sci.* 32: 115–25.

Schilpp, P.A. (ed.) (1974) *The Philosophy of Karl R. Popper,* 2 vols. LaSalle: Open Court. Contains an "Intellectual Autobiography" by Popper, essays by Kuhn, Lakatos, Watkins, Putnam, Ayer, Quine, and others, a reply by Popper, and a bibliography of Popper's writings.

Episodes from the history of science

PARITY CONSERVATION

Gardiner, Martin (1990) *The New Ambidextrous Universe.* New York: Freeman. See, especially, Ch. 22.

Yang, C.N. (1962) *Elementary Particles.* Princeton: Princeton University Press.

QUANTUM MECHANICS

Bohr, Niels (1958) *Atomic Physics and Human Knowledge.* New York: Wiley.

Heisenberg, Werner (1958) *Physics and Philosophy.* New York: Harper.

Jammer, Max (1966) *The Conceptual Development of Quantum Mechanics.* New York: McGraw-Hill.

Kuhn, Thomas S. (1978) *Black Body Radiation and the Quantum Discontinuity, 1894–1912.* Oxford: Clarendon Press.

STELLAR CLASSIFICATION SYSTEMS

Abetti, Giorgio (1952) *The History of Astronomy*, 188–96, 272–3. New York: Abelard-Schuman.

Motz, Lloyd and Weaver, J. H. (1995) *The Story of Astronomy*, Chapter 15. New York: Plenum Press.

Russell, Henry Norris (1914) "Relations Between the Spectra and Other Characteristics of Stars", *Popular Astronomy* 22: 275–94. Reprinted in K.R. Lang and O. Gingerich (eds) *A Source Book in Astronomy and Astrophysics,* 212–20. Cambridge, MA.: Harvard University Press.

VORTEX THEORIES

Aiton, E. J. (1972) *The Vortex Theory of Planetary Motions.* London: MacDonald.

Descartes, René (1647 [1983]) *Principles of Philosophy,* 84–177, (V. R. Miller and R. P. Miller, trans.). Dordrecht: Reidel.

Newton, Isaac (1687 [1962]) *Mathematical Principles of Natural Philosophy*, Vol. 1, 392–6; Vol. 2, 543–7 (A. Motte, trans. [1729], revised by F. Cajori). Berkeley: University of California Press.

Part III

DESCRIPTIVE THEORIES OF SCIENTIFIC PROGRESS

14

NORMATIVE AND
DESCRIPTIVE THEORIES

One may take either a normative approach or a purely descriptive approach to the assessment of scientific progress. All the theories of progress examined in the preceding pages are normative theories. Normative theories provide answers to the question "how *ought* science be conducted in order that progress be achieved?" Incorporation theorists insist that present theories should account for the achievements of past theories. Overthrow theorists insist that the victor in a revolutionary confrontation of theories should resolve difficulties that beset the vanquished.

In the purely descriptive approach to the assessment of progress no recommendations are appended about how science ought be practiced. The aim of descriptive assessment is to discover and display those repeated patterns that are accepted by the practitioners of science as constituting progress.

Whewell and Kuhn based their normative appraisals on descriptions of patterns they professed to see in the history of science. Whewell saw progress as an incorporation of past achievements in present theories. Kuhn saw progress as periods of application and development of dominant theories interrupted by periods of conflict.

Whewell and Kuhn appended normative recommendations to their descriptions of scientific progress. They might have elected not to do so. There is an asymmetry between the normative and descriptive approaches to the analysis of science. The normative approach is parasitic on the descriptive approach. Unless recommended criteria of progress are shown to fit at least some historical episodes antecedently judged important, there is no reason to accept them as criteria applicable to science. On the other hand, it is perfectly possible to describe actual evaluative practice without issuing prescriptive recommendations about how science ought be conducted.

Theories of science specify that which increases when progress is achieved, and/or the mechanisms responsible for such increases. Theories of science may be advanced as descriptive generalizations or as prescriptive recommendations about how science ought be conducted.

15

SCIENTIFIC PROGRESS AND CONVERGENCE UPON TRUTH

One influential suggestion about that which increases when progress is achieved is that it is approximation to truth. Observers of science have posed two questions about the relation of scientific theories to truth:

1 can scientific theories be shown to be true?
2 can it be shown that certain sequences of scientific theories constitute progress toward truth?

The answer to the question 1 clearly is "no." To show that a theory is true, one would have to show that its truth-conditions are fulfilled. But scientific theories make universal claims. And to claim that there is a circulation of blood in *all* human beings, or that *all* bodies exert a $1 / r^2$ force of gravitational attraction, or that *all* gases at moderate temperatures and pressures behave as if they were composed of elastically-colliding point-masses subject to the laws of Newtonian mechanics, is to claim knowledge of unexamined instances. Such knowledge-claims cannot be verified. No amount of evidence can prove that unexamined instances resemble examined instances. Hume was correct about this. Thus some truth-conditions of unrestrictedly general claims cannot be shown to be fulfilled. This is not to say that scientific theories cannot be true, but only that scientific theories cannot be *known* to be true.

Prospects for an affirmative answer to question 2 are more promising. We may be able to establish that successive theories constitute progress toward truth even though we cannot establish that the proximate theory in the sequence is true.

Jay Rosenberg observed that "convergence" is a notion borrowed from mathematics. He contrasted "Weierstrass convergence," in which a sequence approaches a known fixed limit, and "Cauchy convergence," in which each member of a sequence differs from its predecessor by a decreasing amount.[1] Since distances from the fixed limit of the "true" theory are unknowable, "Weierstrass convergence" is not a concept applicable to the history of science. However, it may be possible to find episodes in the history of science that conform to the requirements of "Cauchy convergence."

Given a sequence of theories, T_1, T_2, T_3, if predictions drawn from T_2 are far more accurate than those drawn from T_1, and predictions drawn from T_3 are just slightly more accurate than those drawn from T_2, then the series exhibits predictive convergence. Of course, scientific progress involves more than successful prediction. A sequence of geocentric planetary theories with increasing numbers of epicycles may satisfy the convergence requirement with respect to prediction without qualifying as convergence upon *truth*. A major problem for an application of this mathematical concept to scientific progress is to identify the appropriate measure of the intervals between theories in a sequence.

Peirce on science as a self-correcting enterprise

C.S. Peirce built a case for the "convergence upon truth" thesis. Peirce admired William Whewell's interpretation of the history of science. On Whewell's tributary–river view of scientific progress:

1 the growth of science is an increase in the number of propositions affirmed to be true;
2 the growth of science displays increasing unification, in which ever-more-inclusive theories incorporate increasing numbers of lower-level generalizations;
3 some false propositions contribute to this growth; and
4 in the course of history false propositions are identified and replaced.

Peirce maintained that 4) is true. In the long run, consistent application of the hypothetico-deductive method of science leads to the elimination of falsehoods. According to Peirce, it is this self-correcting aspect of the practice of science that sets it apart from other forms of inquiry.

In a deservedly famous essay—"The Fixation of Belief"—Peirce discussed four methods of inquiry that lead the practitioner from the irritation of doubt to the security of belief.[2] The first three methods—tenacity, authority and the *a priori* method—are widely practiced. However, they are inferior to the method of science. Peirce insisted that only the method of science is subject to control by objective reality independently of the desires and wishes of the investigator.

Peirce acknowledged and defended two realist postulates: 1) there exist real objects that are independent of our opinions about them, and 2) these real objects affect our sense organs according to regular, intersubjectively testable, laws. He admitted that he could not prove that there exist external objects that exist independently of our experience. He pointed out, however, that this realist assumption is assumed in everyday life, that it is consistent with the practice of science, and that acceptance of this assumption has led to a convergence of beliefs within the community of scientists. These considerations fall short of a proof of realism. Peirce noted, however, that the negation of the realist assumption receives no support at all.

Peirce claimed that the method of science is self-correcting. This meant, for Peirce, that in the long run—not tomorrow, nor next year, but ultimately—science reaches a collection of truths purged of all falsehoods. *Prima facie*, this is puzzling. Peirce maintained that science progresses by applications of a hypothetico-deductive method, but that the self-correcting feature of science derives from the nature of induction. It is hard to see how this can be the case.

Larry Laudan pointed out that Peirce distinguished three types of induction: "crude" induction, qualitative induction, and quantitative induction (1903).[3] "Crude" induction is straightforward generalization from samples which contain no negative instances (e.g., "all ravens are black"). Peirce acknowledged that this type of induction is not important within science. Qualitative induction is the entertaining of hypotheses and the eliminating of those whose deductive consequences are not in agreement with observations. Quantitative induction is an inference from a premise about the distribution of properties (events, relations) in a sample to a conclusion about that distribution in the population from which the sample was obtained.

Peirce based his claim about the self-correcting nature of science on the properties of quantitative induction. "Quantitative induction," Peirce declared, "always makes a gradual approach to the truth, though not a uniform approach."[4] As an illustration, Peirce discussed the relation between the properties of samples of grain taken from a ship's hold and the properties of the population as a whole. His conclusion is that

> whatever may be the variations of this ratio [of properties] in experience, experience indefinitely extended will enable us to detect them, so as to predict rightly, at last, what its ultimate value may be, if it have any ultimate value, or what the ultimate law of succession of values may be, if there be any such ultimate law.[5]

This pragmatic justification of induction has been criticized by numerous philosophers. Peirce's "grain example" refers to a finite population. But as P.F. Strawson has emphasized, to extend this analysis to cases of interest in science is to proceed from claim 1 to claim 2 below:

1 The probability that a sample matches a given population increases with the size of the sample.
2 The probability that a population matches a given sample increases with the size of the sample.[6]

Claim 1 is true. In the penultimate sample that includes every grain from the ship's hold except one, the probability is high indeed.

The inference from claim 1 to claim 2 is invalid however. In claim 2 what is "given" is the sample. The sample may or may not be representative of the

100

population. We are ignorant of the ratio of sample size to population size. We have no guarantee that different possible samples of equal size are equally likely to be drawn. Strawson pointed out, in addition, that the transition from claim 1 to claim 2 involves a shift of meaning of "probability." In claim 1 it is a proposition of pure mathematics. In claim 2 it is "a measure of the inductive acceptability of a generalization."[7] Strawson concluded that attempts to justify induction are misguided. He declared that

> to ask whether it is reasonable to place reliance on inductive procedures is like asking whether it is reasonable to proportion the degree of one's convictions to the strength of the evidence. Doing this is what "being reasonable" *means* in such a context.[8]

Laudan directed a quite different criticism at Peirce's self-correction thesis. He maintained that, even if Peirce had made a convincing case for the self-correcting nature of quantitative induction, this would not establish that science is a self-correcting enterprise. Peirce still would have to show that the hypothetico-deductive method that he takes to be essential to science is a self-correcting undertaking. But as Laudan pointed out

> given that an hypothesis has been refuted, qualitative induction specifies no technique for discovering an alternative H' which is (or is likely to be) closer to the truth than the refuted H.[9]

That hypothesis H is shown to be false does not provide a good reason to believe that some other hypothesis H' is true (or closer to the truth). Laudan concluded that

> having set out to show that science is a progressively self-correcting enterprise moving ever closer to the truth ... Peirce finds himself able to show only that one of the methods of science (and that, by Peirce's admission, a relatively insignificant one) was self-corrective.[10]

Nicholas Rescher, conceding the above-mentioned difficulties, sought to extract from Peirce's writings a plausible defense of the self-correction thesis. He maintained that Peirce sought to show that quantitative induction provides a basis for, and renders self-correcting, the hypothetico-deductive method of science.[11]

The method of quantitative induction, which itself is self-correcting, does not apply directly to scientific theories. But it does apply to the successive *applications* of theories. It is in virtue of a monitoring of the successes and failures of predictions (and other applications) that the hypothetico-deductive method of science is self-correcting.

Insofar as this monitoring of predictions is conducted systematically according to the rules of quantitative induction, inadequate theories are refuted, leaving, *in the long run*, only nonrefuted, and presumably true, theories. Peirce argued that if there is a limit of the ratio

$$\frac{\text{successful applications of } T}{\text{total applications of } T}$$

then a continuing survey of the applications of *T* will reveal this limit ... eventually.

Rescher pointed out that Peirce went so far as to define "truth" as the value "1" in the above ratio. Thus when Peirce declared

> the true guarantee of the validity of induction is that it is a method of reaching conclusions which, if it be persisted in long enough, will assuredly correct any error concerning future experience into which it may temporarily lead us.

it is applications of quantitative induction to predictions drawn from scientific theories that he had in mind.[12]

Peirce's self-correction thesis rests on an unproven and unprovable assumption. This assumption is that, in the long run, science achieves all and only true statements about the universe. Given this assumption, the asymptotic approach to the totality of possible *applications* of scientific theories is an asymptotic approach to the truth.

Peirce's optimistic view of the march of science toward ultimate truth is not shared by contemporary defenders of the "pessimistic meta-induction." This pessimistic response to Peirce is based on empirical evidence that important theories that one era takes to be true subsequently are discarded or amended. Galileo's theory of falling bodies, Newton's mechanics, Lavoisier's oxygen theory, kinetic molecular theory and the wave theory of light were once, but are no longer, believed to be true. The proper inductive generalization from the available evidence from the history of science is that it is probable that today's theories, and tomorrow's theories as well, are false. To argue, as Peirce does, that there is an intrinsic convergence upon truth within science, is to fail to base one's judgment on the available evidence.

Duhem and Quine on the limits of falsification

Peirce sought a procedure whose implementation would eliminate false propositions from science. Pierre Duhem argued that there can be no such procedure. Duhem called attention to the logic of falsification. He emphasized that what is falsified by an observation report is a *conjunction* of premises.[13] Consider a litmus paper test for acidity. We predict that the paper will turn red on the basis of the following argument:

102

P_1 All pieces of blue litmus paper, placed in an acid solution, turn red.

P_2 This piece of blue litmus paper is placed in an acid solution.

∴ This piece of blue litmus paper turns red.

If the paper does not turn red, then one or more of the premises is false. The logic of the situation is represented by:

$(P_1 \& P_2) \supset C$
$\sim C$

∴ $\sim(P_1 \& P_2)$

The law (P_1) is not falsified by the negative result $(\sim C)$. Instead, the statement about relevant conditions (P_2) may be false. It may be false that there is blue litmus dye on the paper. It may be false that the solution is acidic. And it may be false that the paper was placed in the liquid.

Duhem noted that the usual context of falsification is more complex. Typically a number of hypotheses are involved in the prediction that a phenomenon occurs. In particular, there often are hypotheses about the operation of instruments that are used to obtain data. This is true even for a simple case like the expansion of a heated balloon. A negative test result $(\sim O)$ falsifies only the conjunction of premises that include a law $(V \propto T)$, statements about relevant conditions $[(T_2 = 2\,T_1)$, mass and pressure are constant], and auxiliary hypotheses about the operation of temperature-measuring and volume-measuring devices. The logic of the situation is:

$(L \& C \& A) \supset O$
$\sim O$

∴ $\sim(L \& C \& A)$

Given a *prima facie* falsifying instance, the theorist may accommodate the instance by abandoning or modifying any of the hypotheses used to make the prediction (L or A). He or she also may retain all hypotheses involved and reject instead the statement about the relevant conditions under which the test was performed (C). Duhem insisted that no observation report ever is decisive against a scientific hypothesis in physical science (Duhem exempted the propositions of physiology from this claim).[14]

Willard van Orman Quine subsequently emphasized that since no experimental result ever is decisive against a single hypothesis, a negative test result can be accommodated by making changes elsewhere in the system of hypotheses and statements about relevant conditions.[15] Suppose observation report O follows from the conjunction of the theory T, auxiliary hypotheses A, and relevant conditions C, viz.,

$$T \& A$$
$$C$$
$$\overline{}$$
$$\therefore O$$

and that ~O is the case. Quine maintained that it always is possible to find auxiliary hypothesis A^* such that

$$T \& A^*$$
$$C$$
$$\overline{}$$
$$\therefore \sim O$$

thereby shielding T from falsification. He granted that A^* may be complex and implausible for other reasons, but the logic of the situation does not require that we take T to be false.[16]

If Duhem and Quine are correct, then Peirce's belief that applications of quantitative induction will weed out false propositions is implausible. A test result that does not agree with what is predicted from a theory merely shows that something is amiss somewhere in the collection of propositions used to make the prediction. Moreover, agreement between theory and observation can be restored in a number of ways. The theorist is not constrained to eliminate as false some one particular proposition. Usually scientists restore agreement with observations by making changes that have minimal repercussions for the theory under test. But this is not always the case. Scientists sometimes restore agreement by rejecting or modifying the basic principles of a theory. It is far from obvious that the various choices that scientists do make converge upon the truth, even in the long run.

Cartwright on the importance of false theories

There is a further difficulty for the self-correction thesis. Nancy Cartwright has called attention to the fact that the laws imbedded in high-level theories are either false or inapplicable. These laws are stated with respect to *ceteris paribus* clauses that, in principle, cannot be fulfilled. For example, Newton's law of inertia describes the motion of a body in the total absence of impressed forces, and Coulomb's law describes the motion of a charged particle subject only to electrical forces. Cartwright observed that

> no charged particle will behave just as the law of universal gravitation says; and any massive object is a counterexample to Coulomb's law.[17]

Strictly speaking, the laws are false of the motions of real bodies. Of course, such laws are true of "uncharged point-masses," "massless charges," "ideal gases," "ideal pendulums," *et al.*, but these "model objects" are not found in the real world.

Thus there is a problem. Scientists know, for instance, that molecules are not elastic point-masses, but they continue to apply the kinetic theory of gases anyway. For gases at moderate temperatures and pressures, predictions derived from the theory are in agreement with observations. It would seem that if predictive accuracy is achieved, scientists are perfectly willing to utilize theories that are known to be false. Successful prediction is an important goal of science. It may be achieved independently of a convergence of theories upon truth.

Rescher on methodological pragmatism and scientific progress

Nicholas Rescher conceded that it is not possible to *demonstrate* that the succession of scientific theories converges upon truth. Nevertheless, he sought to resurrect the "self-correctedness of science" thesis. Rescher claimed that what is subject to self-correction is not theories but the standards and procedures by which they are evaluated. Scientific progress is marked by

> increased refinement of the procedures and methods used in the acceptability-screening processes for truth-candidates.[18]

Rescher maintained that progress is achieved when new evaluative standards and procedures are devised that 1) account for the strengths of the old method, and 2) add new strengths.[19]

To gauge the "strength" of an evaluative procedure it is necessary to consult both "internal factors" and "external factors." Internally, it is required that the method be coherent, self- sustaining and capable of incorporating feedback from its prior variants. In addition, applications of the method must qualify as acceptable theories that are systematic, comprehensive and simple.[20] Rescher emphasized that satisfaction of these internal conditions is insufficient. The method also must warrant theories and laws that increase problem-solving effectiveness and control. He declared that

> we thus envisage a two-fold criteriology of cognitive adequacy (and *ergo* of scientific progress) namely the internal factor of systematization and the external factor of pragmatic efficacy.[21]

Rescher recommended a "Copernican inversion" as a corollary of this position on scientific progress. The Copernican inversion

> proposes that we not judge a method of inquiry by the truth of its results, but rather judge the claims to truth of the results in terms of the merit of the method that produces them (assessing this merit by both internal [coherentist] and external [pragmatist] standards).[22]

Of course, no demonstration is possible that true theories have been produced. But the application of increasingly more meritorious evaluative standards and procedures is held to warrant the *presumption* that later theories are "truer" than earlier ones. Greater truthfulness, on this view, is "a matter of increasingly more firmly rationally warranted presumption."[23]

The program of methodological pragmatism is to extend our confidence in the increasing problem-solving effectiveness of science to scientific theories. This is to be accomplished by reference to the increasing adequacy of evaluative practice. Rescher sought to replace the claim "later theories are more worthy of acceptance because they are closer to truth" by the claim "later theories are closer to truth because they are more worthy of acceptance (since warranted by superior evaluative practice). However, this increasing adequacy of evaluative practice is to be established, in large measure, upon appeal to the acknowledged increasing problem-solving effectiveness of science. Rescher declared that

> we thus envisage a *complex* criterion of merit which stresses the technological/productive side of inquiry in natural science.[24]

The "criterion of merit" is complex, but Rescher concedes that the "technological/ productive side of inquiry" is to be emphasized. He noted that, although the progression of scientific theories displays discontinuity and even incommensurability, there is continuity on the level of increasing problem-solution and control.

There is no doubt that there has been an increase over time of predictive and productive efficacy within science. We have become increasingly successful in manipulating entities and forces in the service of improving adaptation to our environment. There is no dispute about the reality of scientific progress in this sense. However, it is one thing to acknowledge increasing predictive and productive efficacy, and another thing to establish that it is continuing improvement in evaluative practice that is responsible for this increase.

Rescher's discussion in *Methodological Pragmatism* is quite abstract. A natural question is whether it fits the history of science. If there have been methodological innovations, widely accepted by practicing scientists, that were accompanied by subsequent increases in predictive and productive efficacy, this would support Rescher's position. Unfortunately, it would take an extensive examination of the history of science to certify that such innovations have taken place. One would have to show, for a given innovation, that a substantial number of scientists accepted it, and that the appropriate "internal factors" and "external factors" were better satisfied upon application of the innovative methodology than would have been the case had scientists conducted evaluative practice without the innovation. I have not undertaken such an examination. However, the following episodes are *prima facie* qualifying instances:

1 Aristotle required the scientist to advance from "knowledge of the fact" to "knowledge of the reasoned fact," by inducing explanatory principles from the phenomena to be explained and then deducing statements about the phenomena from premises that include these principles. Galileo, by contrast, emphasized the derivation of consequences that "go beyond" the facts that initially gave rise to the inquiry.

   To endorse Galileo's methodology is to retain the "strength" of Aristotle's inductive–deductive procedure and to augment this "strength" by stressing the value of the confirmation of additional consequences of induced explanatory principles. The range of predictive and potentially productive consequences was expanded by adoption of this methodological innovation. Galileo himself cited his own derivation of the parabolic trajectory of a projectile from premises that include the law of falling bodies.

2 Implementation of the inductive method of difference—discussed by William of Ockham, John Herschel and David Hume, and championed by John Stuart Mill—allowed nineteenth-century scientists to set up controlled experiments designed to discover causal relationships. Mill recommended the method of difference as both an investigative procedure and a "rule of proof" of causal connections. This addition to the arsenal of inductive techniques augmented the pragmatic efficacy of science.

3 Similar conclusions are appropriate for the introduction of the methodologies of factor analysis and double-blind testing.

Other proposed methodological innovations have been controversial. For example, Herschel and Whewell promoted the display of "undesigned scope" as a criterion of acceptability for scientific theories. Implicit in this position is the thesis that the prediction of new facts is more important than the accommodation of those facts that the theory initially was formulated to explain.

Observers of science have been divided on this thesis. Some recent studies have concluded that scientists did not give more weight to successful prediction than to accommodation in evaluating the status of important theories. Stephen Brush concluded that scientists gave greater weight to the general theory of relativity's accommodation of the anomalous motion of the perihelion of Mercury than to the novel prediction of the bending of light by the Sun (confirmed by observations at the solar eclipse of 1919).[25] Eric Scerri and John Worrall concluded that scientists were not more impressed by Mendeleeff's novel predictions of the properties of subsequently-discovered elements than by the accommodations he achieved for known elements within his periodic tables.[26]

Karl Popper's methodological falsificationism is another controversial position. Popper sought to redirect the orientation of scientists from the pursuit of confirming evidence for their theories to the construction of tests most likely to falsify them. He insisted that proper scientific methodology is to take the role of antagonist against one's own (and others') theories.

Thomas Kuhn objected that Popper's recommended methodological orientation denigrates "normal science," during which dominant theories are revised and extended to increase their problem-solving effectiveness. According to Kuhn, the practice of methodological falsificationism reduces the pragmatic efficacy of science.[27]

A list of controversial methodological recommendations would include, as well:

1 Descartes' demand that all acceptable explanations of motion specify a pressure (*choc*) responsible for it;
2 Newton's restriction of science to an "experimental philosophy" that includes only statements about phenomena, theories "deduced" from phenomena, and hypotheses whose sole purpose is heuristic;
3 David Bohm's insistence that theories of the quantum domain specify deterministic interactions that underlie probabilistic correlations; and,
4 Niels Bohr's demand that theories of the quantum domain include complementary wave and particle "descriptions" of quantum systems between observations.

It would be a formidable undertaking to determine the extent to which scientists accepted these various methodological recommendations. And it would be equally difficult to assess the subsequent impact of their decisions on the solution of scientific problems. Nevertheless it appears unlikely that these episodes from the history of evaluative practice could be interpreted to provide unequivocal support for Rescher's position.

There is an additional difficulty for Rescher's position. Predictive goals and explanatory goals often conflict. Developments that increase the "external" standing of evaluative practice (e.g., by increasing predictive efficacy) may decrease its "internal" standing (e.g., by decreasing coherence and systematization), and *vice versa*. What counts in a particular evaluative context is not simply that predictive accuracy and explanatory power are acknowledged to be aims of science. Rather, it is the relative emphasis placed on each aim that is most important in the evaluative situation.

There have been evaluative episodes within the history of science in which predictive accuracy is emphasized almost to the exclusion of explanatory power. The tradition of "saving the appearances" in mathematical astronomy is a case in point. Within the tradition that derives from Ptolemy's *Almagest*, the prediction of planetary positions along the zodiac was taken to be the principal aim of astronomy. Andreas Osiander's statement of this aim is well known. According to Osiander, the astronomer

> must conceive and devise, since he cannot in any way attain to the
> true causes, such hypotheses as, being assumed, enable the motions
> to be calculated correctly from the principles of geometry, for the

future as well as for the past .... These hypotheses need not be true nor even probable; if they provide a calculus consistent with the observations, that alone is sufficient.[28]

Predictively successful mathematical models can be formulated for any periodic process. These models may have no explanatory value, however. Copernicus himself piled epicycle upon epicycle in Books II–VI of *De revolutionibus*. But neither Copernicus nor his geostatic-theory rivals held that a planet is in Capricorn today in part because it is moving along an epicycle whose radius is a certain fraction of a deferent circle.

There also have been evaluative episodes within the history of science in which explanatory power is emphasized almost to the exclusion of predictive accuracy. Consider, for example, Darwin's "evolutionary histories" to account for the facts of biogeographical distribution. These histories "explain" by applying the principle of natural selection on the assumption that a number of conditions— an initial dispersion of a parent species, reproductive isolation, diversity of habitats etc.—were realized in the past.[29]

Consider the case of the finches Darwin found on the Galapagos Islands off the coast of Ecuador. The state of affairs to be explained—q—is that a number of closely related species are distributed among the islands, such that a given species may be present on one or more, but not every island. An evolutionary history has been formulated to explain this state of affairs. In the distant past there occurred an initial dispersal of mainland finches to the islands. Once on the islands the ancestral finches encountered diverse living conditions. On some islands fruit was plentiful. On other islands seeds, or particular types of insects, were readily available. Once the initial migration had taken place, birds on a given island mated only with other birds on that island. Over time, separate distinct species emerged to fill the available environmental niches.

This evolutionary history has the form " q because p," but when the implicit generalization is stated the resultant argument can be expressed in deductive-nomological form, viz.,

1    $(x) [(Dx \ \& \ Gx \ \& \ Hx \ \& \ Tx \ \& \ Rx \ \& \ Ix) \supset Ox]$
2    $Da \ \& \ Ga \ \& \ Ha \ \& \ Ta \ \& \ Ra \ \& \ Ia$

    $\therefore Oa$

where,

Dx x is a case in which there was an initial dispersion of mainland finches to the islands.

Gx x is a case in which geographic barriers sufficient to ensure reproductive isolation exists on each island.

Hx x is a case in which each island has a distinctive habitat.

Tx x is a case in which those finches in habitat H_1 that possess trait T^* are more suited to the performance of task K than are finches that lack T^*.

Rx   *x* is a case in which success at task *K* affects positively its possessor's likelihood to survive and reproduce.

Ix   *x* is a case in which *T** is transmitted genetically.

Ox   *x* is a case in which individuals that possess *T** come to become dominant within H_1.

a   the specific case in which e.g., the long-beaked finch *Geospiza scandens* has become dominant in habitat H_1 on James Island.

Evolutionary histories have explanatory value. But the arguments that express these histories invoke a multiply-conditional premise of the form—$(x)[Ax \, \& \, Bx \, \& \, Cx \, \& \, ... \,) \supset \Psi x]$. Only multiply-conditional predictions can be derived from such a premise. If "instance" *a* arises such that *Aa* & *Ba* & *Ca* & ..., then *Ψa* follows. However, Darwin did not apply premises of this form in an effort to predict "new" biogeographical distributions. Instead he stressed the explanatory power of the theory of natural selection.

In some contexts, predictive accuracy and explanatory power are antithetical aims. When these aims do conflict, evaluative decisions are contingent upon judgments about their relative importance. Consider the pressure–volume–temperature behavior of a gas near its critical point. If predictive accuracy is selected to be the more important aim, then the virial expansion is superior to Van der Waals' theory.[30] But if explanatory power is selected to be the more important aim, then the Van der Waals' theory is the superior interpretation.

A pragmatist would agree, of course, that the choice of evaluative criteria is context dependent. If the context is the design of a boiler, then one should apply the predictively more accurate virial expansion to calculate pressure values at high temperatures. If the context is a classroom presentation of gas theory, then one should refer to Van der Waals' Theory, indicating how the pressure–volume–temperature equation can be derived from kinetic molecular theory, modified to accommodate molecules of finite size subject to intermolecular attractive forces.

The tension between the demands of predictive accuracy and explanatory power is reflected in the set of criteria of acceptability for scientific theories compiled by Thomas Kuhn. Kuhn suggested that scientific theories have been, and should be, appraised by reference to standards of:

1 consistency
2 agreement-with-observations
3 simplicity
4 breadth of scope
5 conceptual integration
6 fertility.[31]

Kuhn acknowledged that there are difficulties in the application of these standards. Some of the standards are either vague or ambiguous. "Agreement-with-observations," for instance, is a vague standard. Experimental results that one scientist counts as in agreement with the deductive consequences of a theory a second scientist may judge insufficiently close to count as "agreement-with-observations." "Simplicity" is both vague and ambiguous. Consider the two relations, $y = ax^2 + bx$ and "$y = xz$." Which is the more simple? It depends on which is more important, the power of the independent variables or the number of such variables.

"Fertility" likewise is both vague and ambiguous. A theory may satisfy the criterion "fertility" in either of two ways. The first way is the extension of a theory, initially formulated to account for one type of phenomena, to a second type of phenomena. If the extension is "unexpected" or "striking," the theory gains credit for having displayed "undesigned scope." A good illustration is Einstein's extension of Planck's quantum theory of radiation to explain the photoelectric effect. The quantum theory was formulated initially to account for the observed frequency distribution of radiation from an opening in a heated cavity (black-body radiation). Einstein applied the theory to explain the photoelectric effect, in which light incident upon a metal sets free electrons in the metal.

A second way in which a theory may display fertility is by "pointing toward" modifications of itself. Strictly speaking, it is the progression of theories that is "fertile" in this sense. But one may label "fertile" an initial theory if the scientists who applied it were led to modify it in ways that improved its accuracy or extended its scope. For instance, one may credit as "fertile" the Bohr theory of the hydrogen atom, insofar as Sommerfeld's addition of elliptical orbits was a natural, and successful, extension of the theory.

An additional difficulty is that applications of the standards often yield conflicting evaluations. This is true, for instance, of the criteria "agreement-with-observations" and "simplicity." Consider a set of observation reports on the relationship of properties A and B (Figure 15.1). A theory that implies that the data points be connected by straight lines maximizes agreement with observations. However, a theory that implies that $A \propto 1/B$ would be arguably

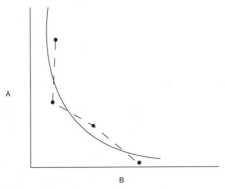

Figure 15.1 Relationship of properties A and B

more simple even though no data-point falls on this curve. Since scientists usually prefer a smooth curve to a linear zigzag function, it is clear that they do not accept agreement-with-observations to be a sufficient condition of the acceptability of theories. Normally, they invoke considerations of simplicity as well. The fact that hypothesis-appraisal usually reflects a tension between agreement-with-observations and simplicity provides support for the conclusion that conflicts between predictive accuracy and explanatory power are common as well.

Given the set of criteria recommended by Kuhn, what is needed is a weighting of their relative importance. There has been no general agreement among methodologists on such weighting. William Whewell, for instance, emphasized breadth of scope. A successor theory receives high marks from Whewell if it accounts for the phenomena explained by its predecessor and additional phenomena as well. Karl Popper, on the other hand, played down this standard. He cautioned that a theory may be used to explain too much and in so doing fail to have falsifiable consequences.

Copernicus claimed that his heliostatic planetary theory achieved "conceptual integration." "Conceptual integration," is achieved when relations that have been accepted as "just facts" are shown to follow from the basic assumptions of some theory. Before Copernicus formulated his theory, the relations of retrograde planetary motions were accepted as "just facts." Copernicus pointed out that his theory *required* that retrograde motion occur more frequently for Jupiter than for Mars and that the extent of retrograde motion be greater for Mars than for Jupiter. He thus converted "mere facts" to "facts required by theory." Copernicus' geocentric opponents were unimpressed. They did not share his conviction that it is important to provide a rationale for the observed ordering of retrograde motions.

Kuhn concluded that, because of these difficulties of interpretation and application, the evaluative criteria he had identified are " an insufficient basis for a *shared* algorithm of choice."[32] He continued to maintain, however, that scientists do apply the several standards in his list in the course of their creation of science. He insisted, however, that evaluative decisions cannot be reduced in practice, or in principle, to prescribed patterns. Kuhn emphasized that evaluative decisions inevitably reflect "idiosyncratic factors dependent on individual biography and personality" as scientists interpret and apply these values.[33]

Unfortunately for the program of methodological pragmatism, predictive accuracy and explanatory power are factors contributing to the "external strength" and "internal strength" of a methodology respectively. The adequacy of a methodology is to be measured by the conjunction of its external and internal strengths. But these strengths are not additive. If one places emphasis on external factors, then evaluative practice justifies "rules of thumb" like the virial expansion. If one places emphasis on internal factors, then evaluative practice justifies theories that make contrary-to-fact conditional claims like "if that physical system conformed to the requirements of this theory, then it would behave in such and such a way."

Rescher's analysis places heavy emphasis on external factors. This leaves open the status of sequences of abstract theories. Methodological pragmatism is no more successful in establishing such sequences to be progressive than prior attempts to demonstrate their convergence upon truth.

Progress, realism and miracles

There are, therefore, serious difficulties for the indirect approach of methodological pragmatism.

This indirect approach seeks to warrant the convergence upon truth of successive scientific theories by reference to improving evaluative practice, which improvement is established, in turn, mainly on appeal to an acknowledged increase in problem-solving effectiveness. But why not base the convergence upon truth of scientific theories directly on increasing predictive efficacy? Consider the argument:

1 Increasing predictive success has been achieved within the history of science.
2 In all cases, if premise 1, then scientific theories have achieved increasing approximation to truth over time.

∴ Scientific theories have achieved increasing approximation to truth over time.

The argument is valid, but premise 2 is false. For instance, within the early history of astronomy, increasingly more complex mathematical theories achieved increasingly more accurate predictions of the paths of the planets along the zodiac. However, this succession of theories did not achieve an increasing approximation to truth. No correspondence was established between the motions stipulated by the theories and the motions of the bodies of the Solar System. If truth is a correspondence between the claims of theory and the properties and relations of physical systems, then these geocentric theories did not achieve progress toward truth.

One response to the failure of the above argument is to shift focus from "approximate truth" to "empirical adequacy." This shift of focus was recommended by Bas van Fraassen.[34] The above argument then may be revised:

1*   Increasing predictive success has been achieved within the history of science.
2* In all cases, if premise 1*, then scientific theories have become increasingly empirically adequate over time.

∴ Scientific theories have become increasingly empirically adequate over time.

Premise 2* is not a tautology. It is possible that increasing predictive success be achieved without appeal to theories at all. But the conclusion established is certainly a weak claim. Most realists insist that successive theories approach truth, such that the structure of the universe is progressively revealed thereby.

Some realists have given support to a "no miracle" argument:

1 Increasing predictive success has been achieved within the history of science.
2 In all cases, if premise 1, and scientific theories do not achieve increasing approximation to truth over time, then the increasing predictive success of science is a miracle.
3 The increasing predictive success of science is not a miracle.

∴ Scientific theories do achieve increasing approximation to truth over time.

Again the second premise is suspect. Geocentric planetary theories achieved increasing predictive success, even though these theories did not achieve an increasing approximation to truth, and no miracle was involved.

Martin Carrier has suggested that the "no miracle" argument be strengthened by allowing "predictive success" to include both the successful extension of a theory to cover both novel regularities (Herschel) and novel relations among known regularities (without specific adjustment for that purpose) (Whewell).[35] Carrier then called attention to two historical episodes in which false, non-referring theories were extended to cover previously unrecognized regularities.

The first episode is Joseph Priestley's prediction that phlogiston, produced by the action of metals on hydrochloric acid, should transform a calx to the corresponding metal. Priestley demonstrated this novel effect experimentally.[36] What is important about this episode is not that Priestley mistakenly took hydrogen to be phlogiston, a presumed component of metals, but that he applied a false, non-referring theory to predict a subsequently confirmed novel relationship. Carrier declared that in this instance

> we have a theoretical prediction of an empirical regularity that was not known to science before.[37]

The second episode features a prediction derived from the caloric theory of heat. Carrier noted that, according to the caloric theory that takes heat to be a fluid, the transition of a substance from the liquid phase to the gaseous phase is due to an accumulation of atmospheres of caloric around the material particle of the substance. Atmospheres of caloric exert mutually-repulsive forces on one another. These repulsive forces are far stronger than the attractive forces between the material particles of the substance. (Figure 5.2)

A gas is elastic. It is compressible, but only if a force is applied to overcome the mutually-repulsive atmospheres of caloric. If a gas is heated, additional caloric is injected into the atmospheres surrounding the material particles and the gas expands.

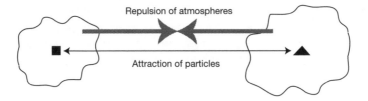

Figure 15.2 The caloric theory model of a gas

Dalton and Gay-Lussac, working independently on the basis of caloric theory, predicted that the rate of increase of volume with temperature at constant pressure should be the same for all gases. This should be the case because 1) the attractive forces between material particles become negligible in the gaseous state, and 2) the force between mutually-repulsive atmospheres of caloric is the same regardless of the nature of the material particles surrounded. Dalton and Gay-Lussac showed experimentally that thermal expansion is the same for various gases, as required by caloric theory. Carrier concluded that this is another instance of

> a confirmed prediction of an empirical law that was previously unknown to the scientific community and furthermore not to be expected given the background knowledge (that is, the state of knowledge without the theory in question).[38]

This episode lacks the dramatic impact of the predictions of the return of Halley's comet, the Poisson white spot, and the bending of starlight around the Sun. Supporters of the caloric theory—LaPlace, Lavoisier, Dalton, Gay-Lussac—did not declare "aha, if caloric theory is true, then the thermal expansion of gases must be independent of the nature of the gas," and then convoke an audience of their peers to witness a test. Nevertheless, Carrier is correct to cite this case as providing novel support for a subsequently discredited, non-referring theory.

Given the historical countercases of predictively successful false theories, there are several response-options available to realists:

1 blunt the force of the anti-realist countercases which divorce predictive success from truth by exhibiting historical episodes acknowledged to be progressive-toward-truth but whose central terms fail to refer;
2 restrict the "convergence upon truth" thesis to theories of "mature sciences," defined so as to exclude geocentric astronomy, phlogiston theory, etc.;
3 restate the "convergence upon truth" thesis as a claim based on *inductive* support; and
4 show that the predictive successes of the anti-realist countercases follows directly from aspects of those theories that are not false.

Clyde Hardin and Alexander Rosenberg have pursued the first option. They observed that there has been a succession of empirically successful theories about "genes," entities that supposedly are carriers of hereditary information. Hardin and Rosenberg pointed out that the functions initially assigned to the Mendelian gene

> are now credited to widely different amounts, highly complex combinations, and incredibly diverse sequences of DNA; indeed in some areas of genetics the term "gene" has pretty much dropped out of sophisticated presentations of the theory in favor of terms that more accurately discriminate between the units of hereditary functions.[39]

Hardin and Rosenberg maintained that Mendelian genetics still qualifies as an "approximately true" theory—the first in a sequence of progressively more adequate theories—in spite of the fact that its central theoretical term "gene" can be said not to refer.

This type of response to the anti-realist challenges has limited impact. Even if there are progressively more truthlike sequences of non-referring theories, there still may be predictively successful theories that fail to converge upon truth, and this remains a problem for realism.

The second response-option seems evasive and somewhat arbitrary. From the standpoint of present-day science we label certain past developments "immature," thereby avoiding troublesome countercases to the convergence thesis.

The first two responses to the anti-realist challenges are directed against the universal generalization: "all predictively successful sequences of theories in a domain converge upon truth." However, one may concede that this generalization is false, and still defend realism. The convergence-upon-truth thesis may be defended as an inductive argument (the third response-option):

x is an episode in which successive theories in a domain achieve increasing predictive success.

∴ It is probable that x is an episode in which theories in a domain achieve increasing approximation to truth.

Countercases are not decisive against this version of the convergence thesis. It may be allowed that there are a few exceptions to the correlation between increasing predictive success and increasing approximation to truth. Only probability is claimed for the convergence thesis.

The fourth response-option, if successful, is the strongest defense of the convergence thesis.

For this response to be successful it must be shown that references to "phlogiston," "caloric," "aether," etc, are irrelevant to the predictive successes of the theories that invoke these concepts. With this project in mind, Philip Kitcher examined several of the anti-realist countercases that had been developed by Larry Laudan.[40]

One of Laudan's countercases to the convergence thesis is the success achieved by geological theories that postulated a structure for the earth in which continents do not move laterally. Laudan emphasized that these theories were highly successful in explaining various features of the geological column. Kitcher's response was to argue that the assumption of the lateral stability of continents played no role in these successful explanations. According to Kitcher, the "lateral stability of continents," like the "aether," is a "presuppositional posit" , rather than a "working posit." As such, it is not involved in explanations of the physical and chemical properties of rock strata.[41]

Kitcher sought to account for the empirical successes of the phlogiston theory by reinterpreting the apparently non-referring terms of the theory. He declared that

> even a brief reading of the writings of the phlogistonists reinforces the idea of true doctrines trying to escape from flawed language.[42]

"Dephlogisticated air," for instance, refers to "the substance breathed by Joseph Priestley and several mice." In Lavoisier's terminology, this is "oxygen."

In some contexts, "phlogiston" refers to "the substance that 'combines' with a calx to form the corresponding metal," e.g.,

$$\text{calx of magnesium} + \text{charcoal} = \text{magnesium} + \text{fixed air}$$
$$\text{(rich in } \varphi) \qquad \text{(calx} + \varphi)$$
$$[2 \text{ MgO} + \text{C} = 2 \text{ Mg} + \text{CO}_2]$$

In other contexts, "phlogiston" refers to "the substance released when hydrochloric acid acts on a metal," e.g.,

$$\text{hydrochloric acid} + \text{magnesium} = \text{phlogiston} + \text{magnesium chloride}$$
$$[2 \text{ HCl} + \text{Mg} = \text{H}_2 + \text{MgCl}_2]$$

The actual referents of the tokens of "phlogiston" and "dephlogisticated air" differ from context to context. When this is taken into account, the empirical successes of phlogiston theories pose no difficulty for realism.

Kitcher's most extended analysis is directed at Poisson's derivation of a subsequently confirmed novel prediction from Fresnel's theory that interprets light to be a wave motion within an aethereal medium. The prediction is that there is a bright spot at the center of the shadow cast when a circular disc is illumined by a point source. Kitcher noted that the successful prediction was derived from premises about the propagation of transverse waves. He held that Fresnel's false belief about a medium through which the waves spread is not essential to the derivation. Kitcher's conclusion about Laudan's countercases is that either the analysis is not sufficiently fine-grained to see that the sources of error are not involved in the apparent successes of past science or there are flawed views about reference.[43]

John Worrall agreed with Kitcher's conclusions about Fresnel's theory. He declared that

> roughly speaking, it seems right to say that Fresnel completely misidentified the *nature* of light, but nonetheless it is no miracle that his theory enjoyed the empirical success that it did; it is no miracle because Fresnel's theory ... attributed to light the right *structure*.[44]

The mathematical form of Fresnel's equations is the same as the mathematical form of the corresponding equations of Maxwell's electrodynamic theory in which "aether" plays no role. Fresnel held that light is a periodic compression and rarefaction of an elastic medium. Maxwell held that light is an oscillating magnetic field. Both took the propagation of light to be rectilinear with two transverse components of varying intensity. The equations developed by Fresnel and Maxwell share a common mathematical form, and it is this form that enabled Poisson to predict the bright spot at the center of the opaque disk's shadow.

Worrall noted that E.T. Whittaker, in his influential *A History of Aether and Electricity* (1910)[45] had claimed that Fresnel first developed a wave theory of light by purely geometrical reasoning, and then superimposed on the theory a model of waves moving through an invisible and imponderable "aether." Worrall disagreed. He maintained that Fresnel's "purely geometrical" reasoning was informed throughout by his commitment to mechanical principles, including Hooke's law and assumptions about the direction-dependent elastic properties of a light-carrying medium.

Fresnel's wave theory achieved predictive successes—the Poisson white spot and the conical refraction patterns inside biaxial crystals. According to Worrall, these predictions were derived from a theory within which general assumptions about wave motion in a medium were essential.

Worrall insisted that his analysis of nineteenth-century aether theories can be accommodated within a realist interpretation of science. However, the relevant "realism" is not a "convergence on truth realism," but a "structural realism." The principal claim of structural realism is that scientific progress is achieved in a domain when there is an isomorphism of structure between successive theories and physical systems. Often this isomorphism of structure is present only under limiting conditions for which there is an asymptotic agreement of calculations for two theories.

To accept structural realism is to raise a question about "truth" and "approximation to truth." That successive theories share a common mathematical form is insufficient to establish progress. As Stathis Psillos emphasized, the mathematical form also must represent correctly the properties and relations of physical systems.[46]

Realist interpretations of science almost always defend (or assume) that truth is a correspondence of theoretical claims and aspects of physical reality. To assert the truth of a theory that introduces terms for hitherto unobserved objects is to assert the existence of these objects. This is why the phlogiston, caloric and aether theories are *prima facie* countercases to the convergence-upon-truth thesis.

We believe that phlogiston, caloric and the aether do not exist. However, there is nothing in the theories about phlogiston, caloric and the aether that precludes the isolation and identification of these putative entities. The same is true of theories about atoms and viruses.

The situation is different, however, for present-day theories about quarks, gravitons and magnetic monopoles. Jarrett Leplin pointed out that the very theories that postulate the existence of these entities do preclude their isolation and identification. For example, if current theory is correct, then the isolated quark cannot exist. It is not subject to isolation and identification. Nevertheless, the term "quark" plays an important role in theories of the nucleus. Quark-triplets are held to be responsible for the exchange of forces within the nucleus.

Leplin noted that explanatory unification has become more important than empirical confirmation in the practice of high-energy physics. Physicists have isolated and identified the W and Z particles posited by the Weinberg–Salam Theory. Leplin conceded that failure to find these particles would have counted against the theory. But the same does not hold for the X particle posited by grand unification theory. The X particle supposedly is involved in the transmutation of a quark into a positron. Leplin observed that

> the trouble is that the X is so massive (10^{14} proton masses) that the right conditions [for identification] require unobtainable energies. The connection between the mass of a force-carrying particle and its range (10^{-29} cm. for the X) is fundamental to the quantum mechanical understanding of the forces being unified, and the connection between mass and energy is fundamental to relativity theory. These constraints are not adjustable. They at once commit the program of unification to specific empirical effects and preclude the observability of these effects.[47]

We appear to have reached a stage in the discipline of high-energy physics in which progress is marked by explanatory coherence rather than successful prediction. The traditional realist position is that progress is convergence upon truth and that convergence upon truth is increasingly more exact correspondence to physical reality. If convergence upon truth is to be established by reference to predictive success alone, developments in high-energy physics make it difficult to show that progress has been achieved in that important domain.

16

LAUDAN ON SCIENTIFIC PROGRESS AS INCREASING PROBLEM-SOLVING EFFECTIVENESS

Larry Laudan's appraisal of the project to show that scientific progress is a convergence upon truth was decidedly negative. He declared that

> no one has been able to say what it would mean to be "closer to truth," let alone to offer criteria for determining how we could assess such proximity.[1]

Laudan concluded that the key to understanding scientific progress is not an "approximation to truth" but the problem-solving ability of its theories. He maintained that science is a sustained attempt to solve problems, and that progress in science is success in this enterprise.

Laudan subdivided the problems that concern scientists into empirical problems and conceptual problems. Empirical problems are "substantive questions about the objects which constitute the domain of any given science."[2] Conceptual problems are theory-related problems. They arise when theory T is seen to be vague, unclear or inconsistent, or when T is seen to conflict with another theory, methodological rule or cognitive aim.[3] Scientists achieve progress within a domain by solving its outstanding empirical or conceptual problems. Whereas Kuhn required for scientific progress either incorporation (during periods of "normal science") or revolution, Laudan required neither. Of course, both incorporation and overthrow *may* increase problem-solving effectiveness.

Particularly important, according to Laudan, is the solution of "anomalous problems," empirical problems "which a particular theory has not solved, but which one or more of its competitors have."[4] Anomalous problems may be solved by a redetermination of observational evidence. An example is the measurement of stellar parallax by Bessel and Struve in 1837. During the seventeenth and eighteenth centuries the supposed absence of parallax was an anomalous problem for heliocentrism, because the rival geocentric theory successfully explained this absence. Of course, heliocentric theorists had explained the failure to observe a parallax by adding an auxiliary hypothesis about the great distance of the Solar System from the nearest star. However, the nineteenth-century measurement of parallax was arguably a better solution of this anomalous problem. Anomalous problems also may be solved by modifying the relevant theory. The corpuscular theory of light, for instance, was modified progressively during the eighteenth and nineteenth centuries to account for the successes achieved by the rival wave theory.[5]

Laudan took a broad view of what counts as a problem. He held that scientists" beliefs about non-existent states of affairs may generate "empirical problems." Laudan included among "empirical problems" the seventeenth-century problem of the properties and behavior of sea serpents, and the nineteenth-century problem of specifying how meat left in the Sun could transmute into maggots.[6] This view of empirical problems accommodates both the search for trans-uranic elements and the search for polywater and N-rays.

Laudan took an equally broad view of conceptual problems. He included among "conceptual problems" relevant to scientific progress "worldview difficulties" in which a theory conflicts with some body of accepted beliefs. These difficulties are not difficulties within science itself, but resolution of the difficulties may have repercussions within science. Laudan suggested that the conflict between Mendelian genetics and Marxist dogma is a worldview difficulty, resolution of which is relevant to scientific progress.[7]

Laudan was generous, as well, about what counts as a "solution" to a problem. He maintained that a theory may "solve" an empirical problem even if it entails only an approximate answer.[8] For instance, he gave Galileo credit for "solving" the problem of falling bodies even though his solution holds only if the ratio of the distance of fall to the distance to the center of the earth is zero.

Laudan also maintained that mathematical models that "save the appearances" may count as solutions to empirical problems. For instance, Ptolemy's epicycle-deferent models were a solution to the empirical problem of the retrograde motion of the planets, despite the fact that he made no claim (in the *Almagest* at least) that planets execute epicyclic motions in physical space. Presumably if a mathematician were to superimpose a power expansion of the form $A = k_1 + k_2B + k_3B^2 + k_4B^3 + \ldots$ upon a set of data points $[A_1, B_1], [A_2, B_2], [A_3, B_3] \ldots$, this would count as a solution to the problem of how A and B are related (if indeed this was believed to be a problem). Indeed Laudan maintained that

> any theory, T, can be regarded as having solved an empirical problem, if T functions (significantly) in any schema of inference whose conclusion is a statement of the problem.[9]

However, the problem-solving model cannot be applied to yield instant-assessment of theory-choice in individual cases. It is only the long-term fecundity of research traditions that is subject to evaluation of problem-solving effectiveness. Research traditions are general assumptions about the entities and processes in a domain of study, and about the appropriate methods to be used for investigating the problems and constructing the theories in that domain.[10]

Any research tradition whose successive theories solve problems within the appropriate domain qualifies as progressive. This includes the research traditions that postulated the existence of phlogiston, caloric and the electromagnetic aether. Laudan conceded that successive theories within these traditions were progressive for a time. Eventually, of course, these research traditions became stagnant.

Laudan claimed that his problem-solving model embodies the "general nature of rationality."

The problem-solving model is not merely the best methodology currently available. Rather this model

> transcends the particularities of the past by insisting that for all times and all cultures, provided those cultures have a tradition of critical discussion (without which no culture can lay claim to rationality), rationality consists in accepting those research traditions which are most effective problem solvers.[11]

It is Laudan's position that the criterion of rational choice among research traditions is the same at all times and all cultures. This is the case despite the fact that specific standards of rationality—methodological rules, cognitive aims and criteria of acceptability—are subject to change.

A theory of scientific progress may be appraised by reference to two requirements: it must "fit" important episodes from the history of science, and it must explain why these episodes developed as they did. Judgments about closeness of fit reflect a tension between agreement with the historical record and simplicity. Theories of scientific progress are idealizations created, in part, to achieve conceptual economy at the expense of detailed descriptive accuracy.

Laudan's problem-solving theory satisfies the first requirement. Given its generous interpretation of what counts as "problems" and "solutions," the theory can be superimposed on almost any development. However, it might seem that the theory achieves a fit with the history of science simply by taking problem-solving to be the same as "that which scientists do." Such an interpretation would be inappropriate because "problem-solving" also is what legislators, artists and automobile mechanics do.

Laudan did not deal with the issue of demarcating the problem-solving that characterizes science from other types of problem-solving. He presupposed, prior to analysis, that scientific domains are known. His approach appeared to be, "given the existence of scientific domains, what is significant about the activities of scientists who work in these domains?" One has to begin an inquiry at some point, and this is a reasonable launch-site.

122

F. Michael Ackeroyd has called attention to an episode from the history of chemistry which may appear to count against the fit achieved by the problem-solving model. The episode in question is a mid-nineteenth-century dispute over the nature of acids.[12]

A research tradition based on the work of Liebig held that acids are hydrogen salts—e.g.,hydrochloric acid and sulfuric acid are taken to be homologues of NaCl and Na_2SO_4. Liebig's theory explains why there can exist acids that do not contain oxygen.

A second research tradition based on the work of Lavoisier and Fourcroy held that all acids contain oxygen. Within the Lavoisier–Fourcroy tradition, the lack of oxygen in hydrochloric acid (HCl) is an unsolved problem. The Liebig theory explains why hydrochloric acid lacks oxygen; the Lavoisier–Fourcroy theory does not.

Ackeroyd pointed out, however, that the Lavoisier–Fourcroy theory solves three problems that beset the Liebig theory:

1 why concentrated and dilute forms of an acid behave differently,
2 why increasing oxygen content is correlated with increasing acidity (e.g., H_2SO_4 is more highly acidic than H_2SO_3), and
3 why some dihydric and trihydric acids are weaker than some monohydric acids (e.g., H_3PO_4 is weaker than $HClO_4$).

Ackeroyd noted that the Liebig theory was dominant during the period 1840–85 despite the disparity in the solved problems/unsolved problems ratio for the two research traditions. Chemists believed that it was more important that the problem of the anomalous status of hydrochloric acid be solved than that the three problems that beset Liebig's theory be solved. The Liebig vs. Lavoisier episode is not evidence that the problem-solving model fails to fit the historical record. It merely shows that comparative problem-solving effectiveness cannot be reduced to a ratio of number of problems solved to number of problems unsolved.

A second episode that may appear to count against the fit achieved by the problem-solving model is late sixteenth-century planetary astronomy. A recurrent pattern in the history of science is the formulation of a theory T_2 that solves some of the problems left unsolved by T_1, but introduces other problems that it does not solve. Consider the initial relationship between Copernicus' heliostatic theory (T_c) and Ptolemy's geostatic theory (T_p). T_c explains why

1 Mercury and Venus never are seen at great angles from the Sun, and
2 the extent of retrograde motion is greater for Mars than for Jupiter than for Saturn, and the frequency of such motions is greater for Saturn than for Jupiter than for Mars.

However, T_c also introduced problems not faced by T_p, for instance

1* the fall of a tower-dropped object is straight to its base,
2* the absence of stellar parallax, and
3* a conceptual tension between Copernicus' qualitative Sun-centered system and his quantitative models which displace the Sun from the center of the planets' orbits.

A similar analysis is appropriate for Darwin's theory of organic evolution (T_D). T_D explains

1 biogeographical distributions,
2 paleontological sequences, and
3 homologous organs.

However, T_D also introduced conceptual problems such as

1* a conflict with the best estimates from physics of the age of the Earth, and
2* a conflict with the dominant Christian understanding of man's position in the universe.

Upon the introduction of Tycho Brahe's revised geocentric theory (1577, published in 1588), it might seem that the geocentric research tradition had won the problem-solving sweepstakes. Brahe developed a geostatic theory with Moon and Sun revolving around the centrally-placed Earth, and Mercury, Venus, Mars, Jupiter and Saturn revolving around the moving Sun (see Figure 16.1). The Tychonic system provided "solutions" to the problems about bodies released from towers and the failure to observe stellar parallax. This system also accounted for the maximum angles from the Sun of Mercury and Venus, and the facts about the retrograde motions of Mars, Jupiter and Saturn. If these were the problems that counted most, then the Tychonic system might be judged superior to Copernicus' theory between 1580 and 1600. Brahe's version of geocentrism both solved problems that had beset the heliostatic research tradition and accounted for problems successfully accounted for by that tradition. It must be conceded, however, that the Tychonic theory was not developed into a system of quantitative astronomy successful in predicting planetary positions. In that respect, the Tychonic system was a promissory note never cashed.

The Brahe episode does not show that the problem-solving model fails to fit the history of science. It shows only that an ultimately nonprogressive research tradition may be superior to its competitors for a time. Laudan himself emphasized that research traditions that invoke the concepts "phlogiston," "caloric," and the "electromagnetic aether" were progressive for a time.[13]

A descriptive theory of progress does not stipulate evaluative standards that can be applied to yield an instant assessment of the rationality of a new development in science. Laudan's problem-solving theory, for instance, lacks

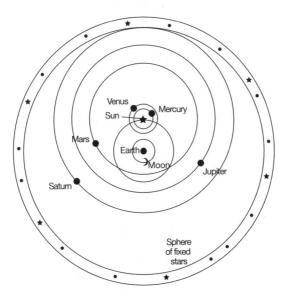

Figure 16.1 Brahe's theory of the Universe

the resources to determine that a problem solved within one research tradition is more important than a problem solved within a second tradition. Nevertheless a judgment may be rendered subsequently based on the problem-solving records of the competing research traditions. This does not preclude the occurrence of periods of superior problem-solving effectiveness by a competitor that eventually becomes stagnant.

Laudan's problem-solving theory also satisfies the second requirement for a descriptive theory of scientific progress. It does provide an explanation of developments in the history of science. It enables the observer of science to explain why science developed as it did. Of course, whether or not a proposed explanation is acceptable to a recipient depends on what the recipient wishes to know. But it is reasonable to accept reference to a string of problem-solutions achieved by a research tradition as an explanation of progress within a scientific domain.

Laudan would not be content with mere descriptive success, however. He subscribed to the position of *normative* naturalism.

17

KITCHER ON CONCEPTUAL PROGRESS AND EXPLANATORY PROGRESS

Despite Kitcher's criticisms of Laudan's countercases to convergent realism, his own theory of progress is quite similar to that of Laudan. Laudan held that progress is achieved when empirical problems or conceptual problems are solved. Kitcher introduced three types of problem-solution—practical, conceptual, and explanatory—that contribute to scientific progress.

Kitcher was not concerned to formulate necessary or sufficient conditions for scientific progress. His orientation is descriptive, focusing on changes in "consensus practices" within communities of scientists. "Practical progress" is achieved through the design and application of scientific instruments. "Conceptual progress" is achieved by the revision of categories to better represent the properties and relations of physical systems. And "explanatory progress" is achieved by means of the improvement or replacement of patterns of explanation.

Kitcher had little to say about practical progress. It is acknowledged on all sides that science has been progressive in this sense. Scientists have utilized a vast array of devices—from the telescope and air pump to particle accelerators and the electron microscope—to extend their abilities to predict and control nature. It is claims about conceptual progress and explanatory progress that are controversial, and Kitcher understandably focused on these areas. He declared that

> conceptual progress is made when we adjust the boundaries of our categories to conform to kinds and when we are able to provide more adequate specifications of our referents.[1]

Thus Copernicus achieved a progressive "boundary adjustment" by including Earth among the planets. And Lavoisier achieved conceptual progress by revising the modes of reference for tokens of Priestley's term "dephlogisticated air."

Kitcher held that certain subsequent modifications of Dalton's schema for the atomic constitution of compounds is a paradigm case of explanatory progress. Dalton formulated an explanatory schema to answer the question "why does one of the compounds between X and Y always contain X and Y in the weight ratio $m : n$?"[2] Dalton's schema assumes that the compound has the formula

$X_p Y_q$, that the atomic weights of X and Y are x and y respectively, and that the weight ratio $X : Y$ is $px : qy$, which is equal to $m : n$.[3]

Dalton's explanatory scheme is an important achievement. However, it leaves unexplained why specific values of p and q are realized in various compounds. The development of valence theory in the nineteenth century enabled chemists to provide a "more fundamental" answer to the question Dalton addressed. The answer is "more fundamental" because valence theory is supported by empirically confirmed periodic relations among the chemical elements. The assignment of valence +1 to sodium and potassium, and −1 to chlorine and bromine is not arbitrary. These assignments receive support from knowledge of the chemical reactions into which these elements enter.

Valence theory, in turn, leaves unexplained why it is that elements have the valences that they have. Molecular orbital theory, which assigns stability to combinations of atoms for which outer electron shells are filled, provides a still more fundamental answer to the original question. And quantum theory provides a yet more fundamental explanation, since it explains why filled outer electron shells confer stability upon molecules.

Kitcher maintained that explanatory progress also was achieved by post-Darwinian developments in evolutionary biology.[4] Darwin explained the biogeographical distribution of species by schemata that feature the idea that natural selective pressure acts upon the individuals in a pool of antecedently given variants. Twentieth-century theorists amended Darwin's explanatory schema to allow for drift, migration, meiotic drive, and other effects, thereby extending the range of "Darwinian" explanations.

Reflecting on these, and other examples, Kitcher suggested that a consensus practice P_2 is explanatorily progressive with respect to practice P_1, provided that

1 P_2 contains a correct explanatory schema that does not occur in P_1, or
2 P_1 contains an incorrect explanatory schema that does not occur in P_2, or
3 P_2 contains an explanatory schema that extends, or otherwise completes, the schemata of P_1.[5]

Reference to "correct" and "incorrect" schemata raises a question about the status of explanatorily progressive developments. Given that there are patterns of conceptual and explanatory progress in the history of science, is this progress evidence that successive scientific theories are convergent upon truth?

Kitcher held that the phase "closer to truth" is properly predicated of some relations between theories. For example, "2" below is closer to truth than "1":

1 "Altruistic alleles are always opposed by natural selection."
2 "Altruistic alleles are always opposed by natural selection except when there is an offsetting inclusive fitness effect."[6]

He acknowledged, however, that there are some cases in which the phrase "closer to truth" is inappropriate, e.g., "light is a wave" versus "light is a particle." In addition, Kitcher conceded that theories that invoke idealizations can be taken as "true" only by convention. We may take claims about "point masses," "massless charges," "elastic collisions," "ideal pendulums," etc., to be true by convention. But then it would appear to be quite arbitrary to take one conventionally-true theory to be "closer to truth" than another. To assign "conventional truth" to theories about idealized entities is to place these theories beyond the scope of the realist program to show that successive theories converge upon truth.

Kitcher sought to defend realism wherever possible. He maintained that the correspondence theory of truth "has roots in everyday practices,"[7] and that the cognitive goal of science is to attain significant truth.[8] But he was sensitive to the tension which arises in the practice of science between the search for true statements about physical systems and the goal of unification of empirical knowledge. He maintained that his project of exhibiting instances of cognitive and explanatory progress within the history of science can be conducted within the framework of a "unificationist realism." This version of realism interprets science to be

> a sequence of practices that attempt to incorporate true statements (insofar as is possible) and to articulate the best unification of them (insofar as is possible).[9]

In response to a complaint by Richard Miller that explanatory unification does not warrant truth claims,[10] Kitcher developed a version of the "no miracle" Argument. He declared that

> we are strikingly good at making science-based interventions in nature. … [and] this success in intervention is incomprehensible unless we suppose that the claims we are putting to work in our practical activities are correct (or, at least, approximately correct).[11]

Kitcher called attention to the successes of geneticists in the design of organisms with selected characteristics—e.g., insulin-producing bacteria. According to Kitcher, such successful interventions are evidence for the truth of claims about genetic structures.[12]

There is a less ambitious version of the "no miracle" argument that is very convincing. This argument is formulated to prove, not a general convergence of scientific theories upon truth, but only that certain important theories are true.

The argument from the multiple determinations of the values of physical constants

1 The values of physical constants determined by application of theories belonging to diverse domains are in agreement.
2 If premise 1, and the theories used in these determinations are not approximately true, then the agreement of these measured values is a miracle.
3 The agreement of the measured values of these constants is not a miracle.

∴ The theories used in these determinations are approximately true.

This is not an argument stated by Kitcher. However, it could be used to advantage in support of unificationist realism.

Jean Perrin, writing in 1912, maintained that the case for the existence of atoms had become overwhelming. Perrin took the agreement among various experimental determinations of the value of Avogadro's number to be a decisive indication that atomic-molecular theory is correct.[13]

The kinetic molecular theory requires that equal volumes of gases contain equal numbers of molecules. A standard volume—22.4 liters, the volume occupied by 32 grams of oxygen at 20°C and 1 atmosphere pressure—thus contains a fixed number of molecules regardless of the element or compound involved. Avogadro's number (N_0) is the number of molecules in the gram-molecular weight of any element or compound—32 grams of oxygen, 28 grams of nitrogen, 18 grams of water, etc.

Avogadro's number is a constant that occurs in equations that describe electrolysis, Brownian motion, black-body radiation, radioactive decay, the scattering of light, and various other phenomena. These processes are quite diverse. Electrolysis is the migration of charged bodies within liquids; Brownian motion is an irregular zigzag movement of the minute particles suspended in a liquid or gas; black-body radiation is an emission of energy from a heated cavity; radioactive decay involves a spontaneous emission of positively charged and negatively charged particles from the nuclei of atoms; and the scattering of light under certain conditions involves a shift in the spectrum of the light (e.g., the scattering that produces the blue color of the sky). That measurements made during the investigation of these processes yield (nearly) the same value of N_0 is not likely to be a coincidence. Perrin took the convergence of experimental results upon a specific value of N_0—6.02×10^{23} molecules / gram-molecular weight—to be decisive evidence for the atomic-molecular theory.

Max Planck advanced a similar argument on behalf of the theory of energy quantization.[14] Planck called attention to the agreement achieved among various determinations of the value of Planck's constant h. This constant occurs in equations for emission and absorption spectra, black-body radiation, the photoelectric effect, the specific heats of solids, the ionization of gases, and various other processes. Planck maintained that the convergence of measurements from these diverse processes on $h = 6.6 \times 10^{-27}$ erg.sec. is decisive evidence for the theory of energy quantization.

Kitcher's proposals for the interpretation of scientific progress were quite modest. His theory of scientific progress depicts scientists working within communities of colleagues and competitors to attain significant truths about the world, truths that are integrated into a systematically unified body of empirical knowledge. Insofar as the pursuit of these goals produces conceptual and explanatory gains, scientific progress is achieved.

18

NORMATIVE NATURALISM

Normative naturalism is the position that evaluative standards and procedures arise within the practice of science, and are to be assessed in the same way that scientific theories are assessed—by reference to claims about the world. The normative naturalist views science and philosophy of science as a seamless whole. He or she is concerned to deny that philosophy of science is a "transcendent" discipline in which transhistorical, inviolable principles are superimposed upon the practice of science.

The *normative* naturalist maintains, nevertheless, that the standards developed within the philosophy of science have prescriptive status. Normative naturalism is a prescriptive enterprise whose acknowledged aim is to uncover standards for the appraisal of scientific theories and explanations, and to specify conditions under which theory-replacement constitutes progress. It is the normative naturalist position that such standards, like scientific theories themselves, have provisional status only. They are subject to correction or abandonment in the light of further experience.

Neurath's "boat image"

Otto Neurath was an early proponent of this position. He maintained that

1 empirical inquiry, the evaluation and/or justification of the results of empirical inquiry, and the selection of standards of appraisal, all are human activities that arise within science itself. No supra-empirical philosophical commentary is either required or appropriate;
2 science itself includes no transempirical inviolable propositions;
3 every proposition within science is corrigible;
4 no propositions within science have foundational status (viz. no subset of propositions is accepted independently of the remaining propositions, such that the non-foundational propositions receive their warrant from the foundational subset);

5 questions about justification (warrant) are appropriate for every proposition that is a candidate for inclusion within science;

6 knowledge claims are subject to acceptance or rejection within socio-political contexts that involve pragmatic considerations about the organization of scientific institutions, the resources of these institutions and the perceived value of the knowledge claims to society as a whole; and

7 a naturalized science, which incorporates the philosophy of science, nevertheless has normative-prescriptive force. Normative claims arise upon application of a principle of coherence. Neurath held that scientists *ought* seek to achieve coherence within the body of scientific propositions. No subset of propositions is epistemologically foundational in the effort to establish coherence, but the recognition of dissonance requires that adjudications be made. Applications of evaluative standards, themselves a product of choices made within science, generate *bona fide* prescriptive recommendations.

Neurath likened the growth of science to the rebuilding of a ship at sea:

we are like sailors who have to rebuild their ship on the open sea, without ever being able to dismantle it in drydock and reconstruct it from the best components.[1]

There are a number of assumptions that underlie the "boat image."[2] One assumption is that science is an ongoing enterprise. At no point does the ship attain the status of "seaworthy for all time." A second assumption is that continual rebuilding is necessary. There are pressures both within science and from the larger community that require responses from the scientific community. If the responses are inadequate the ship may sink. And a third assumption is that there is no transhistorical standpoint (drydock) from which successful responses may be orchestrated. That which contributes to increased seaworthiness is itself learned during the voyage, there is no inviolable axiological dimension within science. Even the most general of evaluative principles are subject to modification in the course of the rebuilding process.

Neurath emphasized that one requirement of anti-foundational naturalism is that sentences that record basic empirical data have the status of provisional hypotheses. An observation report may be accepted. But it also may be challenged for various reasons, and if the challenges are not met, the report may be rejected.

Neurath held that "protocol sentences" that record what is observed include reference to the experience of the observer.[3] An example is, "Fred noted at 5:12 pm. that Fred was aware at 5:11 pm. that the mercury meniscus in the tube before him was on the line 3.6." This report may be excluded from the body of accepted scientific discourse for various reasons: 1) other investigators locate the meniscus at 4.6; 2) Fred was observed to read the meniscus position from a sharp angle; 3) Fred's prior reports of his observations have proved unreliable bases for action; 4) Fred is believed to be deeply committed to a theory that would receive support from the value "3.6"; and 5) Fred is believed to be anxious to please the members of his research group who anticipate the value "3.6." Neurath insisted that the status of an observation report within the language of science depends on decisions about accepting or rejecting various other hypotheses, Observation reports thus cannot serve as a foundational base for the language of science.

Kitcher on the "naturalistic turn"

In an essay published in 1992, Philip Kitcher sought to energize the program of normative naturalism. He noted that normative naturalists occupy an "uncomfortable middle ground" between the prescriptivism of the logical empiricist tradition and the new descriptivism which "abandons or relativizes" normative considerations.[4] Kitcher insisted that

> the ultimate goal of (traditional naturalistic) epistemology is to present a compendium of cognitively optimal processes for all those contexts in which human subjects find themselves.[5]

The basic aim of the normative naturalist program is to show how knowledge of prescriptive standards can be achieved from the empirical study of science. Application of such standards has created, and presumably will continue to create, progress in science.

A preliminary task is to show that normative naturalism is possible. *Prima facie*, there are difficulties. Kitcher acknowledged the following objection to a prescriptive naturalism:

> only if we can arrive at principles that would properly guide inquiry in any world and which can be validated *a priori* will the problem of normative epistemology be solved. For otherwise the dependence of epistemology on information that had to be obtained using admittedly error-prone methods will lead to an unresolvable form of scepticism.[6]

Kitcher argued that this objection would be effective against normative naturalism only if two conditions were fulfilled. First, empirical inquiry reveals that evaluative disputes invariably diverge over time. And second, the further development of cognitive strategies fails to yield a verdict in such cases. If these conditions were fulfilled, then science would not be a progressive, self-correcting enterprise. But since the two conditions are not fulfilled, the above objection to normative naturalism is without force.

Kitcher, in effect, has proposed a burden-of-proof shift. The normative naturalist is not required to show how prescriptive conclusions follow from descriptive surveys. Rather the critic is challenged to prove that a convergence of evaluative practices is not possible. Kitcher declared that

> a strategy for defending traditional naturalism should become evident. With respect to the historical and contemporary cases, the aim will be to show that the case for continued divergence and indefinite underdetermination has not been made out.... All that traditional naturalism needs to show is that resolution is ultimately achieved, in favor either of one of the originally contending parties or of some emerging alternative that somehow combines their merits.[7]

Critics will object that the naturalist must undertake to show much more than this. In particular, the naturalist must show that prescriptive standards follow from empirical inquiry alone without presupposing non-naturalistic, transhistorical principles.

Kitcher was sensitive to this objection as well. He suggested that the challenge be met by formulating a concept of "cognitive virtue" and assigning prescriptive status to those evaluative standards whose applications promote cognitive virtue. On Kitcher's view, to achieve "cognitive virtue" is to achieve a theoretical unification which promotes understanding of the causal structure of the world and leads to successful predictions.

Kitcher's appeal to cognitive virtue is persuasive only if one of the following three options is correct:

1 there is a core meaning of "cognitive virtue" that has informed inquiry throughout the history of science;
2 a concept of "cognitive virtue" has emerged from earlier versions, and this latest concept correctly specifies the aim of science; or
3 successive concepts of "cognitive virtue" are increasingly more adequate interpretations of the aim of science.

The first option is implausible, given scientists' diverse uses of the terms "understanding," "causal structure," and "unification." The second option presupposes that the present concept of "cognitive virtue" will continue to specify the appropriate aim of science. There has been an evolutionary development of the concept, but development has ceased with the formulation of the present version. This is a "presentist" conceit incompatible with a naturalistic philosophy of science. The third option presupposes a linear development of scientific self-understanding. The aim of science, conceived at t_n, is superior to the aim of science, conceived at t_{n-1}. If this linearity could be established, it would provide a warrant for a normative-prescriptive claim—one ought to assess evaluative practice by appeal to the current understanding of "cognitive virtue." Of course, such assessments would be provisional and subject to change with the subsequent development of our understanding of "cognitive virtue."

Laudan on methodological rules as means–end correlations

In the essay "Progress or Rationality? The Prospects for a Normative Naturalism" (1987), Laudan recommended a two-stage program for the appraisal of evaluative standards and methodological rules. The first stage is to restate the standard or rule as a hypothetical imperative of the form (see Table 18.1)

If y is the goal to be achieved, then one ought do x.[8]

Laudan's hypothetical imperatives have prescriptive content. However, this content is expressed only with respect to some goal. Laudan insisted that "the aims of the 'scientific' community change through time."[9] There are no inviolable cognitive aims to serve as the top rung of a justificatory ladder. It is the reticulational model of justification that is correct.

Laudan's hypothetical imperatives are statements of means-end relationships. As such they are subject to empirical inquiry. The second stage of Laudan's program is to determine whether doing x is more likely than its alternatives to achieve y.[10] This second stage requires historical analysis on the part of the methodologist. He or she needs to ascertain which strategies of inquiry have in fact promoted which cognitive aims.

Laudan acknowledged that anti-inductivists will complain that there is no assurance that a past connection between strategies of inquiry and cognitive aims will continue to hold. He recommended acceptance of the following inviolable meta-methodological rule:

If actions of a particular sort, m, have consistently promoted certain cognitive ends, e, in the past, and rival actions, n , have failed to do

Table 18.1 Laudanian hypothetical imperatives

Standard/rule	Hypothetical imperative
"Avoid *ad hoc* hypotheses" (Popper)	"If the goal is to develop risky hypotheses, then one ought avoid *ad hoc* hypotheses."
"Incorporation-with corroborated-excess-content" (Lakatos)	If progress is the goal of a scientific research program, then seek theory T_{n+1} such that 1 T_{n+1} accounts for the previous successes of T_n, 2 T_{n+1} has greater empirical content than T_n and, 3 Some of the excess content of T_{n+1} is corroborated.
Principle of Correspondence (Bohr)	"If inclusiveness and unification are the goals of physics, then formulate theories of the quantum domain which are in asymptotic agreement with classical electrodynamics in the region for which the classical theory has proved effective."

so, then assume that future actions following the rule "if your aim is *e*, you ought to do *m*" are more likely to promote those ends than actions based on the rule "if your aim is *e,* you ought to do *n*."[11]

By accepting this meta-methodological rule, Laudan blocked the potential regress of justificatory arguments for methodological rules,[12] and insured prescriptive content for philosophy of science. Laudan referred to his position as a "normative naturalism." It is naturalistic insofar as the appraisal of methodological rules involves empirical inquiry into means-end correlations. It becomes normative-prescriptive upon application of the inviolable meta-methodological principle. One *ought* adopt just those rules that empirical inquiry reveals to have been effective means-end correlations.

Laudan contrasted this *normative* naturalism with various non-normative retreats into purely descriptive naturalism. He noted with disapproval that

> Quine, Putnam, Hacking and Rorty, for different reasons, hold that the best we can do is to *describe* the methods used by natural scientists, since there is no room for a normative methodology which is prescriptive in character.[13]

Laudan insisted upon a genuine normative-prescriptive role for philosophy of science.

Insofar as normative naturalists are committed to 1) the normative-prescriptive status of evaluative standards, and 2) the corrigibility of these standards in the light of further experience, it would seem that they must accept some inductive principle. Laudan claimed that there are good reasons for adopting the particular principle he recommended. He maintained that the principle "is arguably assumed universally among philosophers of science, and thus has promise as a quasi-Archimedean standpoint."[14] He noted, moreover, that the principle, "appears to be a sound rule of learning from experience."[15]

However, difficulties remain for this version of normative naturalism. Laudan has reinstated a justificatory hierarchy incompatible with his own reticulational model. The meta-methodological inductive principle is at the apex of the hierarchy.

It occupies this position in spite of the fact, recognized elsewhere by Laudan, that some means-end correlations once held to be reliable have ceased to be so. Examples are shown in Table 18.2

It may be objected that to retain the meta-methodological principle in the face of such counterexamples is to accord it inviolable status. To include an inviolable, transhistorical principle within the philosophy of science would be a violation of the program of naturalism. Of course, it is open to Laudan to insist that the principle is a contingent generalization subject to modification. An appropriate modification might be

> apply the meta-methodological principle except in those cases for which a formerly successful means-end correlation has ceased to be successful.

Table 18.2 Means-ends correlations and their failures

Ends	Means	Fails
Understand the motions of bodies	Postulate $1/R^n$ central forces	Electromagnetic induction
Predict correctly orbits of planets	In cases of discrepancy, postulate existence of a hitherto undiscovered planet, e.g., Neptune, Pluto	Orbit of Mercury
Provide a complete explanation of an experimental result	Formulate both a spatio-temporal description and a causal analysis of the result	Quantum phenomena

But then this modified principle would become an inviolable principle, applications of which determine correct evaluative practice. Unfortunately, such a principle is of value only after the fact. One cannot be certain, when initially confronting an evaluative situation, whether this is one of those occasions on which an application of the meta-methodological principle is counter-productive.

Assessment of normative naturalism

There exist normative-prescriptive philosophies of science that include inviolable principles. There also exist descriptive philosophies of science devoid of inviolable principles. The status of normative naturalism, however, is controversial. It is clear that its supporters *intend* to create a normative-prescriptive philosophy of science within which no evaluative principle is inviolable. But can this be accomplished? This depends, in part, on what is taken to be required for normative-descriptive status.

A minimal requirement is that philosophy of science *P* has normative-prescriptive status only if P includes at least one evaluative standard *S* such that

1 competent methodologists believe that at least one application of *S* to a present situation determines *at that time* the correctness of a particular evaluative judgment made in that situation;
2 *S* is held to be applicable to all evaluative situations of the type exemplified in 1); and
3 a justificatory argument is given for *S*.

Standards that satisfy the above conditions include "undesigned scope" (Herschel), "consilience of inductions" (Whewell), "incorporation-with-corroborated-excess-content" (Lakatos), and "express the results of experiments in the quantum domain in the language of classical physics" (Bohr).

Inclusion of requirement 3 denies normative-prescriptive status to philosophies of science whose evaluative recommendations are arbitrary. Larry Laudan endorsed this requirement. In a dispute with John Worrall, Laudan declared

> I thus categorically reject [Worrall's] suggestion that the thesis that the methods of science change in itself gives aid and comfort to relativism. What *does* give comfort to relativism is a failure to address the question: "How are methodological rules or standards justified?"[16]

Laudan criticized Popper, Reichenbach, Carnap and Hempel for failing to formulate appropriate justificatory arguments. He noted that Popper took the methods of science to be conventions, Reichenbach made the selection of aims for science a "volitional decision," Carnap maintained a subjectivist stance on the aims of inquiry, and Hempel failed to discuss the status of methodological rules.[17]

Laudan's own highest-level evaluative principle is the meta-methodological inductive rule. His justification for adopting this rule is rather sketchy. But he does give one. Laudan insisted that the meta-methodological rule "appears to be a sound rule of learning from experience" and it is "accepted universally" by philosophers of science.[18]

Requirement 1 is perhaps more controversial. To accept it is to deny normative-prescriptive status to philosophies of science whose evaluative assessments depend exclusively on observation of future states of affairs. Philosophers of science often endorse "forward-looking" standards, such as

1 T is preferable to T^* only if T proves to be more fertile, and
2 T is preferable to T^* only if T displays greater "fitness," where "fitness" requires both present adaptation and retention of the capacity to adapt to future disciplinary pressures.

A philosophy of science, all of whose evaluative standards are forward-looking, would not satisfy requirement 1.

Inclusion of requirement 1 denies normative-prescriptive status to that extreme form of evolutionary philosophy of science whose *sole* evaluative standard is "fitness." Of course, no one defends such a position. Normative evolutionary naturalists specify additional evaluative principles to provide present estimates of future adaptability. For example, they may adopt an inductive strategy that bases adaptability estimates on information about previous adaptive responses to similar "ecological" (disciplinary) pressures. Such estimates are risky. But they do provide assessments at time t for evaluative decisions to be made at that time, thereby satisfying requirement 1.

Adoption of requirement 1 also may raise questions about the normative-prescriptive status of some versions of normative naturalism. Consider, for instance, Neurath's position. Neurath insisted that every statement within science—including statements recording evaluative decisions, and premises of arguments that justify evaluative decisions—is contingent and subject to exclusion from the corpus of statements accepted within science. There is no transhistorical drydock from which the ship may be rebuilt. Neurath claimed, nevertheless, that the rebuilding process is governed by normative-prescriptive considerations.

Consider the situation of a methodologist in a leaking boat. An evaluative decision is required at the present time. The methodologist may apply an evaluative standard whose prior applications have repaired leaks in the boat. But no two evaluative situations are precisely similar in every respect. The methodologist must judge whether there are sufficient similarities to warrant application of a previously successful standard.

Suppose the methodologist does apply a currently accepted evaluative standard. It would seem that requirement 1 for normative-prescriptive status is satisfied. The methodologist believes that application of the standard at a particular time determines the correctness of the evaluative decision made at that time. This decision may be pronounced incorrect from the standpoint of a later time, but this merely shows that there is a distinction between

1 application of S at t *is believed to* determine the correctness of an evaluative decision at t, and
2 application of S at t *does* determine the correctness of an evaluative decision at t.

According to Neurath, science evolves in response to pressures both from within the discipline and from outside the discipline. Any normative-prescriptive response to such pressures requires a supporting argument. Otherwise the decision is arbitrary. The only supporting arguments consistent with the "boat image" are arguments to show that certain past evaluative decisions have proved effective in repairing leaks in the structure, and that the present leak appears to be similar to earlier leaks. To formulate such arguments is to appeal to an inductive principle: in all situations in which a present evaluative situation resembles earlier evaluative situations, render a decision that is similar to those that proved effective in the earlier situations.

Within a thoroughgoing naturalism of the type defended by Neurath an inductive principle is itself a contingent generalization. But there is considerable evidence against this principle, since evaluative standards and procedures have changed over time.

A case in point is the previously-mentioned standard of explanatory completeness. Prior to the development of quantum mechanics, scientists accepted the explanatory demand that an experimental result be subject to both spatio-temporal description and causal analysis. For investigations in the quantum domain, however, methodologists responsible for the seaworthiness of the boat have raised questions about this explanatory demand. On the

"Copenhagen interpretation", which became the dominant position, one can provide for an experimental result in the quantum domain either spatio-termporal description or causal analysis, but not both. Neils Bohr maintained that the earlier standard of explanatory completeness ought be replaced by a principle of complementarity.

Prima facie, abandonment of the earlier standard of explanatory completeness is evidence that counts against the inductive principle. However, one may choose to salvage the inductive principle by claiming that evaluative situations in the quantum domain are *different in kind* from previously encountered evaluative situations. The quantum domain presents a new type of repair problem to the mariners.

This strategy may be repeated each time an evaluative standard is replaced or modified. But then the critic will ask the naturalist "what sort of evidence would count against the inductive principle?" If no answer is forthcoming, then the critic will justly accuse the naturalist of elevating the inductive principle to inviolable status, thereby repudiating the very program of normative naturalism.

However, the naturalist might respond that "changes in evaluative standards and procedures within the history of science are real and pose difficulties for the methodologist, but these changes have not been sufficiently widespread to lead me to reject the inductive principle. On the other hand, if our experience were so chaotic that no consistent patterns of evaluative success were achieved, then I would be prepared to reject the principle."

A response of this sort might be sufficient to protect a naturalistic philosophy of science from the charge that it incorporates an inviolable principle. However, it remains the case that, because there have been occasions within the history of science in which evaluative standards have been modified, application of the inductive principle sometimes is counterproductive.

139

19

SCIENTIFIC PROGRESS AND THE THEORY OF ORGANIC EVOLUTION

Toulmin on conceptual evolution

The theories proposed by Peirce, Rescher, Laudan and Kitcher are attempts to specify the nature of scientific progress. The dominant theory of the underlying mechanism responsible for progress is an analogical extension of the theory of organic evolution.

Karl Popper was a leading proponent of the evolutionary analogy. He declared that

> science, or progress in science, may be regarded as a means used by the human species to adapt itself to the environment.[1]

On the evolutionary analogy, scientific progress is an "evolution" within which "natural selection" operates on a set of "conceptual variants" such that the "fittest" variants survive. Appeal to this analogy presumably explains scientific progress because we understand what is meant by "variation," "fitness," and "adaptation" in the organic realm.

Stephen Toulmin was one of the first to systematically apply the evolutionary analogy. He suggested in *Foresight and Understanding* (1961) that in science, as in the evolution of biological species, "change results from the selective perpetuation of variants."[2] Subsequently in *Human Understanding* (1972), Toulmin outlined a program for the reconstruction of scientific progress in categories borrowed from the theory of organic evolution.[3] He maintained that scientists often pose the following question:

> given that concepts c_1, c_2, c_3, ... are in some respect *inadequate* to the explanatory needs of the discipline, how can we modify / extend / restrict / qualify them, so as to give us the means of asking more fruitful empirical or mathematical questions in this domain?[4]

To ask such a question is to recognize that "environmental pressures" pose a threat to the continued existence of a hitherto dominant set of concepts.

Scientists formulate research strategies to answer the above question. The resulting conceptual development—reflected in a succession of theories—is a "natural selection" which operates on a set of "conceptual variants." It is the most "fit" among these variants that survive to become subject to subsequent tests of their adequacy. Over time, the history of a scientific discipline displays a pattern. The pattern is a tree of descent, the branches of which are conceptual systems rather than biological species.

A viable theory of progress must account for the persistence of a scientific discipline throughout changes in its content. Toulmin noted that

> each discipline, though mutable, normally displays a recognizable continuity, particularly in the selective factors that govern changes in its content. An evolutionary account of conceptual development accordingly has two separate features to explain: on the one hand, the coherence and continuity by which we identify disciplines as distinct and, on the other hand, the profound long-term changes by which they are transformed or superseded.[5]

Toulmin maintained that the identity-through-change of a scientific discipline is of the same kind as the identity-through-change of a biological species. He declared that

> in both the zoological and the intellectual case ... historical continuity and change can be seen as alternative results of variation and selective perpetuation, reflecting the comparative success with which different variants meet the current demands to which they are exposed.[6]

In support of this thesis, Toulmin drew the analogy shown in Table 19.1.[7]

Hull on selection processes

David Hull sought to show that organic evolution and conceptual change are specific instances of a "general theory of selection processes."[8] The general theory specifies a mechanism by which entities pass on structure over time. The mechanism involves an interrelation among "interactors" and "replicators." Interactors compete with one another in response to environmental pressures. The resultant competitive differential adaptation of interactors causes differential success rates among replicators.

Replicators are entities which give rise to copies of themselves. In the organic realm, "replication occurs primarily at the level of the genetic material."[9] Interactors are entities subject to competition within some specific environment. In the organic realm, "interactors" include not only living organisms, but also genes, chromosomes, cells and kinship groups.[10]

Table 19.1 Toulmin on conceptual change as an evolutionary process

	Organic evolution	Conceptual ehange
Entity subject to change	Species	Scientific discipline
Comprised of	Individual organisms	Concepts, methods and aims
Units of variation	Mutant forms within the population at t_1	Conceptual variants within the discipline at t_1
Units of effective modification	Those t_1 variants dominant within the population at t_2	Those t_1 variants dominant within the discipline at t_2
Mechanism of selection	Differential reproductive pressure	Need for deeper understanding

Within the history of science, replicators are concepts and beliefs, and interactors are individual scientists and individual research groups. "Concept-replicators" are individual entities, but they exist in various contexts of interrelatedness. Beliefs also are individual entities, and include commitments to methodological principles and standards of appraisal.

Hull maintained that the history of science, like the history of organic forms, is the result of selective pressure operating on a set of variants. The history of science is a history of "lineages," theories that change over time while retaining self-identity. Theories, like species, are entities determined by phylogeny, and not by possession of a common structure or set of properties. What counts is descent and not sameness of content.

Hull noted that, on a phylogenetic understanding of theory-life, "unappreciated precursors do not count."[11] Thus, Patrick Matthew's unnoticed formulation of the principle of natural selection (1831) is not part of the lineage of natural-selection theory. Hull concluded that a "phylogenetic" reconstruction of Darwinian evolutionary theory reveals a tree of descent whose branches include "Darwin's Darwinism, late nineteenth-century Darwinism, neo-Darwinian Darwinism, the new synthesis Darwinism, and so on."[12]

Hull's descriptive philosophy of science is robust. He maintained that we may increase our understanding of evaluative practice within science by reference to the general theory of selection processes. Indeed, he claimed that otherwise puzzling aspects of evaluative practice are readily understood when viewed from the standpoint of the general theory of selection processes.

One such puzzle is the success of science in policing the activities of its members.[13] The great majority of professional organizations are ineffective at imposing discipline upon their errant members. Science is a striking exception to the general rule. On Hull's model, an individual scientist is an interactor subject to the pressure of selection. His or her "fitness" is established by publishing results that subsequently are acknowledged and utilized by other scientists. It is not in the long-term self-interest of a scientist to falsify or fabricate data, or to distort the conclusions reached by other scientists. Consequently, scientists collectively are quick to condemn and punish those occasional miscreants who undermine the process by which lineages are created.

A second puzzle is the vehemence of priority disputes among scientists. If the goal of science is the formulation of increasingly more powerful theories, what does it matter who receives credit for them? On the general theory of selection processes it matters greatly. Theories are phylogenetic entities. An interactor's fitness is measured by his or her contribution to such lineages. Any challenge to an interactor's role in the creation of a lineage is a serious threat indeed. Given Hull's evolutionary model, it is not surprising that priority disputes often are heated controversies.

Is the evolutionary analogy appropriate?

An acceptable theory about the mechanism(s) responsible for scientific progress 1) describes recurrent patterns of progress in the history of science, and 2) explains why these patterns occur. The evolutionary analogy fails the first test.

It is true that there exist competing concepts and theories in science, and that some survive over time and some do not. On the evolutionary analogy, this is the result of responses to pressures that arise within and upon the discipline. Successful responses are those that increase fitness such that difficulties are overcome without compromising future fertility.

Unfortunately for the evolutionary-analogy program, there are important disanalogies between organic evolution and the growth of science. L.J. Cohen pointed out two such disanalogies.

In the first place, a biological species is a population of similar individuals, each of which "instantiates" the species.[14] But a scientific discipline is not a population of this kind. According to Toulmin, a discipline comprises concepts, methods and aims. Even if we restrict our attention to concepts, it is obvious that the concept of "mass" does not instantiate physical theories in the way in which Tabby instantiates the species *Felis domestica*.[15] To speak, as Toulmin does, of a "population" of concepts, is to ignore the interrelatedness of concepts. Cohen conceded that some concepts may have a few variant forms which are in competition with one another. But he insisted that

> the great bulk of the "concepts, methods and aims" within a rational discipline at any one time manage to be quite   different from one another and yet not be in competition, but in systematic association, with one another.[16]

Moreover, the identity-though-time of a biological species is markedly dissimilar to the identity-through-time of a scientific discipline. A biological species retains its identity provided that a set of individuals with similar characteristics at time t_2 resembles in relevant respects another set of individuals with similar characteristics at time t_1. But the identity-through-change of a scientific discipline cannot be of this type. In order to solve conceptual problems within a discipline we need a set of interrelated concepts, not a population of concepts with similar characteristics. Hence changes within a discipline involve a restructuring of an "evolving" concept's relations to other concepts and not just a replacement of concepts similar to c_1 by concepts similar to c_2.

In the second place, conceptual evolution, unlike organic evolution, is "coupled"—there is a connection between the factors responsible for the generation of variants and the factors responsible for the selection of variants. Conceptual variants are not "mutations" that arise in a spontaneous, random manner. Scientists invent conceptual variants to solve specific disciplinary problems that are responsible both for the generation and for the selection of concepts. By contrast, in organic evolution, mutation and selection are "uncoupled." As Cohen put it,

> the gamete has no clairvoyant capacity to mutate preferentially in directions preadapted to the novel ecological demands which the resulting adult organisms are going to encounter at some later time.[17]

Toulmin and Hull had taken note of this "coupled–uncoupled" contrast. But they maintained that evolutionary biology and conceptual change share enough points of similarity for the analogy to be useful. Cohen disagreed. He insisted that the lack of coupling between the generation of variants and the selection of variants is an *essential* feature of the Darwinian theory, and that it ought to be part of any account of conceptual change that claims to be "Darwinian."

In addition, there is a third disanalogy not emphasized by Cohen. Biological evolution within a phylogenetic tree is from trunk to branches. Such descent-with-modification inverts Whewell's "tributary–river" pattern of the historical development of science, within which progress is from "branches" to "trunk." Whewell's pattern reflects scientists' concern to achieve theoretical unification, and the history of several sciences displays this pattern. Whewell's interpretations of developments in astronomy and optics to 1830, for example, are sound. If the evolutionary analogy requires increasing speciation over time, then its application to the history of science entails some distortion of the historical record. This is not to deny that there is, in the history of science, "increasing speciation" *qua* proliferation of known lower-level regularities.

Campbell and Popper on blind variation and selective retention

Donald Campbell sought to overcome objections to the evolutionary analogy by shifting attention from "random mutations" to "blind trials." He acknowledged that scientific beliefs, unlike biological variants, are not produced randomly. The scientist has in mind a problem to be solved and a history of prior attempts to find a solution. However, if scientific progress results from the selective retention of blind trials, then the core of the evolutionary analogy may be retained. Every random trial is a blind trial, but a trial may be blind without being random.

In Campbell's usage, a "blind trial" is a trial that satisfies three conditions: 1) the trial is independent of environmental conditions; 2) a successful trial is no more likely to occur at one point in a series of trials than at any other point in the series; and 3) no trial in a sequence of trials is put forward as a "correction" of a prior trial. Campbell claimed that

> a blind-variation-and-selective-retention process is fundamental to all inductive achievements, to all genuine increases in knowledge, to all increases in fit of system to environment.[18]

Campbell thus maintained that the goal-directed decisions of scientists to entertain specific hypotheses are "blind" forays into the unknown, and that those hypotheses that prove "nonadaptive" under testing are eliminated.

Aharon Kantorovich agreed. He maintained that

> many creative leaps and breakthroughs in science result from serendipitous processes which represent the blind discoveries in science … And even those discoveries which do not seem to be serendipitous include subconscious stages of blind variation and selection.[19]

Kantorovich expanded the meaning of "serendipity" to include not only cases in which a scientist, seeking to explain A, instead succeeds in explaining B, but also cases in which a scientist, seeking to explain A, does succeed in explaining A, but also explains B.

Kantorovich held that "science can make significant progress only by serendipity."[20] On this view, the scientist who seeks to explain A, and succeeds only in explaining A, fails to contribute significantly to scientific progress. This is an extreme position, a position that would diminish the significance of a great number of explanatory successes in science, among them:

1 Galileo's arguments to show that sunspots are on the surface of the Sun,
2 Leverrier's explanation of the perturbation of the orbit of Uranus (due to Neptune), and
3 Darwin's explanation of the restricted habitat of marsupials (confined mostly to Australia).

Of course, these successful explanations invoke lawful generalizations that have other applications. But this fact is not sufficient to establish "serendipity" for these cases. There may be progressive instances in the history of science that fit the "selection from a set of blind variations" picture, but it is wrong to make serendipity a necessary condition of scientific progress.

Karl Popper endorsed Campbell's version of the evolutionary analogy. He held that the conjectures of scientists are analogous to variations and that refutations are analogous to the selective retention of variants. On this view, the "phylogeny" of science is the lineage of theories that survive the rigors of severe testing.

Popper's opposition to inductivism is well known. He repeatedly insisted that there can be no successful algorithm for theory-formation. Popper likened the position of the theorist to the

> situation of a blind man who searches in a dark room for a black hat which is—perhaps—not there.[21]

The theorist, like the blind man, proceeds by trial and error, coming to learn where the hat is not, without ever reaching a certainty immune from rejection from the force of further experience.

Popper is correct to emphasize the role of creative imagination in the formulation of scientific hypotheses. The problem-situation does not dictate a solution to the theorist. However, neither are hypotheses formulated independently of the problem-situation. Popper's "black-hat image" is quite misleading. Scientific conjectures are "blind" only in the sense that the outcome of subsequent testing is unknown. They are not "blind" in Campbell's sense of being "independent of the environmental conditions of the occasion of their occurrence."[22]

There is a further difficulty in Popper's particular use of an evolutionary analogy. Popper insisted that scientists ought to formulate bold, content-increasing conjectures that run a high risk of falsification. But the Darwinian picture of descent-with-modification is a gradual accretion of small adaptations. Popper claimed explanatory value for an "evolutionary analogy" that includes pious references to "Darwinian theory." But he also introduced "Lamarckian" emphases and "saltation effects" seemingly inconsistent with Darwin's emphasis on accretion. Of course, there have been disputes over the specific content of Darwinian theory, in particular on Darwin's alleged "Lamarckian backsliding." Nevertheless Michael Ruse has concluded that

> Popper has been no more successful than others in making traditional evolutionary epistemology plausible. The growth of science is not genuinely Darwinian.[23]

In order that Campbell's "selective-retention-of-blind-variants" theory of scientific progress achieve success, two conditions must be fulfilled. The first condition is that the evolutionary analogy—amended to require selective retention of "blind" variants—must fit important episodes from the history of science. The second condition is that the "fit" has explanatory force.

Kepler's work on the orbit of Mars is a promising candidate for Campbellian reconstruction. Kepler hypothesized a number of ovoid orbits for Mars ("blind trials") before hitting upon an ellipse. The "blind trials" picture also may be superimposed upon various programs to "save the appearances." The list of such programs includes Babylonian astronomy (the use of linear zigzag functions to calculate the day on which the next new moon appears), Ptolemy's mathematical models for calculating the zodiacal positions of the planets, the nineteenth-century algebraic chemistries of Benjamin Brodie and Josiah Cooke, and contemporary econometric modeling of macroeconomic forces.

The modified evolutionary analogy is less promising as an account of theories about underlying mechanisms. It remains to be shown that Descartes' vortex theory, the kinetic molecular theory of gases, molecular-orbital theory and plate tectonics theory are results of the selective retention of blind trials.

Ron Amundson has insisted that the adequacy of "selection explanations" depends on the degree to which certain "central conditions" are met. These central conditions place restrictions on variation and sorting. Variations must be spontaneous, abundant and heritable modifications that are "nondirected with respect to the environmental needs of the organism."[24] And, given a pool of such variants, there must be a

> preferential persistence of those variations which happen to be suited to the environmental needs of the organism or species—and (most importantly) this sorting mechanism is itself nonpurposive.[25]

Amundson maintained that the above conditions are necessary conditions of explanatory success for analogical applications of the theory of natural selection. He noted that challenges to proposed selection explanations often take the form of a denial that the requisite central conditions are met.

Campbell's "blind-variation-and-selective-retention" theory of scientific change would appear to be subject to two principal challenges. In the first place, the generation of variant hypotheses is neither random nor blind. Rather, hypotheses are put forward in response to recognized inadequacies within the scientific environment. In the second place, the sorting process that results in a decision to reject (or accept) a high-level hypothesis involves judgments about background knowledge, auxiliary hypotheses, experimental procedures, and sometimes even metaphysical principles. Amundson declared that

> the process of rejecting a "falsified" hypothesis is often more like the literary critic's negative assessment of a poem than like the cold wind's freezing of the baldest polar bear.[26]

Campbell sought to blunt this type of criticism by acknowledging the existence of "shortcuts" for the blind-variations-and-selection process. The formulation of hypotheses designed to address perceived deficiencies within a scientific domain may serve as a shortcut for the method of blind trials. Campbell insisted that such shortcuts themselves are inductive achievements. He declared that we have acquired a

> wisdom about the environment achieved originally by blind variation and selective retention.[27]

Purposefully generated (nonblind) hypotheses may be part of a "phylogenetic lineage" the earlier members of which *were* generated by the "blind-variation-and-selective-retention" process.

Does the evolutionary analogy have explanatory value?

Campbell's introduction of "shortcuts" raises a question about the explanatory force of his version of the evolutionary analogy. Does it have explanatory force to argue that scientists endorse goal-directed hypotheses today because at some point in the past our ancestors engaged in blind trials upon which selection operated? And, in general, do any interpretations that invoke the principle of natural selection qualify as genuine explanations?

No doubt the "survival of the fittest" picture can be abused. If a biologist were to identify "those individuals most fit to survive at time t" and "those individuals that in fact have survived at time $t + \Delta t$" then the "evolutionary account" is a mere redescription of what happens. Mere redescription is not normally accorded explanatory value.

To explain change as "survival of the fittest" the scientist needs a theory that can be applied at time t to yield an estimate about fitness *at that time*. The biologist does have access to such theories. Estimates of relative fitness of variants under specified environmental conditions often can be given at that time. These estimates are based on knowledge about anatomy, physiology, social structure, the pressures of predation, ecological changes, etc. For example, given a decrease in the temperature of an environment, a variant with a denser coat of fur is more fit that its fellows. And given a flooding of former land areas amphibians are more fit than land mammals. "Fitness," in such contexts, is a measure of the propensity of individuals to survive and reproduce. On a propensity interpretation of "fitness," judgments about fitness do have explanatory value. Such judgments are not reducible to an identification of those that are fit with those that in fact have survived subsequently.

If the evolutionary analogy is to provide an explanation of scientific progress, the methodologist needs to show that the comparative fitness of theories at time t can be assessed at that time. Otherwise the "survival of the fittest theories" is merely the sequence of theories that actually survived. What is required are standards of evidential support, problem-solving effectiveness, inclusiveness, completeness, and the like. Such standards have been proposed. No doubt they are controversial. But, given such standards, there is no barrier to genuinely explanatory applications of an evolutionary analogy. There remain, however, the above-mentioned important disanalogies between biological evolution and theory-choice.

Ruse on the evolutionary origins of evaluative standards

Michael Ruse, who has been critical of the evolutionary-analogy view of scientific progress, has proposed instead an "evolutionary-origins" view. The "evolutionary-origins" view attributes the growth of science to the application of epigenetic rules that have proved adaptive within the course of evolutionary history. On this view, science develops as it does because certain methodological rules and evaluative principles have become encoded in our genes. Acting on these rules and principles presumably proved adaptive for our proto-human ancestors.

Ruse called attention to three "genetically hard-wired" rules that have evolved in *Homo sapiens*: the partitioning of the visible spectrum into discrete colors, the "deep-structure" of language (Chomsky), and the prohibition of incest. These rules presumably have become genetically encoded because they confer adaptive advantage in the struggle for existence.

Pattern recognition and successful prediction not only are basic survival strategies for *Homo sapiens*, but also are important foundations of the edifice of science. Ruse suggested that progress in science depends on these and other epigenetic rules:

1 formulate only internally consistent theories,
2 utilize the resources of mathematics in the construction of theories,
3 seek "severe tests" of theories (Popper), and
4 accept theories that prove "consilient" (Whewell).[28]

In support of the epigenetic status of consilience, Ruse contrasted the responses of two hominids to evidence of the presence of tigers. Hominid #1 takes the existence of feathers, blood, paw marks in the mud, and growls from the bushes to establish a consilience of inductions, and flees. Hominid #2 views the same evidence but fails to see the importance of consilience. Ruse then asked "which one of these was more likely to be your ancestor?"[29]

Because it was adaptive for our ancestors to act on judgments of consilience, today consilience is a criterion of acceptability for scientific theories. Consilience is an epigenetic rule that has become embedded in scientific evaluative practice as a result of responses to natural selective pressures in the course of the evolutionary history of *Homo sapiens*. The evolutionary-origins view thus provides a partial explanation of scientific progress.

Perhaps there are additional procedural directives, measures of evidential support, or standards of theory-comparison that have become "hard-wired" as a result of evolutionary development. A survey of scientific practice might reveal such principles.

Larry Laudan and associates have conducted such a survey, although not from the perspective of an evolutionary-origins theory of scientific evaluative practice.[30] The principal aim of the group was to test theories of scientific progress—Kuhn, Lakatos, Laudan, *et al.*—against the "empirical record."

The empirical record comprises a set of case studies of episodes from the history of science.[31] The Laudan Group sought to test, not entire theories of scientific change, but rather specific empirical claims about innovation, theory-choice and responses to perceived anomalies.

The case-studies are alleged to provide support for the following claims about scientific evaluative practice:

1   guiding assumptions [which include both substantive assumptions about the world and guidelines for theory construction and theory modification] are accepted … because they have exhibited an ability to generate theories which possess considerable problem-solving success,

2   scientists award high marks to theories that can turn apparent counter-examples into confirming instances,

3   theories are expected to solve some of the problems unsolved by their rivals and predecessors, and

4   a scientific revolution does not consist in the wholesale replacement of one set of guiding assumptions by a wholly different set. Rather scientists work their way gradually from one framework to the other so that guiding assumptions change neither rapidly nor in holistic bundles.[32]

These are not the only claims about methodological practice to receive support from the case studies. But they are representative of the complete set. The methodological directives—"identify and solve problems," "seek to convert apparent counter-examples into confirming instances," "apply theories to problems unsolved by other theories"—may well be epigenetic rules. But these rules are not much more specific than the directives about pattern recognition and prediction. The methodologist is directed to identify and solve problems, a process that involves theory-comparison and a distinction between instances that provide evidential support and instances that do not.

It is the claim of the Laudan Group that these methodological rules governing problem-solving fit scientific evaluative practice. This claim is grist for the mill of the evolutionary-origins program only if it can be established that these rules have become embedded in scientific evaluative practice as a result of evolutionary adaptation. If this can be done, then the evolutionary-origins theorist may claim to have made a modest contribution to an explanation of scientific progress.

Ruse compared epigenetic rules to Hume's "dispositions." Hume had observed that we organize our lives by reading "necessary connections " into nature. We act on the expectation that correlations experienced in the past will continue to hold in the future. Ruse accepted Hume's account of the dispositions involved in our commerce with the world and appended to the Humean account a theory about the origin of these dispositions.

Hume denied that a rational justification can be provided for our expectations of regularity. Past uniformity does not entail the future continuation of that uniformity. Ruse accepted this Humean claim as well. He suggested that the only "justification" for implementing epigenetic rules is that these rules did arise during the course of human evolution. Ruse acknowledged that to provide a theory about the origin of a rule is to fall short of providing a justification for continuing to implement the rule.

Ruse developed the evolutionary-origins view as a descriptive theory of scientific progress. He did not issue normative-prescriptive recommendations about the conduct of scientific inquiry. Other evolutionary naturalists have drawn normative conclusions about how science ought be practiced. Normative-prescriptive content may be added to the evolutionary-origins view by endorsing the move from

1 the application of methodological rule *R* and evaluative standard *S* were adaptive responses to former ecological pressures *P*.
2 *R* and *S* *ought to be* applied by scientists today.

The normative version of the evolutionary-origins view is subject to an important limitation however. In biological evolution, "long-run fitness" is a balance between successful adaptation to present environmental conditions and the retention of the capacity to respond creatively to future changes in these conditions. In a particular case, successful adaptation may be achieved at the expense of a loss of adaptability. That this has occurred becomes evident only with the passage of time.

Given a specific evaluative situation, the normative evolutionary naturalist stipulates that a particular decision is correct only if it promotes fitness in the long run. But how can one know at the time a decision is made that it will do so? One may appeal to the fact that similar decisions in the past proved to have survival value. However, it is always possible that the ecologically unique present situation requires a different decision.

The most adequate appraisals are those rendered long after the fact. Survival is the best indicator of long-run fitness. It is survival that establishes a continuing retention of adaptive capacity in the face of changing conditions. The major conceptual innovations of Newton and Einstein pass this test. These innovations participate in lineages to which subsequent scientists have contributed. Judgments about contemporary changes are much less secure.

This is not an objection to evolutionary naturalism as a *descriptive* theory of scientific progress. Scientific theories are subject to modification and replacement, and so too are the judgments issued by the philosopher of science. What initially appeared to be a "fit" response may turn out subsequently not to be such. It is no more realistic to expect certainty in philosophy of science than it is to expect certainty in science.

PART III: DESCRIPTIVE THEORIES
OF SCIENTIFIC PROGRESS

Suggestions for further reading

Theorists of scientific progress

CHARLES SANDERS PEIRCE

Peirce, Charles S. (1935) *Collected Papers, Vol. VI, Scientific Metaphysics* (C. Hartshorne and P. Weiss, eds). Cambridge, MA: Harvard University Press.
—— (1958) *Collected Papers,Vols. VII and VIII, Science and Philosophy* (A. Burks, ed.). Cambridge, MA: Harvard University Press.
—— (1958) *Values in a Universe of Chance* (P.P. Wiener, ed.). New York: Doubleday Anchor. Includes the influential essays "The Fixation of Belief" and "How to Make Our Ideas Clear."

Foss, Jeff (1984) "Reflections on Peirce's Concepts of Testability and the Economy of Research," *PSA 1984, Vol. 1*, 28–39. East Lansing: Philosophy of Science Association.
Laudan, Larry (1973) "Peirce and the Trivialization of the Self-Correcting Thesis" in R.N. Giere and R.S. Westfall (eds) *Foundations of Scientific Method: The Nineteenth Century*, 275–306. Bloomington: Indiana University Press.
Murphey, Murray G. (1993) *The Development of Peirce's Philosophy*. Indianapolis: Hackett.
Rescher, Nicholas (1978) *Pierce's Philosophy of Science*. Notre Dame: Notre Dame Press.
—— (1977) *Methodological Pragmatism*. Oxford: Oxford University Press.

PIERRE DUHEM

Duhem, Pierre (1914 [1962]) *The Aim and Structure of Physical Theory,* 2nd edn (P.P. Wiener, ed.). New York: Atheneum.
—— (1969) *To Save the Phenomena* (E. Doland and C. Maschler, trans.). Chicago: University of Chicago Press.
—— (1996) *Essays in the History and Philosophy of Science* (R. Ariew and P. Barker, eds). Indianapolis: Hackett.

Ariew, R. and Barker, P. (eds) (1990) "Pierre Duhem: Historian and Philosopher of Science", *Synthese* 83: 179–453.
Harding, Sandra (ed.) (1976) *Can Theories Be Refuted? Essays on the Duhem–Quine Thesis*. Dordrecht: Reidel. Essays by Grünbaum, Hesse, and Laudan are particularly helpful.
Krips, Henry (1982) "Epistemological Holism: Duhem or Quine?", *Stud. Hist. Phil. Sci.* 13: 251–64.
McMullin, Ernan (1997) "Review of Duhem, *Essays in the History and Philosophy and Science*", *Brit. J. Phil. Sci.* 48: 606–9.
Quinn, Philip L. (1974) "What Duhem Really Meant" in R.S. Cohen and M. Wartofsky (eds) *Boston Studies in the Philosophy of Science, Vol. XIV*, 33–56. Dordrecht: Reidel.

NANCY CARTWRIGHT

Cartwright, Nancy (1983) *How the Laws of Physics Lie*. Oxford: Oxford University Press.
—— (1989) *Nature's Capacities and Their Measurement*. Oxford: Clarendon Press.
—— (1999) *The Dappled World: A Study of the Boundaries of Science*. Cambridge: Cambridge University Press.

Giere, Ronald N. (2000) "Review of Cartwright, *The Dappled World*," *Phil. Sci.* 67: 527–30.
Kline, A. David and Matheson, Carl A. (1986) "How the Laws of Physics Don't Even Fib," *PSA 1986, Vol. 1*, 33–46. East Lansing: Philosophy of Science Association.

NICHOLAS RESCHER

Resner, Nicholas (1977) *Methodological Pragmatism*. Oxford: Oxford University Press.
—— (1978) *Peirce's Philosophy of Science*. Notre Dame: Notre Dame Press.
—— (1978) *Scientific Progress*. Pittsburgh: University of Pittsburgh Press.
—— (1990) *A Useful Inheritance* (Savage, MD: Rowman & Littlefield.

Altschuler, Bruce (1979) "Review of *Methodological Pragmatism*", *Phil. Rev.* 88: 490–6.
Haack, Robin (1979) "Review of *Methodological Pragmatism*", *Mind* 88: 292–6.

PHILIP KITCHER

Kitcher, Philip (1989) "Explanatory Unification and the Causal Structure of the World" in P. Kitcher and W. Salmon (eds) *Scientific Explanation*, 410–515. Minneapolis: University of Minnesota Press.
—— (1992) "The Naturalists Return," *Phil. Rev.* 101: 53–114.
—— (1993)*The Advancement of Science*. Oxford: Oxford University Press.

Miller, Richard W. (1995) "The Advancement of Realism", *Phil. Phenom. Res., LV*: 637–45.
Shanahan, Timothy (1997) "Kitcher's Compromise: A Critical Examination of the Compromise Model of Scientific Closure, and its Implications for the Relationship Between History and Philosophy of Science", *Stud. Hist. Phil. Sci.* 28: 319–38.
Shapere, Dudley (1995) "Kitcher on Advancing Science", *Phil. Phenom. Res., LV*: 647–51.

DAVID HULL

Hull, David (1982) "The Naked Meme" in H.C. Plotkin (ed.) *Learning, Development and Culture*, 273–327. New York: Wiley.
—— (1988) *Science as a Process*. Chicago: University of Chicago Press.
—— (1989) *The Metaphysics of Evolution*. Albany; SUNY Press.
—— (1990) "Conceptual Selection," *Phil. Stud.* 60: 77–87.

Cain, Joseph Allen and Darden, Lindley (1988) "Hull and Selection", *Biol. & Phil.* 3:165–71.

Dupre, John (1990) "Scientific Pluralism and the Plurality of the Sciences; Comments on David Hull's *Science as a Process*", *Phil. Stud.* 60: 61–76.

Oldroyd, David (1990) "David Hull's Evolutionary Model for the Progress and Process of Science", *Biol. & Phil.* 5: 473–87.

Ruse, Michael (1989) "David Hull Through Two Decades" in M. Ruse (ed.) *What the Philosophy of Biology Is.* 1–15. Dordrecht: Reidel, 1989.

Sterelny, Kim (1994) "Science and Selection", *Biol. & Phil.* 9: 45–62.

DONALD T. CAMPBELL

Campbell, Donald T. (1987) "Blind Variation and Selective Retention in Creative Thought as in Other Knowledge Processes" in G. Radnitsky and W. W. Bartley III (eds) *Evolutionary Epistemology, Rationality, and the Sociology of Knowledge*, 91–114. La Salle: Open Court.

—— (1987) "Evolutionary Epistemology" in G. Radnitsky and W.W. Bartley III (eds) *Evolutionary Epistemology, Rationality, and the Sociology of Knowledge*, 47–89. La Salle: Open Court.

—— (1988) "A General 'Selection Theory' as Implemented in Biological Evolution and in Social Belief-Transmission-with-Modification in Sciences", *Biol. & Phil.* 3: 171–7.

Amundson, Ron (1989) "The Trials and Tribulations of Selectionist Explanations" in K. Hahlweg and C.A. Hooker (eds) *Issues in Evolutionary Epistemology*, 413–32. Albany: SUNY Press.

Hahlweg, Kai and Hooker, C.A. (1989) "Evolutionary Epistemology and the Philosophy of Science," in K. Hahlweg and C.A. Hooker (eds) *Issues in Evolutionary Epistemology*, 23–44. Albany: SUNY Press. A discussion of the views of Toulmin, Popper and Campbell, among others.

Popper, Karl, R. (1987) "Campbell on the Evolutionary Theory of Knowledge" in G. Radnitsky and W.W. Bartley III (eds) *Evolutionary Epistemology, Rationality, and the Sociology of Knowledge*, 115–20. La Salle: Open Court.

MICHAEL RUSE

Ruse, Michael (1973) *The Philosophy of Biology*. London: Hutchinson.

—— (1986) *Taking Darwin Seriously*. Oxford: Blackwell.

—— (1995) *Evolutionary Naturalism*. London: Routledge.

Bradie, Michael (1990) "Should Epistemologists Take Darwin Seriously?" in N. Rescher (ed.) *Evolution, Cognition and Realism*, 33–8. Lanham, MD: University Press of America.

O'Hear, Anthony (1997) *Beyond Evolution*. Oxford: Clarendon Press.

Episodes from the history of science

CALORIC THEORY

Brush, Stephen G. (1976) *The Kind of Motion We Call Heat,* Vol. 2, Chapter 9. Amsterdam: North-Holland.

Carrier, Martin (1991) "What Is Wrong with the Miracle Argument", *Stud. Hist. Phil. Sci.* 22: 23–36 .

Roller, Duane (1950) *The Early Development of the Concepts of Temperature and Heat: The Rise and Fall of the Caloric Theory. Harvard Case Studies in Experimental Science*, Vol. 3. Cambridge, MA: Harvard University Press.

DARWIN'S THEORY OF NATURAL SELECTION

Darwin, Charles (1859 [1968]) *The Origin of Species*, 1st edn. Harmondsworth: Penguin.

Browne, Janet (1995) *Charles Darwin, Voyaging: A Biography*. Princeton: Princeton University Press.

Ghiselin, Michael T. (1969) *The Triumph of the Darwinian Method*. Berkeley: University of California Press.

Hull, David L. (ed.) (1973) *Darwin and His Critics*. Chicago: University of Chicago Press. Includes responses to Darwin's work by Hooker, Sedgwick, Owen, Jenkin, von Baer, Agassiz, and others.

Kohn, David (ed.) (1985) *The Darwinian Heritage*. Princeton: Princeton University Press. An extensive collection of essays on Darwin and the development of Darwinian theories. Contains a useful bibliography.

Ruse, Michael (1979) *The Darwinian Revolution*. Chicago: University of Chicago Press.

Weiner, Jonathan (1994) *The Beak of the Finch*. New York: Vintage. A survey of twentieth-century studies of selective pressures and the course of evolution of Galapagos' finches.

CONCLUSION

An examination of historical episodes generally regarded to be progressive reveals that some fit an incorporation model and some fit an overthrow model. Kuhn was correct to identify two types of progress within the history of science. There are periods of "normal science" within which progress is achieved by accretion and incorporation, and there are periods of "revolutionary science" within which progress is achieved by the replacement of one "disciplinary matrix" by another. Kuhn was correct, as well, to insist that there is no algorithm that determines the conditions under which theory-replacement is progressive.

Kuhn was wrong, however, about certain of the features of the two patterns of progress. It is not the case that revolutionary overthrow always is an holistic, all-at-once replacement of one taxonomy by another. It is false of the history of science that a high-level theory is rejected only if a viable competing theory is available. And it is not the case that high-level theory-replacement invariably is preceded by an accumulation of anomalies. This is not to deny that some cases of theory-replacement do involve a holistic taxonomic change that resolves a prior accumulation of anomalies.

There have been numerous attempts to establish necessary or sufficient conditions of "progressive incorporation" or "progressive overthrow." If the preceding analysis is correct, then these efforts have been largely unsuccessful. Nearly every proposed condition is open to countercases such that either we must admit that the condition is neither necessary nor sufficient, or we must revise significantly our understanding of the history of science. This is true of consilience, undesigned scope, incorporation-with-corroborated-excess-content, asymptotic agreement of calculations, the testimony of "crucial experiments," and the resolution of anomalies.

One exception is the convergence of diverse experimental determinations upon a single value. Perrin and Planck advanced strong arguments for such convergence as a sufficient condition of progressive theory-replacement. The convergence of various determinations of the value of Avogadro's number on 6.02×10^{23} molecules/ gram molecular weight warrants as progressive the transition from theories of the macroscopic domain to the atomic-molecular theory of its microstructure. And the convergence of various determinations of the value of Planck's constant on 6.6×10^{-27} erg-sec. warrants the transition from classical electromagnetic theory to the theory of the quantization of energy. I know of no plausible countercase in which convergence of this kind is achieved in the case of a transition judged not to be progressive on other grounds.

Unfortunately, opportunities to apply the convergence condition are rare within the history of science. The overwhelming majority of questions about scientific progress must be resolved without appeal to a convergence of the results of diverse experimental determinations. Moreover, what is warranted by the convergence criterion is transitions between one *type* of theory to a second. For example, the criterion warrants a transition from theories about relations among the thermodynamic properties of macroscopic systems to theories about an underlying microstructure of the systems. The criterion also warrants a transition from theories in which electromagnetic energy is distributed continuously to theories in which energy is quantized. This, of course, falls short of providing a warrant for the truth of specific theories about molecular interactions or energy quantization.

Scientists do base judgments about scientific progress on such criteria as consilience, asymptotic agreement of calculations, resolution of anomalies, etc., even though the satisfaction of no one of them is either necessary or sufficient for scientific progress. It always is relevant to ask questions that invoke the above criteria, for instance:

1 Has consilience been achieved within a domain?
2 Are the anomalies that beset T_1 overcome by T_2?
3 Is the replacement of T_1 by T_2 accompanied by a display of undesigned scope?
4 Do calculations derived from T_2 agree asymptotically with those of its (partially) successful predecessor T_1?

Answers to the above questions are important to an assessment of progress in science, even though no affirmative answer determines that a sequence of theories is progressive.

After decisions are reached about which historical episodes are progressive, observers of science then may ask:

1 what is the nature of the "goodness" that is increased when progress is achieved, and
2 what is the underlying mechanism responsible for this progress?

One influential answer to question 1 is to take progress to be successive approximation to truth. It is tempting to seek to extend the truth of confirmed predictions (results that agree with predictions within a specified experimental error) to the approximate truth of the theories involved in the predictions. It might seem that if a sequence of theories displays increasingly more accurate predictions, then that sequence converges upon truth.

Unfortunately, predictive success does not establish the truth of theories. Sequences of theories whose central terms fail to refer have achieved increasingly more accurate predictions. Moreover, we know that many important theories can be true only of their model-objects—"point-masses," "massless charges," *et al.*—objects that cannot be found in the physical world.

A second influential answer to question 1 is to equate progress and increasing problem-solving effectiveness. At the level of the practical applications of scientific knowledge it is incontrovertible that the science of the year 2000 has solved problems not solved by the science of the year 1900. And there are no practical applications of scientific knowledge of year 1900 that cannot be duplicated in year 2000. The growth of science displays an increase in the number and range of successful practical applications. Science surely is progressive in this sense of "problem-solving."

Whether or not there is theoretical progress that parallels this increasing success in practical applications remains to be shown. Laudan's problem-solving model provides an inclusive interpretation of scientific progress. But it is only the long-term records of research traditions that are properly spoken of as "progressive" or "nonprogressive." The model lacks the resources to verify that individual theory T_2 (which solves problems $p_1, p_2,$ and p_3) is more progressive than theory T_1 (which solves problems $p_1, p_2,$ and p_4). There is no standard within the problem-solving model for gauging the relative importance of problems. Nor is there a standard for individuating problems. Hence one cannot base judgments of relative problem-solving effectiveness on the number of problems solved. The problem-solving model does not warrant judgments that establish instant rationality, but it does present a comprehensive descriptive theory of scientific progress applicable to the history of science.

Is there a satisfactory theory about a mechanism responsible for scientific progress? Some observers of science have recommended an evolutionary analogy, which attributes scientific progress to a "Darwinian selective pressure" operating on a pool of variant conceptual options. Just as Adam Smith's "invisible hand" insures that economic individuals pursuing self-interest produce a communal economic good, so also individual scientists, seeking to participate in the lineages of successful theories, contribute to scientific progress.

An evolutionary analogy that is based on the theory of natural selection does not fit the enterprise of science. Within science, the production of variants and the selection of variants are not uncoupled processes (contrary to the case of natural selection). What remains of the analogy is merely that scientists, like individual biological entities, respond to pressures (seek to solve problems) such that the most "fit" problem-solutions survive. In this weak form, the "Evolutionary Analogy" is a descriptive theory of scientific progress rather than a theory about a causal mechanism responsible for progress. It adds nothing to the problem-solving model.

The evolutionary-origins theory is a second version of an "evolutionary" explanation of scientific progress. On the evolutionary-origins theory, evaluative standards whose applications lead to progress are held to have become genetically encoded in present-day scientists as a result of past responses to environmental pressures that proved adaptive for our remote ancestors.

The evolutionary-origins theory makes attributions of causal relatedness across millions of years. It is open to the objection that to trace a sequence of stages (even if it could be done in detail) is not the same thing as to establish that an earlier stage is the cause of a later stage. More specifically, it needs to be shown how changes in evaluative practice from Aristotle to the present time are effects of temporally-remote responses to threats to survival and reproductive success. The prospects for success in such an undertaking are not high.

NOTES

INTRODUCTION

1 See, for instance, Niiniluoto (1980) 426–7.
2 Kuhn (1957), 264–5.

1 WHEWELL'S "TRIBUTARY–RIVER" IMAGE OF
SCIENTIFIC PROGRESS

1 Whewell (1857) Part I, Book V, 272; 338.
2 Ibid. Part I, Introduction, 3.
3 Whewell, (1847) Part II, Book XI, 3.
4 Ibid. Part II, Book XI, 18–9.
5 Ibid. Part I, Book III, 177–85.
6 Ibid. Part I, Book III, 248.
7 Whewell (1857) Part I, Book V, 271–336; Part II, Book VII, 99–221; Whewell (1847) Part II, Book XI, 118.
8 Priestley (1767) Vol. II, 1–2.
9 Whewell (1857) Part I, Book V, 285.
10 Whewell used the term "induction" for both the process of generalization and the results of generalization.
11 Whewell (1847) Part II, Book XI, 85.
12 Simplicity is difficult to assess, even in the case of mathematical relations. We may judge "$y = x$" to be simpler than "$y = x^2$" or "$y = xz$", but be uncertain about the relative simplicity of "$y = x^2$" and "$y = xz$". Is it the order of the equation or the number of variables that is more important?
13 Whewell (1847) Part II, Book XI, 65.
14 Herschel (1830) 33–4; 171–2.
15 Ibid. 33–4.
16 Ibid. 171–2; Whewell (1857) 250–1.
17 A persuasive example from twentieth-century science is Einstein's application of Planck's hypothesis of energy quantization, initially formulated to account for black-body radiation, to the photoelectric effect.
18 Whewell (1847) Part II, Book XI, 67–8.

2: BREWSTER ON HOW NOT TO DO HISTORY OF SCIENCE

1 Brewster (1837) 119.
2 Ibid. 122.
3 Ibid. 121.
4 Ibid. 144.

3: MILL'S OBJECTIONS TO WHEWELL'S HISTORICISM

1 Mansel (1851) 257.
2 Mill (1872) Book IV, Ch. II, § 4; 429–30.
3 Ibid. Book IV, Ch. II, § 5; 431.
4 Ibid. Book III, Ch. XIV, § 6; 330.
5 This is Hume's "official position." Hume also defended a subjunctive conditional view of causal relatedness— *c* and *e* are causally related provided that if *c* had not occurred, *e* would not have occurred either. (Hume 1740, 79).
6 Mill (1872) Book III, Ch. V, § 6; 221.
7 Ibid. Book III, Ch. XXII, § 3; 380.
8 The limitations of Mill's inductive methods as instruments for discovering causal connections were set forth by W.S. Jevons (1890) and John Venn (1907), among others.
9 Mill (1872) Book III, Ch. IX, § 5; 280.
10 Ibid. Book III, Ch. IX, § 6; 283.
11 Ibid. Book III, Ch. XI, § 3; 304.
12 Ibid. Book III, Ch. II, § 4; 194.
13 Venn (1907) 354.
14 Mill (1872) Book III, Ch. IX, § 6 ; 283.
15 Ibid. Book III, Ch. IX, § 6; 284.
16 Ibid. Book III, Ch. VIII, § 3; 258.
17 Ibid. Book III, Ch. XIV, § 4; 324.
18 Ibid. Book III, Ch. XXI, § 3; 373.
19 Ibid. Book III, Ch. XXI, § 3; 374.
20 Hume (1740) 37.

4: PROGRESS THROUGH REDUCTION

1 What counts as "logical empiricism" depends on which philosophers and scientists are selected as its representatives, and, in some cases, on the particular stage of the career of the representative. I believe that the above characterization would have been accepted by Carnap, Frank, Hempel and Nagel in the early post-World War II period. Recent interpretations of the historical development of logical empiricism include Giere and Richardson (1996), Coffa (1991) and Friedman (1991).
2 Nagel (1961) 351–8.
3 $(P + a/V^2)(V - b) = kT$, where a is a measure of intermolecular attractive force, and b is a correction term to account for the finite volume of the molecules.
4 Nagel (1961) 336–7.
5 Feyerabend (1962) 46–8.
6 Feyerabend (1965a) 267–71; (1970a) 220–1; (1970b) 84.
7 Ibid. 271–2.
8 Feyerabend (1962) 77.
9 Ibid. 78.
10 Spector (1978) 40–1.

11 Putnam (1965) 206–7.
12 Feyerabend (1965b) 229–30.
13 $T = 2\pi\sqrt{l/g}$, where T is the period and l is the length of the pendulum.
14 $(T_1 / T_2) = (d_1 / d_2)^{3/2}$, where T is the period and d is the mean distance of a planet from the Sun.
15 Nagel (1974) 101.
16 Feyerabend (1962) 59.
17 Feyerabend (1965c) 180.
18 Nagel (1974) 110.
19 Shapere (1966) 55–6.
20 Achinstein (1964) 504–5.
21 Ibid. 499.
22 Feyerabend (1965a) 267.
23 Ibid. 267.
24 Ibid. 268–9.
25 Shapere (1966) 64.
26 Feyerabend (1965c) 216–7.
27 Feyerabend (1970b) 91.
28 Feyerabend (1965c) 214.
29 Ibid. 198.
30 Ibid. 212.
31 Shapere (1966) 60.
32 Ibid. 60.
33 Feyerabend (1970b) 91.
34 Nickles (1975), 181–201.

5 LAKATOS' VERSION OF THE "PROGRESS IS INCORPORATION" THESIS

1 Lakatos (1971).
2 Ibid. 100–1.
3 Lakatos (1970) 116–8.
4 Applications of Arrhenius' theory revealed that colligative-property measurements agreed with conductance measurements in the case of weak electrolytes, but not in the case of "strong" (nearly completely dissociated) electrolytes.
5 Debye and Hückel hypothesized that the motions of ions in solutions of strong electrolytes subject to an applied electromotive force are retarded by two effects: 1) the distortion of the oppositely-charged ionic atmosphere, and 2) an electrophoretic effect that arises when an ion moves against the direction of flow of an oppositely moving medium.
   Onsager added Brownian-motion effects to the ionic-atmosphere distortion and electrophoretic effects to account for conductance measurements in dilute solutions of strong electrolytes.
6 Galileo (1632 [1962]) 21.
7 See Shea (1972) 85–7.
8 Lakatos (1970) 138–40.
9 Dumas (1857) 709.
10 Einstein's addition of a "$1/r^4$" term to the law of gravitational attraction was required by the axioms of general relativity theory. It was not an *ad hoc* adjustment made solely to remove the anomaly of Mercury's motion. In the 1830s some scientists also had suggested the addition of a "$1/r^4$" term to the Newtonian law. By so doing, they sought to account for the anomalous motion of the newly discovered planet Uranus. This nineteenth-century tinkering with the law of gravitational attraction was an *ad hoc* adjustment held to be

applicable only to the region of the Solar System beyond the orbit of Saturn. (See Grosser, 1962, 46–9.)

11 Hoyle (1975) 497.
12 Lakatos (1971) 104–5.
13 Feyerabend (1970a) 219–23.
14 LaPlace subsequently accounted for unidirectional motions by postulating that the Solar System was formed by condensation from a rotating nebula of gas. LaPlace's hypothesis was not an integral part of the original Newtonian research program.
15 Lakatos (1971) 109.
16 Ibid, 105.
17 Ibid. 108–22.
18 Among these case studies are: Zahar (1973), Fricke (1976), Gay (1976), Musgrave, (1976a), and Elkana (1973).
19 Clark (1976).
20 Musgrave (1976b).
21 Ibid. 466.
22 Frankel (1979) 57.
23 Ibid. 58.
24 Ibid. 30–9.
25 Ibid. 66.
26 Musgrave (1976b).

6 PROGRESS AND THE ASYMPTOTIC AGREEMENT OF CALCULATIONS

1 Lakatos (1970) 116.
2 Hutten (1956) 165–8; Agassi (1963) 26.
3 See, for instance, Van Name (1952) 45–9.
4 See, for instance, Jammer (1966) 17.
5 Ibid. 23.

7 I.B. COHEN ON THE IDENTIFICATION OF SCIENTIFIC REVOLUTIONS

1 I.B. Cohen (1985) 40.
2 Ibid. 41–7.
3 Kuhn (1957); I.B. Cohen (1985) 105–25.
4 Weismann (1904), vol. 1, Chs. II, III; Mayr (1982) 507–8.
5 Sedgwick (1973) 159–66; Owen (1973) 175–213.
6 Grant (1971) 83–90; Rosen (1959) 4–33.
7 Kuhn (1957) 5–7.
8 de Solla Price (1959) 197–218.
9 Lakatos and Zahar (1975) 354–83.
10 Gough (1988) 15–33.
11 Siegfried (1988) 34–50.
12 I.B. Cohen (1985) 236.
13 Hall (1962).
14 Kuhn (1977) 31–65.
15 Kuhn (1970b).
16 I.B. Cohen (1985) 135–45, 151–60, 187–94, 283–300, 301–15, 352–66, 427–34.

8 KUHN'S TAXONOMIC CRITERION

1 Kuhn (1987) 19.
2 Ibid. 20.
3 C.E. Perrin (1988) 121.
4 Kuhn (1987) 19.
5 Geoffroy (1968) 67–75.
6 See, for instance, Abetti (1952) 188–96, 272–3; Struve and Zebergs (1962) 186–208; Motz and Weaver (1995) 257–78.
7 See, for instance, Moore (1950) 453–5.
8 Examples include the water molecule and the HSO_3^- ion.
9

```
     Cl        H              Cl   H
     ..        ..             ..   ..
Cl : B   +   : N : H  ——→  Cl : B : N : H
     ..        ..             ..   ..
     Cl        H              Cl   H
    acid      base
```

9 TOULMIN'S "IDEALS OF NATURAL ORDER"

1 Toulmin (1961) 79.

11 KUHN'S THREE-BEAT PATTERN

1 Kuhn (1970b).
2 Ibid. 174–5.
3 See, for instance, Heidelberger (1976).
4 I.B. Cohen (1985) 123–4.
5 Kuhn (1970b) 77.
6 Lakatos (1970) 119 .
7 Eddington (1959) 93.
8 Galileo's law states that the acceleration of a body falling *in vacuo* to the earth's surface is constant. But according to Newtonian gravitation theory, since the distance between a falling body and the center of mass of the earth changes, so too does the gravitational force on the body and its acceleration. Galileo's law holds approximately, because the distance of fall typically is but a small fraction of the earth's radius.
9 Yang (1962) 53–8.

12 LAUDAN'S RETICULATIONAL MODEL OF SCIENTIFIC CHANGE

1 Laudan (1984) 63.
2 See Aiton (1972) 209–14.
3 Born (1956) 48.
4 Actually, no measurements are made on the electron or photon between the slit and the photographic plate upon which the particle makes impact.
5 Bohr (1958) 45.
6 Holton (1986) 68–76.
7 Laudan (1984) 104.
8 See, for instance, Doppelt (1986) 225–52.
9 Quinn (1986) 335.

13 POPPER ON PROGRESS THROUGH OVERTHROW-
WITH-INCORPORATION

1 Popper (1981) 93–4.
2 Popper (1959) 78–84; (1972) 13–17.
3 Ibid. 43–8, 100–11.
4 Ibid. 108–9.

15 SCIENTIFIC PROGRESS AND CONVERGENCE UPON
TRUTH

1 Rosenberg (1988) 171–3.
2 Peirce (1958) 91–112.
3 Laudan (1973) 289–92.
4 Ibid. 290.
5 Peirce (1935) 32.
6 Strawson (1952) 254.
7 Ibid. 254–5.
8 Ibid. 257.
9 Laudan (1973) 298.
10 Ibid. 291.
11 Rescher (1978) 1–17.
12 Ibid. 10–11.
13 Duhem (1914 [1962]) 180–200.
14 Ibid. 180–3.
15 Philosophers sometimes speak of " the Duhem–Quine thesis." However, they disagree about its content. Representative positions are included in Harding (1976). The essays in this volume by Grünbaum and Laudan are instructive on this issue.
16 Quine (1953) 41–4.
17 Cartwright (1983) 57.
18 Rescher (1977) 175.
19 Ibid. 175.
20 Ibid. 176.
21 Ibid. 177.
22 Ibid. 179.
23 Ibid. 183.
24 Ibid. 186.
25 Brush (1995) 133–45.
26 Scerri and Worrall (2001) 407–52.
27 Kuhn (1970a) 1–23.
28 Osiander (1959) 24–5.
29 Michael Ghiselin has emphasized Darwin's use of multiply-conditional explanations to account for coral-reef formation, biogeographical distributions, homologous organs, vestigial organs and various other phenomena (Ghiselin 1969).
30 The virial expansion is $PV = A + BP + CP^2 + DP^3 + \ldots$ Where $A, B, C, \ldots$ are empirically determined, temperature-dependent coefficients that are specific to the gas in question. Van der Waals' equation is $(P + a / V^2)(V - b) = kT$, where a is a measure of intermolecular attractive forces, and b is a corrective term to account for the finite volume of the molecules.
31 Kuhn (1977) 322–3.
32 Ibid. 331.
33 Ibid. 329.
34 van Fraassen (1980).

35 Carrier (1991) 28.
36 Priestley believed that metals were composite substances composed of a calx and phlogiston (e.g. zinc = [calx of zinc (ZnO) + phlogiston]. He interpreted the action of hydrochloric acid on a metal to be a liberation of the phlogiston bound to the calx, and the reduction of the calx to its metal to be a union of the calx with phlogiston. On current theory the reactions are:

$$Zn + 2\ HCl = H_2 + Zn^{++} + 2\ Cl^{-}$$
$$ZnO + H_2 = Zn + H_2O$$

Priestley observed that water appeared in the second reaction, but attributed it to a condensation of moisture present initially in the "inflammable air" (phlogiston).
37 Carrier (1991) 30.
38 Ibid. 31.
39 Hardin and Rosenberg (1982) 606–7.
40 Kitcher (1993) 149.
41 Ibid. 142.
42 Ibid. 100.
43 Ibid. 143.
44 Worrall (1989a) 117.
45 Whittaker (1951).
46 Psillos (1995) 27.
47 Leplin (1997) 182.

16 LAUDAN ON SCIENTIFIC PROGRESS AS INCREASING PROBLEM-SOLVING EFFECTIVENESS

1 Laudan (1977), 11.
2 Ibid. 15.
3 Ibid. 49.
4 Ibid. 17.
5 Newton himself added an auxiliary hypothesis about "fits of easy transmission and reflection" to account for the colors produced by pressing together thin glass plates. Subsequently, proponents of the corpuscular theory accounted for diffraction by subjecting the emitted particles to complex laws of attraction and repulsion; for polarization by postulating that emitted particles have asymmetrical "sides"; and for double refraction by subjecting particles to different forces along different axes of the crystal.
6 Ibid. 16.
7 Ibid. 63–4.
8 Ibid. 23–4.
9 Ibid. 25.
10 Ibid. 81.
11 Ibid. 130.
12 Ackeroyd (1993) 785–8; (1990) 437–9.
13 Laudan (1984) 120–4.

17 KITCHER ON CONCEPTUAL PROGRESS AND EXPLANATORY PROGRESS

1 Kitcher (1993a) 96.
2 Ibid. 107.

3 In the case of "fixed air," for instance, the weight ratio C : O is 1 : 2.66, and the atomic weights are C = 12 and O = 16. Since $12p : 16q = 1 : 2.66$, $p = 1$ and $q = 2$, and the molecular formula is CO_2.
4 Kitcher (1993a) 110.
5 Ibid. 111.
6 Ibid. 120.
7 Ibid. 130.
8 Ibid. 157.
9 Ibid. 172.
10 Miller (1955) 642–3.
11 Kitcher (1955) 659.
12 Kitcher (1993b) 170–1.
13 J. Perrin (1913 [1922]), 215–7.
14 Planck (1919 [1966]) 496–500.

18 NORMATIVE NATURALISM

1 Neurath (1983) 92.
2 Cartwright, Cat, Fleck and Uebel (1996) identify three separate "boat images" within Neurath's writings. The version quoted above is from Neurath's essay "Protocol Statements" (1932) included Cohen and Neurath (1983).
3 Neurath (1959) 202–8.
4 Kitcher (1992) 77.
5 Ibid. 76.
6 Ibid. 79.
7 Ibid. 97–8.
8 Laudan (1987) 24.
9 Ibid. 23.
10 Ibid. 25.
11 Ibid. 25.
12 Viz. to justify methodological rule R, appeal to rule R^* that states how a methodological rule is to be tested; to justify R^* appeal to rule R^{**} that states how selection is to be made from alternative ways of testing rules, etc.
13 Laudan (1987) 19.
14 Ibid. 26.
15 Ibid. 26.
16 Laudan (1989) 370.
17 Ibid. 370–1.
18 Laudan (1987) 26.

19 SCIENTIFIC PROGRESS AND THE THEORY OF ORGANIC EVOLUTION

1 Popper (1981) 73.
2 Toulmin (1961) 110.
3 Toulmin (1972).
4 Toulmin (1974) 394.
5 Toulmin (1961) 130.
6 Ibid. 141.
7 Ibid. 121–3, 135–44.
8 Hull (1988) 409; (1989) 96.

9 Hull (1989) 221.

10 Ibid. 221.

11 Ibid. 233.

12 Ibid. 234–7.

13 Hull (1988) 301–19.

14 Hull held that species are singular entities rather than collections of individuals. His position is unaffected by this criticism.

15 L.J. Cohen (1973) 48–9.

16 Ibid. 49.

17 Ibid. 47.

18 Campbell (1987) 91.

19 Kantorovich (1993) 148.

20 Ibid. 157.

21 Popper (1974) 1061.

22 Campbell (1987) 92–3.

23 Ruse (1986) 65.

24 Amundson (1989) 417.

25 Ibid. 417.

26 Ibid. 428.

27 Campbell (1987) 91.

28 Ruse (1995) 157–65; (1986) 149–60.

29 Ruse (1995) 169.

30 Donovan, Laudan, and Laudan (1988).

31 Included are studies on Galileo (M. Finocchiaro), Newton (B.J.T. Dobbs), vortex theory (B. Baigrie) the chemical revolution (C.E. Perrin), molecular geometry (S. Maieskopf), benzene theory (A.J. Rocke), fermentation theory (W. Bechtel), polywater (A.M. Diamond), Ampère's electrodynamics (J.R.H. Hofmann), Brownian motion (D. Mayo), plate tectonics (H. Frankel, R. Nunan), Planck's quantum hypothesis (J. Nicholas), nuclear magnetic resonance theory (H. Zandvoort), and electroweak unification (M.J. Hones).

32 Donovan, Laudan, and Laudan (1988) 29–41.

REFERENCES

Abetti, Giorgio (1952) *The History of Astronomy*. New York: Abelard-Schuman.

Achinstein, Peter (1964) "On the Meaning of Scientific Terms", *J. Phil.* 61: 504–5.

Ackeroyd, F. Michael (1990) "The Challenge to Lakatos Revisited", *Brit. J. Phil. Sci.* 41: 437–9.

—— (1993) "Laudan's Problem Solving Model", *Brit. J. Phil. Sci.* 44: 785–8.

Agassi, Joseph (1963) "Between Micro and Macro", *Brit. J. Phil. Sci.* 14: 26–31.

Aiton, E.J. (1972) *The Vortex Theory of Planetary Motions*. London: MacDonald.

Amundson, Ron (1989) "The Trials and Tribulations of Selectionist Explanations" in K. Hahlweg and C.A. Hooker (eds) *Issues in Evolutionary Epistemology*. Albany: SUNY Press.

Bohr, Niels (1958) *Atomic Physics and Human Knowledge*. New York: Wiley.

Born, Max (1956) *Physics in My Generation*. London: Pergamon.

Brewster, David (1837) "Whewell's *History of the Inductive Sciences*", *Edinburgh Review* 66: 110–51.

Brush, Stephen G. (1995) "Dynamics of Theory Change: The Role of Predictions", *PSA 1995 Vol. 2*. East Lansing: Philosophy of Science Association.

Campbell, Donald T. (1987) "Blind Variation and Selective Retention in Creative Thought as in Other Knowledge Processes", *Psych. Rev.* 67: 300–400. Reprinted in G. Radnitzsky and W.W. Bartley III (eds) *Evolutionary Epistemology, Rationality, and the Sociology of Knowledge*. LaSalle: Open Court.

Carrier, Martin (1991) "What Is Wrong with the Miracle Argument?" *Stud. Hist. Phil. Sci.* 22: 23–36.

Cartwright, Nancy (1983) *How the Laws of Science Lie*. Oxford: Oxford University Press.

Clark, Peter (1976) "Atomism *versus* Thermodynamics" in C. Howson (ed.) *Method and Appraisal in the Physical Science*. Cambridge: Cambridge University Press.

Coffa, J. Alberto (1991) *The Semantic Tradition from Kant to Carnap*. Cambridge: Cambridge University Press.

Cohen, I. Bernard (1985) *Revolution in Science*. Cambridge, MA: Harvard University Press.

Cohen, L. Jonathan (1973) "Is the Progress of Science Evolutionary?" *Brit. J. Phil. Sci.* 24: 41–61.

de Solla Price, Derek, J. "Contra-Copernicus: A Critical Re-Estimation of the Mathematical Planetary Theory of Ptolemy, Copernicus and Kepler" in M. Clagett (ed.) *Critical Problems in the History of Science*. Madison: University of Wisconsin Press.

Donovan, Arthur, Laudan, Larry and Laudan, Rachel (1988) *Scrutinizing Science*. Dordrecht: Kluwer.

Doppelt, Gerald (1986) "Relativism and the Reticulational Model of Scientific Rationality", *Synthèse* 69: 225–52.

Duhem, Pierre (1914 [1962]) *The Aim and Structure of Physical Theory*, 2nd edn. (P.P. Weiner, trans.). New York: Atheneum.

Dumas, J.B.A. (1857) *Compt. Rend.* 45: 709.

Eddington, A.S. (1959) *Space, Time and Gravitation*. New York: Harper & Row.

Elkana, Yehuda (1973) "Boltzmann's Scientific Research Program and Its Alternatives", in Y. Elkana (ed.) *Some Aspects of the Interaction of Science and Philosophy*. New York: Free Press.

Feyerabend, Paul K. (1962) "Explanation, Reduction and Empiricism" in H. Feigl and G. Maxwell (eds) *Minnesota Studies in the Philosophy of Science*, vol. III. Minneapolis: University of Minnesota Press.

—— (1965a) "On the 'Meaning' of Scientific Terms", *J. Phil.* 62: 266–74.

—— (1965b) "Reply to Criticism: Comments on Smart, Sellars and Putnam" in R. Cohen and M. Wartofsky (eds) *Boston Studies in the Philosophy of Science,* vol. II. New York: Humanities Press.

—— (1965c) "Problems of Empiricism", in R. Colodny (ed.) *Beyond the Edge of Certainty*. Englewood Cliffs: Prentice-Hall.

—— (1970a) "Consolations for the Specialist" in I. Lakatos and A. Musgrave (eds) *Criticism and the Growth of Knowledge*. Cambridge: Cambridge University Press.

—— (1970b) "Against Method: Outline of an Anarchistic Theory of Knowledge" in M. Radner and S. Winokur (eds) *Minnesota Studies in the Philosophy of Science*, vol. IV. Minneapolis: University of Minnesota Press.

Fox, Robert (1974) "The Rise and Fall of Laplacian Physics", *Hist. Stud. Phil. Sci.* 4: 89–136.

Frankel, Henry (1979) "The Career of Continental Drift Theory: An Application of Imre Lakatos' Analysis of Scientific Growth to the Rise of Drift Theory", *Stud. Hist. Phil. Sci.* 10: 21–66.

Fricke, Martin (1976) "The Rejection of Avogadro's Hypothesis" in C. Howson (ed.) *Method and Appraisal in the Physical Science*. Cambridge: Cambridge University Press.

Friedman, Michael (1991) "The Re-evaluation of Logical Empiricism", *J. Phil.* 88: 505–19.

Galilei, Galileo (1632 [1962]) *Dialogue Concerning the Two Chief World Systems* (Stillman Drake trans.). Berkeley: University of California Press.

Gay, Hannah (1976) "Radicals and Types: A Critical Comparison of the Methodologies of Popper and Lakatos and Their Use in the Reconstruction of Some 19th Century Chemistry", *Stud. Hist. Phil. Sci.* 7: 1–51.

Geoffroy, Etienne François (1968) "Concerning the Different Affinities Observed in Chemistry Between Different Substances" in H.M. Leicester and H.S. Klickstein (eds) *A Source Book in Chemistry , 1400–1900*. Cambridge, MA: Harvard University Press.

Ghiselin, Michael (1969) *The Triumph of the Darwinian Method*. Berkeley: University of California Press.

Giere, R.N. and Richardson, A.W. (1996) *Origins of Logical Empiricism, Minnesota Studies in the Philosophy of Science*, vol. XVI. Minneapolis: University of Minnesota Press.

Gough, J.B. (1988) "Lavoisier and the Fulfillment of the Stahlian Revolution", *Osiris, Second Series* 4: 15–33.

Grant, Edward (1971) *Physical Science in the Middle Ages*. New York: Wiley.

Grosser, Morton (1962) *The Discovery of Neptune*. Cambridge, MA: Harvard University Press.

Hall, A. Rupert (1962) *The Scientific Revolution — 1500–1800*, 2nd edn. Boston: Beacon Press.

Hardin, Clyde and Rosenberg, Alexander (1982) "In Defense of Convergent Realism", *Phil. Sci.* 49: 604–15.

Harding, Sandra (1976) *Can Theories Be Refuted?* Dordrecht: Reidel.

Heidelberger, Michael (1976) "Some Intertheoretic Relations Between Ptolemaic and Copernican Astronomy", *Erkenntnis* 10: 323–36. Reprinted in Gary Gutting (ed.) *Paradigms and Revolutions*. Notre Dame: University of Notre Dame Press.

Herschel, John F.W. (1830 [1966]) *A Preliminary Discourse on the Study of Natural Philosophy*, 1st edn. New York: Johnson Reprint, 1966.

Holton, Gerald (1986) *The Advancement of Science, and its Burdens*. Cambridge: Cambridge University Press.

Hoyle, Fred (1975) *Astronomy and Cosmology*. San Francisco: Freeman.

Hull, David (1988) *Science as a Process*. Chicago: University of Chicago Press.

—— (1989) *The Metaphysics of Evolution*. Albany: SUNY Press.

Hume, David (1740 [1927]) *An Enquiry Concerning Human Understanding*. Chicago: Open Court.

Hutten, Ernest H. (1956) *The Language of Modern Physics*. London: George Allen and Unwin.

Jammer, Max (1966) *The Conceptual Development of Quantum Mechanics*. New York: McGraw-Hill.

Jevons, W. Stanley (1890) *Pure Logic and Other Minor Works*. London: Macmillan.

Kantorovich, Aharon (1993) *Scientific Discovery: Logic and Tinkering*, Albany: SUNY Press.

Kitcher, Philip (1955) "Author's Response", *Phil. Phenom. Res.* 55: 659.

—— (1992) "The Naturalists Return", *Phil. Rev.* 101: 53–114.

—— (1993a) *The Advancement of Science*. Oxford: Oxford University Press, 1993.

—— (1993b) "Knowledge, Society and History", *Canad. J. Phil.* 23: 155–77.

Kuhn, Thomas S. (1957) *The Copernican Revolution* Cambridge: Harvard University Press.

—— (1970a) "Logic of Discovery or Psychology of Discovery?" in I. Lakatos and A. Musgrave (eds) *Criticism and the Growth of Knowledge*. Cambridge: Cambridge University Press.

—— (1970b) *The Structure of Scientific Revolution,* 2nd edn. Chicago: University of Chicago Press.

—— (1977) *The Essential Tension*. Chicago: University of Chicago Press.

—— (1987) "What Are Scientific Revolutions?" in Lorenz Kruger, Lorraine J. Daston and Michael Heidelberger (eds) *The Probabilistic Revolution, Vol. 1: Ideas in History*. Cambridge, MA: MIT Press.

Lakatos, Imre (1970) "Falsification and the Methodology of Scientific Research Programmes" in I. Lakatos and A. Musgrave (eds) *Criticism and the Growth of Knowledge.* Cambridge: Cambridge University Press.

—— (1971) "History of Science and its Rational Reconstructions" in R. Buck and R.S. Cohen (eds) *Boston Studies in the Philosophy of Science,* vol. VIII. Dordrecht: Reidel.

—— and Zahar, Elie (1975) "Why Did Copernicus' Research Program Supersede Ptolemy's?" in Robert S. Westman (ed.) *The Copernican Revolution.* Berkeley: University of California Press.

Laudan, Larry (1973) "Peirce and the Trivialization of the Self-Correcting Thesis" in R.N. Giere and R.S. Westfall (eds) *Foundations of Scientific Method: The Nineteenth Century.* Bloomington: Indiana University Press.

—— (1977) *Progress and its Problems.* Berkeley: University of California Press.

—— (1984) *Science and Values.* Berkeley: University of California Press.

—— (1987) "Progress or Rationality? The Prospects for a Normative Naturalism", *Amer. Phil. Quart.* 24: 19–31.

—— (1989) "If it Ain't Broke, Don't Fix It", *Brit. J. Phil. Sci.* 40: 369–75.

Leplin, Jarrett (1997) *A Novel Defense of Scientific Realism.* Oxford: Oxford University Press.

Mansel, H.L. (1851) *Prolegomena Logica.* Oxford: W. Graham.

Mayr, Ernst (1982) *The Growth of Biological Thought.* Cambridge: Harvard University Press.

Mill, John Stuart (1872 [1970]) *A System of Logic,* 8th edn. London: Longman.

Miller, Richard W. (1955) "The Advancement of Realism", *Phil. Phenom. Res.* 55: 637–45.

Moore, Walter J. (1950) *Physical Chemistry.* New York: Prentice-Hall.

Motz, Lloyd and Weaver, J.H. (1995) *The Story of Astronomy.* New York: Plenum Press.

Musgrave, Alan (1976a) "Why Did Oxygen Supplant Phlogiston? Research Programmes in the Chemical Revolution", in C. Howson (ed.) *Method and Appraisal in the Physical Science.* Cambridge: Cambridge University Press.

—— (1976b) "Method and Madness?" in R.S. Cohen *et al.* (eds) *Boston Studies in the Philosophy of Science,* vol. 39. Dordrecht: Reidel.

Nagel, Ernest (1961) *The Structure of Science.* New York: Harcourt, Brace & World.

—— (1974) "Issues in the Logic of Reductive Explanations", in *Teleology Revisited.* New York: Columbia University Press.

Neurath, Otto (1959) "Protocol Sentences" in A.J. Ayer (ed.) *Logical Positivism.* Glencoe: Free Press.

—— (1983) "Protocol Statements" in R.S. Cohen and M. Neurath (eds) *Otto Neurath: Philosophical Papers.* Dordrecht: Reidel.

Newton, Isaac (1730 [1952]) *Opticks.* New York: Dover.

Nickles, Thomas (1975) "Two Concepts of Intertheoretic Reduction', *J. Phil.* 70: 181–201.

Niiniluoto, Ilkka (1980) "Scientific Progress", *Synthèse* 45: 426–62.

Oersted, H.C. (1963) "Experiments on the Effect of a Current of Electricity on the Magnetic Needle" in W.F. Magee (ed.) *Source Book in Physics.* Cambridge, MA: Harvard University Press.

Osiander, Andreas (1959) "*Preface* to Copernicus, *De revolutionibus*" in E. Rosen (ed.) *Three Copernican Treatises*. New York: Dover.

Owen, Richard (1973) "Darwin on the Origin of Species" in David Hull (ed.) *Darwin and His Critics*. Chicago: University of Chicago Press.

Peirce, Charles S. (1935) "Necessity Considered as a Postulate" in C. Hartshorne and P. Weiss (eds) *Collected Papers, Vol. VI: Scientific Metaphysics*. Cambridge, MA: Harvard University Press.

—— (1958) "The Fixation of Belief" in Philip P. Weiner (ed.) *Values in a Universe of Chance*. Garden City: Doubleday Anchor Books.

Perrin, C.E. (1988) "The Chemical Revolution: Shifts in Guiding Assumptions" in A. Donovan, L. Laudan and R. Laudan (eds) *Scrutinizing Science*. Dordrecht: Kluwer.

Perrin, Jean (1913 [1922]) *Atoms* (D. Hammick, trans.) London: Constable.

Planck, Max (1919 [1966]) "The Origin and Development of the Quantum Theory", Nobel Prize Award Address, 1919. Reprinted in H.A. Boorse and L. Motz (eds) *The World of the Atom*. New York: Basic Books.

Popper, Karl (1959) *The Logic of Scientific Discovery*. New York: Basic Books.

—— (1972) *Objective Knowledge*. Oxford: Clarendon Press.

—— (1974) "Replies to my Critics" in P.A. Schilpp (ed.) *The Philosophy of Karl Popper*. LaSalle: Open Court.

—— (1981) "The Rationality of Scientific Revolutions" in Ian Hacking (ed) *Scientific Revolutions*. Oxford: Oxford University Press.

Priestley, Joseph (1767 [1966]) *The History and Recent State of Electricity*. New York: Johnson Reprint.

Psillos, Stathis (1995) "Is Structural Realism the Best of Both Worlds?" *Dialectica* 49: 15–46.

Putnam, Hilary (1965) "How Not to Talk About Meaning" in R. Cohen and M. Wartofsky (eds) *Boston Studies in the Philosophy of Science,* vol. II. New York: Humanities Press.

Quine, Willard van Orman (1953) "Two Dogmas of Empiricism" in *From a Logical Point of View*. Cambridge: Cambridge University Press.

Quinn, Philip (1986) "Comments on Laudan's 'Methodology: Its Prospects' " *PSA 1986 Vol. 2*. East Lansing: Philosophy of Science Association.

Rescher, Nicholas (1977) *Methodological Pragmatism*. Oxford: Oxford University Press.

Rescher, Nicholas (1978) *Peirce's Philosophy of Science*. Notre Dame: University of Notre Dame Press.

Rosen, Edward (1959) *Three Copernican Treatises*. New York: Dover.

Rosenberg, Jay F. (1988) "Comparing the Incommensurable: Another Look at Convergent Realism", *Phil. Stud.* 54: 169–93.

Ruse, Michael (1986) *Taking Darwin Seriously*. Oxford: Blackwell.

—— (1995) *Evolutionary Naturalism*. London: Routledge.

Scerri, Eric R. and Worrall, John (2001) "Prediction and the Periodic Table", *Stud. Hist. Phil. Sci.* 32A: 407–52.

Sedgwick, Adam (1973) "Objections to Mr. Darwin's Theory of the Origin of Species", in David Hull (ed.) *Darwin and His Critics*. Chicago: University of Chicago Press.

Shapere, Dudley (1966) "Meaning and Scientific Change" in R. Colodny (ed.) *Mind and Cosmos*. Pittsburgh: University of Pittsburgh Press.

Shea, Wlliam (1972) *Galileo's Intellectual Revolution*. New York: Science History Publications.

Siegfried, Robert (1988) "The Chemical Revolution in the History of Chemistry", *Osiris,* Second Series 4: 34–50.

Spector, Marshall (1978) *Concepts of Reduction in Physical Science*. Philadelphia: Temple University Press.

Strawson, Peter F. (1952) *Introduction to Logical Theory*. New York: Wiley.

Struve, Otto and Zebergs, Velta (1962) *Astronomy of the Twentieth Century*. New York: Macmillan.

Toulmin, Stephen (1961) *Foresight and Understanding*. New York: Harper Torchbooks.

—— (1972) *Human Understanding*, vol. I. Oxford: Clarendon Press.

—— (1974) "Rationality and Scientific Discovery" in K. Schaffer and R. Cohen (eds) *Boston Studies in the Philosophy of Science,* vol. XX. Dordrecht: Reidel.

van Fraassen, Bas (1980) *The Scientific Image*. Oxford: Clarendon Press.

Van Name, F.W. (1952) *Modern Physics*. New York: Prentice Hall.

Venn, John (1907) *The Principles of Empirical or Inductive Logic,* 2nd edn. London: Macmillan.

Weismann, August (1904) *The Evolution of Life*. London: Edward Arnold.

Whewell, William (1847 [1967]) *Philosophy of the Inductive Sciences*, 2nd edn. London: Cass.

—— (1857 [1967]) *History of the Inductive Sciences*, 3rd edn. London: Cass.

Whittaker, E.T. (1951) *A History of the Theories of Aether and Electricity*. London: Nelson.

Worrall, John (1989a) "Structural Realism", *Dialectica* 43: 99–124.

—— (1989b) "Fix It and be Damned: A Reply to Laudan", *Brit. J. Phil. Sci.* 40: 376–88.

Yang, C.N. (1962) *Elementary Particles*. Princeton: Princeton University Press.

Zahar, Elie (1973) "Why Did Einstein"s Programme Supersede Lorentz's?" *Brit. J. Phil. Sci.* 24: 95–123, 223–61.

INDEX OF NAMES

Achinstein, Peter   32–3
Ackeroyd, F. Michael   123
Adams, John C.   42
Agassi, Joseph   52
Airy, George B.   48
d'Alembert, Jean   77
Ampère, André   168
Amundson, Ron   147
Arago, François   22–3
Aristotle   16, 21, 63, 68, 77, 90, 107, 159
Arrhenius, Svante   40–1, 72, 162
Avogadro, Amedeo   74, 129, 156

Baigrie, Brian   168
Bailly, Jean-Sylvain   65
Balmer, Johann   51
Bartholinus, Erasmus   17
Bechtel, William   168
Bessel, Friedrich 48, 120
Bohm, David   108
Bohr, Niels   1, 40, 51–2, 55, 66, 77, 84–6,
   108, 134, 136
Boltzmann, Ludwig   53, 68
Born, Max   84
Boyle, Robert   8, 24, 29, 90
Brahe, Tycho   41, 124
Brewster, David   Ch. 2
Brodie, Benjamin   147
Broglie, Louis de   86
Brønsted, J. N   72
Brush, Stephen D.   107

Campbell, Donald   144–8
Carnap, Rudolf   137, 161

Carrier, Martin   114–15
Cartwright, Nancy   90, 104, 167
Cat, Jordi   167
Cauchy, A.L.   98
Charles, Jacques   29, 90
Chomsky, Noam   149
Clairaut, Alexis   48, 65
Clark, Peter   48
Clausius, Rudolf   48
Coffa, J. Alberto   161
Cohen, I. Bernard   Ch. 7, 68, 74, 78
Cohen, L. Jonathan   143–4
Cooke, Josiah   147
Copernicus, Nicolaus   2, 12, 65–6, 67, 68–70,
   75, 78, 90, 105, 109, 112, 123–4, 126
Coulomb, Augustin   51, 104

Dalton, John   48, 67, 75, 115, 126–7
Darwin, Charles   45, 65, 67, 75, 109–10, 124,
   127, 142, 144, 145, 146, 158, 165
Davy, Humphrey   68
Debye, Peter   41, 162
Descartes, René   10, 44, 67, 75, 78, 82–4, 90,
   108, 147
Diamond, Arthur M.   168
Dobbs, B.J.T.   168
Duhem, Pierre   102–4
Dumas, J.B.A.   42

Eddington, Arthur S.   79
Ehrenfest, Paul   53
Einstein, Albert   43, 52, 55, 67, 75, 79, 86,
   111, 151
Euler, Leonhard   48

Feyerabend, Paul   Ch.4, 43–4
Finocchiaro, Maurice 168
Fleck, Lola   167
Fontenelle, Bernard 65
Fourcroy, Antoine   123
Frank, Philipp   161
Frankel, Henry   49, 168
Fresnel, Augustin   14, 15, 117–18
Freud, Sigmund   67, 75
Friedman, Michael   161

Galileo   10, 24, 30, 36, 41–2, 66, 67, 78, 80,
    90, 102, 107, 121, 145, 164, 168
Gay-Lussac, Louis   29, 90, 115
Geoffroy, Etienne-François   70
Ghiselin, Michael   165
Giere, Ronald   161
Gough, J.B.   66–7
Grant, Edward   66
Grünbaum, Adolf   165

Hacking, Ian   135
Hall, A. Rupert   67
Hall, Asaph   48
Halley, Edmund   115
Hamilton, William R.   77
Hardin, Clyde   116
Harvey, William   67
Heisenberg, Werner   84
Hempel, Carl   137, 161
Herschel, John   15, 20, 107, 114, 136
Herschel, William   68, 70
Hertzsprung, Ejnar   70–2
Hess, Harry   49
Hofmann, James R.   168
Holmes, Arthur   49
Holton, Gerald   86
Hones, Michael J.   168
Hooke, Robert   17, 118
Hoyle, Fred   43
Hückel, Erich   41, 162
Hull, David   141–4
Hume, David   20, 27, 98, 107, 150
Hutten, Ernest   52
Huygens, Christiaan   10, 17

Jammer, Max   55
Jeans, James 53–4

Jevons, W. Stanley 161
Joule, James   48

Kant, Immanuel   19
Kantorovich, Aharon   145
Kaufmann, Walter   86
Kepler, Johannes   8, 11, 13–14, 24, 25–6,
    44, 78, 83, 147
Kitcher, Philip   117–18, Ch. 17, 132–3, 140
Krönig, August   48
Kuhn, Thomas S.   2, 65, 66, 67, Ch. 8,
    Ch. 11, 82, 87, 88, 97, 108, 110–12, 120,
    150, 156

LaGrange, Joseph L.   48, 77
Lakatos, Imre   1, Ch. 5, 51, 66, 79, 134,
    136, 150
Lamarck, Jean Baptiste   145
LaPlace, Pierre S.   15, 24, 73, 75, 115
Laudan, Larry, 1, Ch. 12, 100–1, 117,
    Ch. 16, 126, 134–7, 140, 150, 158, 165
Lavoisier, Antoine   12, 66–7, 69–70, 90,
    102, 115, 117, 123, 126
Lee, T.D.   80–1
Leibniz, G.W.   83
Leplin, Jarrett   119
Lewis, G. N.   72
Leverrier, Urbain   42–3, 145
Liebig, Justus   123
Lowry, Thomas M.   72
Lyell, Charles   67
Lysenko, Trofim   45

Maieskopf, Seymour   168
Malus, Etienne   17
Mansel, H.L.   19
Marx, Karl   121
Matthew, Patrick   142
Matthews, Drummond   49
Maxwell, James C.   48, 67, 118
Mayo, Deborah   168
Mayr, Ernst   65
Mendel, Gregor   77, 116, 121
Mendeleeff, Dmitri   40, 107
Meyer, O.E.   48
Michelson, A.A.   79
Mill, John Stuart   Ch. 3, 107
Miller, Richard   128

Molières, Joséph P. de 83–4
Morley, Edward W. 79
Moseley, H.G.J. 40
Musgrave, Alan 48–50

Nagel, Ernest 1, Ch. 4, 161
Neurath, Otto 130–2, 138
Newcomb, Simon 48
Newton, Isaac 2, 8–11, 13–14, 23, 24–6,
    30, 36, 38–9, 42, 44, 46, 48, 51, 52, 63,
    65, 66, 67, 68, 69, 70, 73–4, 75, 77, 78,
    79–80, 82–4, 86, 90, 98, 102, 104, 108,
    151, 164, 166, 168
Nicholas, John M. 168
Nickles, Thomas 36–7
Nunan, Richard 168

Ockham, William of 107
Onsager, Lars 41, 162
Osiander, Andreas 108–9
Owen, Richard 65

Pascal, Blaise 22
Peirce, Charles Sanders 1, 99–102, 104,
    140
Perrin, C.E. 69, 168
Perrin, Jean 129, 156
Pickering, Edward, C. 71
Planck, Max 53–5, 68, 111, 129, 156–7,
    168
Poisson, Simeon, D. 15, 115, 117–18
Popper, Karl R. 1, 39, 45, 46, Ch. 13,
    107–8, 112, 134, 137, 140, 145, 149
Price, Derek 66
Priestley, Joseph 11–12, 114, 117, 126, 166
Prout, William 42–3
Psillos, Stathis 118–19
Ptolemy, Claudius 10, 12, 66, 68, 78, 84,
    108, 121, 123–4, 147
Putnam, Hilary 31, 135

Quine, Willard van Orman 103, 135
Quinn, Philip 87

Rayleigh, Lord (J.W. Strutt) 53–4
Reichenbach, Hans 137
Rescher, Nicholas 101–2, 105–13, 140
Richardson, A. W. 161
Rocke, A. J. 168

Rorty, Richard 135
Rosen, Edward 66
Rosenberg, Alexander 116
Rosenberg, Jay 98
Ruse, Michael 145, 149–51
Russell, Henry Norris 70–2

Salam, Abdus 119
Scerri, Eric 107
Schrödinger, Erwin 52, 85
Secchi, Angelo 70–2
Sedgwick, Adam 65
Siegfried, Robert 66–7
Shapere, Dudley 32, 34–5
Smith, Adam 158
Snel, Wilibrod 24
Sommerfeld, Arnold 40, 74, 111
Specter, Marshall 30–1
Stahl, Georg E. 66
Steno, Nicolaus 73
Strawson, Peter 100–1
Struve, Otto 120

Toulmin, Stephen Ch. 9, 140–4

Uebel, Thomas E. 167

Van der Waals, Johannes 29, 48, 53, 110,
    165
Van Fraassen, Bas C. 113
Venn, John 24, 161
Vine, Fred 49

Wegener, Alfred 49
Weierstrass, Karl 98
Weinberg, Stephen 119
Weismann, August 65
Whewell, William 1, Ch. 1, Ch. 2, Ch. 3, 38,
    97, 99, 107, 112, 114, 136, 144, 149
Whittaker, Edmund T. 118
Wien, Wilhelm 53–4
Wilson, Tuzo 49
Worrall, John 107, 118, 137

Yang, C. N. 80–1
Young, Thomas 14, 17

Zahar, Elie 66
Zandvoort, Henk 168

INDEX OF SUBJECTS

a priori judgments   9, 19, 132
acids   70, 72, 102–3, 123, 162n., 164n.
action-at-a-distance   84, 87
ad hoc hypotheses   14, 18, 41, 134, 162
adaptability   151
adaptation   106, 140, 146, 151, 159
aether   86, 116, 117, 118, 119, 122, 124
agreement, method of   20–1
Almagest (Ptolemy)   108, 121
anomalies   40, 42, 46, 48, 50, 76, 77, 78, 120, 150, 157
Aristotelian physics   63, 68, 77, 78, 90, 107
asymptotic agreement of calculations   1, Ch. 6, 134, 156–7
atomic number   40
auxiliary hypotheses   38, 42, 50, 86, 89, 103–4, 120–1, 147, 166n.
Avogadro's number   129, 156

basic statements   89
biogeographical distribution   109–10, 127
black-body radiation   53–4, 78, 111, 129, 160n.
blind trials   144–8
Bohr's theory of the hydrogen atom   32, 33, 40, 51, 55, 77, 111
Boyle's law   8, 24, 29, 90
Brownian motion   129, 162n. 168n.

caloric theory   86, 114–15, 116, 119, 122, 124
calx   12, 67, 114, 117, 166n.
Cartesian physics   75
cause   8–10, 20, 21–2, 25, 86, 133, 136, 138–9, 158, 159, 161

ceteris paribus clause   104
Charles' law   29, 90
chemical revolution   66–7, 75, 168n.
cognitive aims   Ch. 12, 108, 122, 128, 143, 145
cognitive virtue   133
colligation of facts (Whewell)   8, 11, 24
colligative properties   40–1
comets   41
Commentariolus (Copernicus)   66
complementarity, principle of   84–6, 108, 139
completeness   84, 148
composition of forces   10, 23
conceptual integration   110, 112
concomitant variations   20, 22
consilience   1, 11, 13, 15, 16, 136, 149, 156, 157
consistency   13, 36–7, 87, 110, 120, 149
contact action   108
continental drift   49
convention   137
convergence upon truth   1, Ch. 15, 120
convergent realism   126
Copenhagen interpretation   85, 134
Copernican revolution   65–6, 67, 78, 90, 112, 123–4
corpuscular theory of light   14–15, 121, 166n.
correspondence, rules of   51]
correspondence principle   52, 134
Coulomb's law   51, 104
critical point   48, 110
crucial experiment   103, 156

De revolutionibus (Copernicus)   66, 78, 109

descent, tree of   144, 146

descriptive progress   2

descriptive theory of science   97, 124, 135, 136, 151, 158

difference, method of   20–2, 25, 107

diffraction   85

disciplinary matrix   77, 80, 156

DNA   63, 116

elective affinity   10, 70,

electrolysis   129

electrolytes   40–1

electromagnetic theory   31, 46, 51, 54–5, 87, 118, 134, 157

electron charge   32

electron spin   32, 40

electroweak interactions   80–1, 168n.

empirical adequacy   113–14

epicycle   10, 12, 84, 99, 109, 121

epigenetic rules   149–51

equant point   10

evolution, theory of   140, *see also* evolutionary histories

evolutionary histories   109–10, 148, 149, 165n.

exemplar   77

"experimental philosophy" (Newton)   86, 108

explanatory overlap   43–4, 46

explication of conceptions (Whewell)   8, 28

facts (vs. ideas)   7–8, 10–11, 14, 16

falling bodies, law of   21, 30, 36, 80, 90, 102, 107, 121, 124, 164n.

falsification   39, 46, 89, 90, 102, 146

falsificationism   45–6, 79, 107

fertility   37, 110–11

fitness   140–2, 143, 148, 151, 158

"fits of easy transmission and reflection" (Newton)   14, 17, 166n.

force   19, 23

Foresight and Understanding (Toulmin)   140

Gay-Lussac's law   29, 90

gene   116, 141

general relativity theory   30, 78, 79–80, 107, 162

gravitons   119

heat, theory of   15

heuristic, positive   47–8, 50

Hooke's law   118

Human Understanding (Toulmin)   140

hypothetico-deductive procedure   23–4, 99–101

ideal gas theory   53, 104

ideals of natural order (Toulmin)   Ch. 9, 76

incommensurability   32, 33, 106

"incorporation-with-corroborated-excess-content" (Lakatos)   1, 39, 42, 46, 51, 134, 136

induction   11, Ch. 3, 45, 77, 100, 102, 115, 116, 135, 137, 138–9, 148, 161n.

inductivism   45–6, 146

inertial homogeneity of matter   70

interactors (Hull)   141–3

inviolable principles   130, 131, 134–6

isotopes   43

justification, context of   25–6, 36, 44–7, 136–9

Kepler's laws   8, 13–14, 24, 25–6, 31, 44, 83, 147

kinetic molecular theory   29, 48, 53, 90, 102, 105, 110, 129, 147

length   30

lineages   142, 143, 148, 151, 158

Logic of Scientific Discovery (Popper)   89

logical empiricism   28, 132, 161n.

magnetic monopole   119

magnetic vortex theory   13

Mars, orbit of   147

mass, conservation of   80

meaning variance   34

Mercury, anomalous motion of 42–3, 46, 48, 77, 78, 79, 107

meson   34

miracle argument, no   114, 128

modus ponens   25
modus tollens   25
molecular orbital theory   127, 147
mutation   142, 144

N-rays   121
natural selection   45, 65, 110, 127, 140, 142, 148, 158
naturalism   Ch. 18
necessary truth   9–10, 150
Newtonian mechanics   13–14, 23, 30, 31, 33, 36, 38–9, 42–3, 44, 48, 52, 63, 65, 66, 67, 68, 70, 75, 77, 78, 79, 80, 84, 86, 90, 98, 102, 104, 108, 168n.
"normal science" (Kuhn)   68, Ch. 11, 88, 108, 120
normative claims   45, 86, 87, 97, 125, Ch. 18, 151

observation language   34–5, 79, 103, 131–2
Opticks (Newton)   67
original horizontality, principle of   73
oxygen theory   12–13, 77, 78, 90, 102, 117, 123

paradigm   Ch. 11
parity, conservation of   80
periodic tables   40, 77
"pessimistic meta-induction"   102
phlogiston theory   12–13, 77, 78, 86, 90, 114, 115, 116, 117, 119, 122, 124, 166n.
photoelectric effect   55, 111, 129, 160n.
phylogeny   142, 143, 144, 146, 148
Planck's constant   129, 157
plate tectonics theory   49, 75, 147, 168n.
point-mass   46, 98, 104, 105, 128, 158
Poisson white spot   118
polarization   17–18, 25
polywater   121, 168n.
Principia (Newton)   65, 67, 86
principles, inviolable   130, 133, 134, 135–6, 139
probability   100–1, 108, 116
problem-solving   1, 105–6, 113, Ch. 16, 126, 148, 150, 158
protective belt (Lakatos)   38–9
protocol sentence   131–2

Prout's hypothesis   42, 43
Ptolemaic planetary models   10, 12, 66, 68–9, 78, 84, 108, 121, 147

quantum theory   30, 31, 52, 54–5, 78, 84, 86, 108, 111, 119, 127, 134, 136, 138, 139, 157, 160n. 168n.
quarks   119

radioactive decay   63, 80, 129
rational reconstruction   45, 46, 48, 49, 50
rationality   122
realism, scientific   118–19, 128
realizability   87
reduction   1, Ch. 4, 38
refraction, double   14, 17
relativism   137
replicators (Hull)   141–3
research programmes   Ch. 5
residues, method of   20, 22–3
"reticulational model" (Laudan)   Ch. 12
retrograde motions of planets   112, 123
"revolutionary science" (Kuhn)   Ch. 8, Ch. 11, 88

"saving the appearances"   13, 66, 84, 108, 113, 121
serendipity   145–6
simple enumeration   26–7
simplicity   13–15, 86, 105, 110–12, 122, 160n.
solar system   13–14, 41, 163n.
special relativity theory   31, 52, 79, 80, 85–6
speciation   144
species   143–4, 168n.
stars, classification of   70–2
statistical mechanics   29, 36, 54
stellar parallax   120, 124
structural realism   118–19
Structure of Scientific Revolutions (Kuhn)   67, 77
superconductivity   63
System of Logic (Mill)   25

tautology   114
taxonomic change, holistic   Ch. 8, 76, 82, 150

temperature   8, 29, 30, 71, 89, 105, 115, 148

theory-agnosticism   2

thermodynamics   29, 30, 36, 53

tributary–river model (Whewell)   11, 13–14, 16, 17, 18–19, 38, 99, 144

Tychonic system (Brahe)   124–5

uncertainty relations   86

unconditional relations   20–1, 25, 26

underlying mechanisms   3, 140, 147, 157, 158

undesigned scope   15–16, 107, 111, 136, 156, 157

unification, explanatory   14, 99, 128, 129, 133

uniformity of nature   26, 27

Uranus   145, 162n.

valence theory   127

Van der Waals' theory   29, 48, 53, 110, 161n., 165n.

variation   140, 142, 143, 144, 145, 146, 148, 158

virial expansion   110, 112, 165n.

viscosity   48

vital force   8, 10

vortex theory   44, 82–4, 90, 147, 168n.

Vulcan   43

wave theory of light   14–15, 18, 77, 85, 102, 117–18, 121, 127

worldview difficulties   121